ROUTLEDGE LIBRARY EDITIONS:
MANAGEMENT

Volume 47

IMAGINATIVE MANAGEMENT CONTROL

IMAGINATIVE MANAGEMENT CONTROL

RONALD OGDEN

LONDON AND NEW YORK

First published in 1970 by Routledge & Kegan Paul Limited

This edition first published in 2018
by Routledge
2 Park Square, Milton Park, Abingdon, Oxon OX14 4RN

and by Routledge
711 Third Avenue, New York, NY 10017

Routledge is an imprint of the Taylor & Francis Group, an informa business

© 1970 The Estate of Ronald Ogden

All rights reserved. No part of this book may be reprinted or reproduced or utilised in any form or by any electronic, mechanical, or other means, now known or hereafter invented, including photocopying and recording, or in any information storage or retrieval system, without permission in writing from the publishers.

Trademark notice: Product or corporate names may be trademarks or registered trademarks, and are used only for identification and explanation without intent to infringe.

British Library Cataloguing in Publication Data
A catalogue record for this book is available from the British Library

ISBN: 978-1-138-55938-7 (Set)
ISBN: 978-1-351-05538-3 (Set) (ebk)
ISBN: 978-0-8153-6576-1 (Volume 47) (hbk)
ISBN: 978-1-351-26064-0 (Volume 47) (ebk)

Publisher's Note
The publisher has gone to great lengths to ensure the quality of this reprint but points out that some imperfections in the original copies may be apparent.

Disclaimer
The publisher has made every effort to trace copyright holders and would welcome correspondence from those they have been unable to trace.

IMAGINATIVE MANAGEMENT CONTROL

RONALD OGDEN

LONDON
ROUTLEDGE & KEGAN PAUL

First published in 1970
by Routledge & Kegan Paul Limited
Broadway House, 68–74, Carter Lane
London, E.C.4
Printed in Great Britain
by Willmer Brothers Limited
Birkenhead
© *R. Ogden* 1970
No part of this book may be reproduced
in any form without permission from
the publisher, except for the quotation
of brief passages in criticism
SBN 7100 6584 1

CONTENTS

ACKNOWLEDGMENTS *page* x

PREFACE xi

1 THE NEED FOR CONTROL IN MODERN BUSINESS 1
meaning of control – accounting and control – financial control – marketing control – management as control – management decisions – the role of management – capital – budgetary control – profits – dividends – industrial finance – production control – the smaller company – future of the small business

2 THE FUNCTIONS OF MANAGEMENT 18
management breakdown – management objectives – definition of 'need' – the role of profits – secondary objectives – marketing concept – business structures – holding companies – functions of directors – an overseas example – production department – sales department – supply department – decentralization

3 HUMAN RELATIONS IN MANAGEMENT 34
business as an organism – incentives – human variations – leadership – the foreman/supervisor – method study – group psychology – selection of supervisors – graduate foremen – span of control – junior management – management development – management recruitment – character – the 'management grid' as an assessment of character – dynamic group – value of 'grid' assessment – personnel control – line and staff – discipline – importance of human relations – opinion surveys – new methods in human relations

CONTENTS

4 THE CONTROL OF PEOPLE 50
treating people as human beings – living with trade unionism – conflict or identity of objects – labour management relations – communication in industry – self-control – the glacier experiment – labour participation – joint consultation – the new industrial revolution – changing role of management – role of consultants – the management team – the manager as consultant – management training – role of the B.I.M. – internal training centres – management: a science and an art

5 MOTIVATION AND COMMUNICATION 66
authority and interdependence – multiple roles – work or drudgery – work can be fun – misconceptions about incentives – participation – centralization and decentralization – attitude surveys – danger of false opinions – importance of individuality – building a team – communication and management – human relations and communication – dangers of obsolete thinking – the operational group – delegation and development – communication and delegation – management by integration – target setting – self-assessment – theory and practice

6 COMMONSENSE OF MANAGEMENT 85
dangers of mystiques – operational research – management assessment – bases of new techniques – human and electronic mind – use of statistics in business – laws of probability – ratios and units – information passing – language and communication – language of mathematics – computer application – management and the computer – management and design – design and research – packaging and design

7 CUSTOMER RELATIONS AND ADVERTISING 102
hypnotism and advertising – informative advertising – the function of advertising – advertising media – the account executive – public relations – product and consumer relations – protection of the consumer – quality control – importance of the image – opinion surveys and image analysis

CONTENTS

8 INNOVATION AND EXPANSION 112
varieties of business – the typical business – value of the smaller business – necessity for profit – relevant questions – brain-storming – organization and methods – innovation – example of a small business – break-even chart – cash position – diminishing returns – discounted cash flow – decision trees

9 THE MARKETING CONCEPT 131
profitability and the market – brand availability – brands and brand names – brand loyalty – availability and marketing – the middle-man – science of marketing – market research – design and packaging – coupons and stamps – the marketing manager – division of markets – the multiple store – fixed prices – marketing overseas

10 SCIENCE AS AN AID TO MANAGEMENT 142
scientific method – science and business – operations research (OR) – a practical example – operations research applied to business – questioning – variables – cybernetics – working model – queueing theory – stochastic method – product variety – decision theory – mathematics and management – the importance of concepts – OR and human relations –

11 MANAGEMENT ACCOUNTING 158
basic control – capital – the balance sheet – profit and loss account – double entry – trial balances – change in values – business is dynamic not static – cost accounting – unit cost and break-even point – standard costing – auditing – credit – budgeting

12 PLANNING 174
need for planning – suspicion of planning – swedish example of planning – attention to detail – budgeting and planning in the private sector – planning for the optimum – servicing – stock control – long- and short-term planning – the planning department – organization change – short-term planning – long-range planning – planning in a world situation – new developments – the

CONTENTS

smaller firm and planning – what is our business? – expansion – planning and takeovers – what are we selling? – planning tools – use of consultants – value of consultants – conclusion

APPENDICES

A	Network analysis and planning	191
B	Trees of decision	206
C	Linear programming	213
D	Stock or inventory control	216

SELECT BIBLIOGRAPHY 220

INDEX 223

FIGURES

1	Normal distribution curve or Gaussian Probability Curve *page*	91
2	Break-even chart	119
3	Cash position graph	124
4	Sales per quarter	165
5	Critical path method	194
6	Decision tree	208
7	Simplified decision tree	211
8	Linear programming graph	214

TABLES

1 (*a* and *b*)	123
2 (*a* and *b*)	210

PREFACE

This book is not intended to be a textbook of modern management techniques. There are many such books available and some are referred to in these pages. This book is rather an assessment of the art and science of management in the light of modern developments. It is written in the belief that there are certain principles of good management which need to be known and observed by successful managers, and that managers require some background knowledge in order to be effective managers.

It is the result of some 35 years experience in the practice, observation and teaching of management techniques, including five years in the services, both military and civil, where effective management is essential if chaos is not to ensue.

The book is not intended for the pundits of management but mainly for two types of reader: first, the student of management who wants to get an idea of what it is all about; and second, the manager in the small to medium-sized business, who may be unaware of certain modern management developments and wants to know more about them.

It is certainly not meant to be exhaustive and much has, of necessity, been omitted. I am fully aware of its shortcomings, some of which are due to the fact that it has been written in such spare time as has been available from a full-time and fairly demanding job, coupled with a certain amount of other writing. Its object is to stimulate thought and imagination rather than to lay down strict rules of conduct.

My own interest in management started some forty years ago when I was an undergraduate studying economics at Cambridge – in those days the phrase was 'scientific management'. Its high priests were Taylor and Gantt, and among the lectures I attended at Cambridge were those of Professor Sargant Florence, author of *The Economics of Fatigue and Unrest*. It was at Cambridge that I learnt that management is primarily concerned with people. Later I came to know Colonel Urwick, the pioneer of scientific manage-

PREFACE

ment in England; it was he who first enunciated to me the apothegm that 'the first syllable of management is *Man*'.

This led me to realize that, however scientific our management may be, it is primarily concerned with the humanities. This may be the reason why Professor Peter Drucker, author of *The Practice of Management*, has said that we cannot afford illiterate managers and that the best vocational courses for managers are courses in poetry and short story writing. The basis of management, as of human relationships in business, is effective communication, and for effective communication an understanding of the proper use of words is essential.

Managers also need to be psychologists, in the widest sense of that much misused word. I do not mean that they must be fully versed in the writings of Freud, Jung and Adler. What I mean is they should understand people and the motives which actuate them. This is still not fully realized and, a great deal of the industrial conflict of today, which is costing industry untold millions in loss of profits and markets, is largely due to lack of knowledge of psychology on the part of management. There is still a tendency to ride rough-shod over the feelings and aspirations of people and then to be surprised at the resentment and discontent which is engendered. People are neither machines nor animals to be driven on by sticks or cajoled with carrots. They are thinking, feeling organisms – possessed with intelligence and immortal souls. They cannot be reduced to cyphers in a ledger or mere appendages to machines without causing resentment and rebellion.

I do not believe, with many, that the answer to all our industrial problems is to hand all business over to the state. The state can prove just as hard a taskmaster as the individual entrepreneur, with the added handicap of being amorphous and impersonal.

No – the answer to our problems lies in more intelligent management, a better understanding of the problems which managers have to face and solve in a highly scientific and sophisticated age. In this book I have tried to put forward some suggestions as to how management can tackle these problems.

While the opinions expressed in this book are entirely my own – though some are based on the writings of far wiser and more experienced writers – I must acknowledge my gratitude to a number of people for the help they have given me in getting my material into some sort of logical shape and sequence. Among these

PREFACE

is Mr Ralph Glasser, the editor of the British Library of Business Studies series. To his patience and industry and assistance in editing and revision I owe much. I must also thank Mr John Wilkins for his help in checking through the book in its final stages and for pointing out repetitions and non sequiturs as well as typing errors. His experience as a sub-editor, proof reader and journalist has been invaluable. I must also acknowledge my debt to a number of authors and their publishers whose works have been quoted in the text and included in the bibliography. 'History repeats itself, historians repeat each other', as Philip Guedalla once wrote. The same must apply to writers on management. This is not only inevitable but salutary. There is now growing up a body of thinking on management subjects, based on the experience of managers and on management research, which, used rightly, can be of great value. Acknowledgements, where possible, have been made in the text – but my debts to such classic writers as F. W. Taylor, Henry Gantt, Mary Parker Follett, Elton Mayo, Lyndall Urwick and Peter Drucker will be obvious.

I wish to thank the following:

Mr. Peter Hardie-Bick for permission to quote from his article in *Management in Nigeria*, July–August 1967, and Mr. E. L. Buesnel from whose course for training Unilever personnel much of the material for this article was drawn; Management Publications Ltd. and Mr. David T. T. Frost for permission to quote from his article in *Management Today*, July–August 1966; Mr. Robert Dorfman for the example of linear programming in 'Linear Programming, a Graphical Illustration' in *Managerial Economics and Operations Research* edited by Edwin Mansfield (New York: Norton & Co., 1966); Mr. J. C. Beresford for the formula from his chapter on stock control in *Operational Research in Management* edited by K. Pennycuick, R. T. Eddison and B. H. P. Rivett (London: The English Universities Press, 1962).

CHAPTER 1

The need for control in modern business

Meaning of control

Business, whether we like it or not, is the means whereby we live. Until comparatively recently business was looked upon as not entirely respectable. I am told that among some undergraduates of the older universities this is still the case. Napoleon referred to England contemptuously as 'a nation of shopkeepers'. Later, in spite of his contempt, England's customers included the greater part of the world. Now we have many rivals in the shopkeeping business, but we still need to be good shopkeepers if we are going to live, and our shop includes workshops as well as shop-windows.

Personally I look forward to the day when business will be largely automatic. Then we can really start to live. But until that day comes – and it appears to be coming fairly rapidly – we must run our businesses as efficiently as possible, whether they be 'big business', with international connections throughout the world, or small businesses supplying a mainly local market; and if business is going to be efficient it has to be efficiently controlled.

What do we mean by control? Let us consider the pilot of an air-liner. He sits at what are called 'the controls'. These enable him not only to operate the aircraft – to go up or down, faster or slower, or to left or right – they also give him information about his height, his speed and his direction. In a large modern air-liner the pilot has to delegate some of these controls to others: to his navigator, his engineer. He is, however, in over-all control of the aircraft and if he gets the wrong information or pulls or pushes the wrong control he and his aircraft are in trouble. So, in business, the management is in control whether it be the chairman, the board of directors, the general manager or merely the proprietor of a small business. Somebody has to be in control, to operate 'controls' and use them for information and action.

THE NEED FOR CONTROL IN MODERN BUSINESS

Accounting and control

The most obvious business control is accounting. Management has to know whether its business is making a profit or a loss. It has to know what it is spending and what it is getting back. Unless it is making a profit, that is getting back more than it is spending, the business will eventually founder. Thus profit is essential to the survival of any business. In order to make a profit a business has to satisfy a market – it has to satisfy the requirement of a body of consumers at the price they are willing to pay; a price moreover which will yield a profit to the business. High volumes of sales do not necessarily mean that a business is making a profit, if the price at which an article is being sold does not cover the total costs of producing and distributing that article.

This is where accounting comes in. Basically the accountant's job is to analyse the costs of the business. Thus 'cost control' is one of the foremost tools of management. Without it management is blundering in the dark, whether it be operating a large international company of the size of I.C.I. or a small village grocery store or motor repair shop.

Financial control

Cost control, however, is only one of many controls required by business today. It is part of a wider system of control usually called 'financial control'. This includes many other factors which will be analysed later in this book. Briefly, however, financial control means the examination of all those factors which go to make up the financial activities of a business.

To start a business as well as to carry it on, capital is required. This applies equally to a nationalized industry like British Rail or the Coal Board as it does to a local hairdressing establishment. Equipment has to be purchased, premises rented, bought or built, staff has to be hired, raw materials purchased and reserves built up for emergencies.

All these need to be controlled. For this reason further controls are needed, such as budgetary control, or forecasting future capital requirements; and stock control, to determine the amount of stocks which should be held, the safeguarding of stocks from deterioration, the turnover of stocks, insurance, storage and so on. As a business grows there becomes necessary some form of staff control, which includes questions of pay, of holidays, of working conditions, of performance evaluation, of promotion, of redundancy and retirement.

Marketing control

Since the object of business is to satisfy a market, however, it is in this field of sales and marketing that some of its most important controls have to operate, and that the maximum amount of information is obtained and acted upon. Many people go into business believing that a market exists for their products because they see a large number of buyers for the product. Too often they find that, though a market may exist, it is already satisfied, and that the only way they can create a market for their own products is by selling them cheaper than their competitors or providing a better-quality article. This they may be unable to do except at a financial loss.

On the other hand potential markets may exist which their competitors have not exploited. But to find such markets requires research and analysis. An established business needs to be constantly on the watch for changes in markets, such as alterations in taste or variations in demand. A market is not a static entity; it is constantly changing and developing, expanding or diminishing. A successful business cannot be static either. It is an essentially dynamic entity, constantly adapting itself to new conditions, new needs and changing circumstances. In order to keep itself fully and quickly informed of these changes, effective controls are necessary. A sales force is not merely a channel for unloading goods upon the market, it should be a sensitive source of up-to-date information about market conditions as a whole. It should constantly be feeding information back to management on changes in consumer tastes, new sources of demand and market developments of every sort. All this information has to be tabulated and stored, to be readily available as a guide for appropriate action and adjustment by other departments of the business.

In order to sell a product successfully a salesman himself must have the maximum information about the market as well as knowing the psychological techniques of salesmanship. He must know what his competition consists of, and something of the methods his competitors employ. He must know something of social psychology and social economics. Above all he must know his own product, its advantages and its limitations. All this comes under the general heading of sales control, together with sales administration, the organization of the sales force and the training of salesmen.

Management as control

It will already be seen that control in business entails a good deal more than sitting in an office chair and issuing orders. A business is always exploring and conquering new ground, like a successful military operation; it can never be content with past gains, but, having consolidated its position, must be ready to advance on a new objective. Also, like a military unit, it must be wisely and effectively controlled. The task of this control lies with management, and, in complicated modern business, the responsibilities of management are great.

It is often said that a manager is born and not made. Today it is recognized that, though a man may possess potential management qualities, they need development to be effective. No doubt there are many people who, lacking the basic qualities of management, will never make good managers; but such are the complications of modern business that a good manager today needs something more than leadership qualities, courage, imagination and tenacity to manage a business effectively. He also needs considerable knowledge of the various techniques of management. These include accounting, business economics, market research, statistics, industrial psychology, quality control, operational research and the various technical sciences with which his business is concerned, whether they be chemical, constructional or mechanical.

It is clear, therefore, that education in a number of skills is essential for a good manager. He does not have to be an expert in all of them, but he must know how to appreciate the work of the specialist and know enough about it to be able to judge the importance and quality of the specialist's work. He must also be able to talk to the specialist to some extent in his own language, appreciate his point of view, and assess it in its correct relationship to other specialist opinions.

The manager must also know a good deal about the world in which he lives and in which his business operates, about its social and economic background and about new trends and developments which are likely to affect his business. This is the justification for the amount of attention which is being paid today to management education and training. But it is doubtful if any amount of management education can produce the character which is basic to management. What this character consists of will be discussed below, but suffice it to say that if it does not exist in embryo it can never be developed, though much can probably be done to eliminate those factors which inhibit it. Experience also helps, but even experience may merely consist of continually repeating the same mistakes. A manager must be a man who can recognize his own mistakes and learn to avoid repeating them. He must also be capable of commanding men through respect and not through fear. Above all he must possess intelligence, which is the power to act realistically in terms of unfamiliar circumstances. A knowledge of management theory is no substitute for intelligence. Intelligence is the power of discrimination as to when and when not to apply a theory; it is the power to assess a situation clearly and apply the appropriate knowledge.

To sum up, a manager is a person who, while possessing the basic qualities of leadership, has acquired sufficient knowledge of business practices to be able to apply them effectively. Business today can afford neither the purely intuitive manager nor the purely theoretical manager. The modern manager must be a mixture of the two because he can never possess *all* the knowledge required to assess a situation fully. He must therefore use imagination and foresight and have the courage to take calculated risks: but he must be capable of calculating them and not merely of acting by guesswork. For this he needs knowledge and training, and a capacity for clear analysis as well as for positive action.

Management decisions

The manager's main function is decision-making; and to make decisions in modern business one must have a maximum of information. When information is incomplete, however, as it only too often is, in spite of controls, a manager often has to make decisions on insufficient evidence, and he must be able to persuade his colleagues that his decisions are the right ones. It is here that integrity is important because unless he is known for his integrity he cannot command the respect and authority to carry his colleagues with him and gain co-operation from his staff, particularly if he has to make decisions which he cannot support with adequate evidence.

Because a manager is human, he is bound, at times, to make the wrong decisions. If he does he must have the courage and humility to admit his error and not blame someone else – a common practice of bad management. This in itself will be evidence of his integrity and it will command respect and loyalty. The manager who is always 'passing the buck' loses the respect of his colleagues, his staff and superiors. He is in fact a bad manager. The manager who tries to substitute theory for realistic action is as dangerous as the manager who ignores theory, knowledge and intelligence and acts exclusively on hunches. Both intuition and knowledge have their place in management and one of a manager's requirements is to know when each is appropriate and the relation of each to the other.

Thus while *controls* are necessary in business to keep managers informed about facts they can never be a substitute for *control*, which implies personal managerial qualities, which can only be observed in action and must be innate in character.

The role of management

The role of management in modern industrial society is to organize the resources at its disposal in order to supply the needs of the consuming public as efficiently as possible and at prices which they are willing to pay. These resources consist broadly of capital, raw materials and labour. Each of these has a number of sub-divisions.

Capital and 'capitalist' have become almost words of opprobrium in some sections of modern society, but without capital no business enterprise is possible whether under communism or a system of free enterprise. In a communist or socialist state capital is obtained either by taxation or appropriation. Under free enterprise it is contributed voluntarily by those who have a surplus of wealth, either through saving or inheritance, to invest in productive activity. Such people expect payment for the loan of their surplus wealth which they receive – or hope to receive – in the form of dividends or interest. Marx called this the 'unearned increment' and looked upon it as rightfully the property of the worker. Its justification is however that it is (a) the reward of saving, (b) payment for risk, or (c) payment for the hire of essential resources.

The idea popularized by Marx, and still widely believed by many, that the manual worker is the only creator of wealth, is based on a fallacy. Work is useless without capital resources and management, without raw materials, organization and marketing machinery. Emerson's legendary creator of the ideal mousetrap would have been ineffective without resources with which to make it and methods by which to market it. Living, as Emerson suggests, in the middle of the jungle he had first to inform the public of its existence, which today is known as advertising. It is doubtful, in fact, if anyone would have beaten a path to his door and more likely that the path-beating would have taken place in the other direction in order to allow some form of primitive transport – a donkey for instance, or a mule – to convey his mousetraps to the nearest town. This would have been the start of his marketing operation.

An historical case in point was the inventor of the spinning mule, Samuel Crompton, who lived in the days when spinning and weaving were domestic industries carried on in the homes of the operatives themselves. Being of an ingenious turn of mind he invented a greatly improved spinning device combining the advantages of the existing spinning jenny with that of the spinning frame – which was the reason for its name.

Though a shy and retiring man Crompton took the results of his invention, a far finer thread than had hitherto been spun in England, to the local market at Bolton and soon caused a stir by its excellence. Hitherto such fine thread had only been spun in India, but now it was available for making the fine muslins for which thread had formerly to be imported. Naturally he was able to charge much higher prices for his product than his rival spinners and, when spinning factories were opened, his mule became the main form of spinning machinery; with certain modifications it still remains so.

Unfortunately Crompton, though a brilliant inventor, was a poor business man; after a fruitless struggle for recognition of his services to the British cotton industry, he died in penury. Arkwright, his contemporary, was an indifferent inventor but a better business man, and by filching and exploiting other people's inventions eventually became a millionaire. Had Crompton possessed more capital and more management ability, he too might have made a fortune. In fact it was the application of these factors by others to his invention which made it the basis of Britain's cotton industry for succeeding generations. No doubt Marx saw this as an example of capitalist exploitation. In fact it was an example of capitalist development, by more competent business management, of the inventor's original idea.

Capital

Capital is generally thought of as money or purchasing power, but of course if it remains merely money it is useless. It must be used to purchase buildings, machinery, equipment and other 'fixed capital assets'. It must also be used to hire labour, for management and to purchase raw materials. Only a small proportion remains in the form of money or credit to fall back on in case of emergency.

Few businesses start making a profit immediately, and resources are needed to carry a business over the interim period of initial establishment, and to subsidize those losses which it is likely to make until it has fully established a market for its goods or services. Even Crompton, with the small resources at his disposal, had to wait until his invention was completed before he could start reaping the benefit from it in the greatly improved yarn he was able to market. His troubles began when he started to market his products and to try to cope with the demand which their great superiority created. It is said that Arkwright himself sent spies to Crompton's garret near Bolton to try to discover his secret, and eventually Crompton was forced to disclose it and part with it for a few thousand pounds to people who soon turned it into millions. Had he been a better businessman and been able to raise capital to develop his invention, he and not others would have reaped the rich rewards of his invention. His case is a warning for all, that, however ingenious or superior a product or an invention may be, it is management skills which are necessary to develop it profitably and successfully.

Industrial history is full of stories of men like Crompton who, with no resources but their ingenuity have (unlike him) become successful businessmen and built up great organizations. One, of course, was Richard Arkwright, another was Henry Ford, another was William Lever and yet another William Morris. Realizing the need for capital, these men took steps to find it: they may have borrowed it from banks, or found friends or relations to help them, but somehow or other they found it; and having found it they used it wisely and constructively to build up successful businesses.

The factor which made these men successful, whereas Crompton was a failure, was that they also had a flair for business management – or if they did not have it themselves, as had been said of both Ford and Morris, were able to recognize and hire people who had. Crompton, being somewhat withdrawn, with few friends, of a rather suspicious nature, and a poor judge of people, failed to find those people who could have helped him to develop his invention for his own benefit. Some people may say that Crompton's story is now out of date. Perhaps so; but it still illustrates the principle that hard work and ingenuity are not enough to make a successful businessman.

Budgetary control

Capital, as we have seen, takes many forms, each of which, in a modern business, involves control. It is just as dangerous to be over-capitalized as to be undercapitalized. Capital costs money, it has a market value. Thus to have capital lying idle involves an unnecessary drain on resources. On the other hand insufficient capital is a prevalent source of failure in businesses which might otherwise be successful. If capital is not available for the replacement of obsolete or outworn machinery or to develop new products to meet changes in demand, a business is heading for disaster. This is why reserves are important, and why budgeting is necessary.

Budgetary control is essential for a successful business. No business can live from hand to mouth, hoping that capital will be available when it is needed. No business can afford to overspend its capital and then find it has nothing to fall back on in time of emergency or necessary development. It must allocate its capital carefully between the various calls upon it. It must observe a proper balance between fixed capital, working capital and reserves. A business, as we have seen, is never static – it is a constant flow of activities, all of which have to be financed; and it is to enable the management to observe the correct rate and allocation of resources, through the various channels involved, that financial control is necessary.

Raw material ties up capital and prevents it being used for other purposes. In a cigarette factory tobacco has to be stored for a year at least and sometimes two years before it can be used. This represents a considerable freezing of capital resources apart from costs of storage, insurance and other charges involved in the prevention of deterioration. A large paper-making firm may have to spend millions of pounds laying down forests for timber which will not materialize as raw material for more than fifty years. A greengrocer's shop has to calculate carefully how much fresh stock to lay in daily without incurring the risk of rapid loss through deterioration. The same applies to a fishmonger or a butcher. With modern methods of refrigeration these risks have been greatly reduced, but refrigeration plants cost money and represent a capital investment.

If capital is not available what other methods can be used, such as loans or hire purchase? All this has to be carefully calculated by small and large businesses alike.

Time is an important factor in financial and budgetary control, because time, as has so often been said, is money. Risk is also an important factor and the whole vast business of insurance has grown up to safeguard business against risk. But insurance also costs money and has to be taken account of in costs.

Reserves are a form of insurance and reserves can be invested. Many firms invest considerable surpluses in order to safeguard themselves against lean years, as a means of bolstering up their revenue if profits should for some reason fall. These investments also provide securities on which money can be borrowed if urgently needed.

Profits

Profits, obviously, are necessary to keep a business alive, but what is done with profits is a vital factor of financial control. Profits are what is left over after all current expenses have been paid – these expenses of course include what are known as 'overheads' or fixed recurring charges which have to be met irrespective of turnover. Such overheads include rent of premises or land, maintenance of machinery and buildings, transport charges, management salaries, storage and power. There are also many other overheads such as lighting, heating, water supply and insurance. The distinction can be made between gross profits, which exclude overheads from costs, and nett profits which include them.

In calculating the costs of a unit all charges have to be included, and this is done in modern cost-accounting with varying degrees of accuracy. In a cigarette factory the actual cost of producing one thousand cigarettes is calculated in terms of all the expenses involved, from the purchase of the tobacco up to the final delivery to the distributor. Proportions of overheads (see Chapter 10) are allocated in accordance with carefully calculated principles, and the prices of brands are fixed on that basis. Ultimately however, it is only in the final annual accounts that profit or loss can be confirmed.

Unforeseen circumstances may – and frequently do – arise which knock previous calculations sideways. Taxation is one obvious example. If inland revenue or import duties are imposed by the government, costs may vary considerably. If floods disrupt railway transport or ships are late or cargoes lost, costs may also vary considerably. Labour troubles and 'go-slow' tactics may also affect costs seriously. All this adds to the complications of financial control but it does not eliminate its necessity or, in the long run, affect its validity. Adjustments have constantly to be made. The ultimate profit and loss account will obviously reflect these variations, and a forecast profit may easily turn into a loss, or even vice versa. On the findings of financial control not only prices but also wages must ultimately be fixed. In those industries where labour charges form a high proportion of costs, correct wage fixing may be an important factor in determining profit and loss. But wages, like prices, involve human, psychological and social factors. You cannot offer a man a wage which he will not accept any more than you can ask a customer to pay a price which he cannot afford.

Dividends

To return to the allocation of profit, however, there are many ways in which this can be distributed. An obvious one is the payment of dividends to those who have invested their money in the enterprise. These dividends, as we have seen, represent compensation to those who have risked their money, or foregone the use of their savings, in order to make the enterprise possible. It is possible and likely that the present shareholders of a public company may have bought their shares on the stock exchange and played no part in the launching of the enterprise. In a private company, however, owing to the limitations on sale of shares, it is probable that most of the shares are held by those who helped to start the business. The same applies to a simple partnership with no limitation of liability.

In a public company dividend policy is linked up with several factors including that of good standing in the eyes of the investing public in the event of a need to raise further capital. If its shares are standing high on the market, as the result of a generous record of dividends, the public will be more anxious to invest in any new issue it produces. A good example of this was a recent issue of shares by Imperial Chemical Industries, which, in spite of a drastic squeeze in purchasing power due to Government policy of deflation, was heavily over-subscribed. A company with a record of low dividends will not find it so easy to raise fresh capital.

Dividends, however, contrary to common opinion, constitute only a small proportion of the ultimate destination of profits. A far larger proportion of profits are generally 'ploughed back' into the business in the form of various reserves or sinking funds towards repayment of long-term loans. Reserves, as we have seen, are essential, not only to meet emergencies but also for necessary development. But reserves which are shown on a balance sheet may in fact not exist at all – they may have already been used in essential capital development. They must, however, be shown as a debt owed by the company to its shareholders since, if the money had not been put to reserve it would have been paid back to them in dividends or as repayment of their investment.

Industrial finance

Today a large proportion of new development is financed by long-term loans, often advanced by governments or government finance corporations formed to develop the national resources of the country concerned. A British company setting up a project in one of the 'developing' countries of Africa or Asia may, for instance, seek aid from the Commonwealth Development Corporation or from the National Development Funds put up by a foreign country. Such loans generally carry a fixed rate of interest and are repayable over a certain period, and this entails the establishment of a sinking fund for the gradual repayment of the principal. In

Britain the larger insurance companies lend funds for capital development as well as the merchant banking houses. The 'Big Five' banks seldom advance money on long term but are available for short-term loans. Merchant bankers both in the U.K. and Europe are more accommodating.

Finance is also raised by debentures, which are long-term loans carrying a fixed rate of interest. They claim a priority of payment over preference or ordinary shares and are secured on the property of the company. Preference shares, as their name implies, can claim dividend payment before ordinary shares, but only to a limited percentage; they may or may not involve voting rights at shareholders' meetings. Ordinary shares, while carrying voting rights, have to take their chance of earning dividends after all other claimants have been satisfied. If the company does well, its owners (ordinary shareholders) benefit by a higher dividend than the owners of preference shares or debentures; if the company does badly the ordinary share dividend may be 'passed' and the share value will fall on the Stock Exchange, being considered to be an unprofitable buy.

One of the objects of financial control is to decide, among these many forms of financing an enterprise, which is the most appropriate, and in what proportions each should be used and can be used. In certain cases new issues of shares are restricted to existing shareholders, and are known as issues of 'right'.

Production control

Production raises a whole host of problems which the new science of method or work study can do much to solve. Production control involves the saving of unnecessary time and effort, the saving of unnecessary expense, the simplification of processes, the maximum utilization of labour, the avoidance of labour disputes, the establishment of effective management relations, the most effective methods of training, the elimination of waste and the avoidance of time lost through accidents. The control of quality and the standardization of products are also important factors in production control.

Management also has to determine, in this context, the advantages or disadvantages of diversification. Is the market for its product a seasonal one? If so, how can labour and equipment be utilized in those periods when demand falls off? It was no mere chance which drove Walls, who were originally sausage and meat-pie manufacturers, to turn their activities to ice-cream manufacture during the summer months. Why has Imperial Tobacco Company started making potato crisps and BAT gone in for paper making and toiletry? What drove Lever Bros., who were soap makers, to become fishmongers and producers of tinned vegetables? What persuaded George Kent and Company of Luton to change from making knife cleaners to making electrical switchgear and various other engineering products? The answer to the last question is, of course, stainless steel.

The small manufacturer is even more vulnerable to changes of taste or to new inventions, to alterations in demand. George Kent saw the red light early enough to be able to adapt themselves to new conditions. Their management was fully alert to a changing situation, so were the management of Walls, now part of the Unilever Group. The small company with smaller resources must be even more alert than the larger companies to safeguard itself against change. What was good enough for a manager's father and his grandfather will not automatically be good enough for the manufacturer of today, when change is rapidly accelerating under the pressure of technological development.

The smaller company

What has been said above applies mainly to the larger public company, but the same principles apply to the private company or partnership – or even to the one-man business. Obviously the methods of finance will not be so complicated or varying, but the same degree of control needs to be exercised over the use of finance in the small company as in the large one. To the small business a variety of methods are available both in raising initial capital and the day-to-day financing of operations.

Many large companies have grown out of comparatively small ones: Morris Motors, now part of British Leyland Motor Holdings, started, as everybody knows, out of a small bicycle shop in Oxford where William Morris, later Lord Nuffield, built his first Morris car. Many small shops have blossomed and become multiple chain stores or world-famous department stores. They have done so because they satisfied, under carefully calculated control, a need of the consumer community. The small businessman can no more afford to neglect methodical control of his business than can Unilever, or I.C.I., or the Imperial Tobacco Company. He can, in fact, afford to neglect principles of control rather *less*, because he has fewer reserves to fall back on and his margin of profit is probably smaller. Whereas a big company can, to some extent, absorb mistakes and write them off as trading losses, the same mistakes made by a small company may easily drive it into bankruptcy.

Obviously the first essential of any company, be it large or small, must be an effective accounting system. This must do much more than indicate whether a business is making a profit or a loss, though this is obviously its first function. An accounting system, for instance, must show which lines of production are more profitable and which are only marginal, or even unprofitable altogether. It is a bad but not uncommon practice in business to allow the more profitable lines to carry the less profitable ones. Obviously if one's accounting system is not geared to showing the difference between them no action can be taken and the management can only work by guesswork.

Sooner or later, however, it will get caught out.

Financial control can prevent this happening. There may be reasons for carrying less profitable or even unprofitable lines, reasons concerned with prestige or non-financial policy; but a businessman should at least *know* what he is doing and why he is doing it, rather than blunder on in the hope that things will turn out right in the end.

Financial control, again, must determine such questions as policy in regard to loans and bank overdrafts. Too often in a small business the servicing of capital is looked upon as something which does not enter into costs, being to some extent variable. In fact these costs may make all the difference between profitability and loss. Rent of premises is also a subject of financial control. A high rent for a tobacconist shop in a populous locality, may in fact be less expensive in terms of turnover than a low rent in a less populated district. The carrying and storage of stocks is also something upon which there must be a carefully worked-out policy. Storage costs money, but inadequate stocks when they are needed may lose considerable business. What is the optimum figure? What information is available? What are the seasonal changes in demand? What lines move faster than others? What safeguards are in operation against loss by deterioration, theft or fire?

A small manufacturing business has much the same problems to face as a retailer. The main problem is how to allocate its resources so as to obtain the maximum profit on capital: how much for instance to spend on advertising, how much on the sales force, on marketing, on transport, on labour, on financial control itself? Many of these things can only be found out by trial and error, by experience and exploration. The information produced by experience and exploration must be carefully codified and tabulated in order to be available when major decisions are required.

Future of the small business

Some people may think there is no room for the smaller company today. This may be true of the small company which is content to remain a small company, but if a man has a good product for which substantial public demand can be created, he may have to *start* on a small scale, but he should be able to build up his business into a larger one. An outstanding example of this is Dexion, a comparatively recent invention which started with quite a small capital and now has ramifications throughout the world. Dexion consists of metal angle strips perforated with holes which can be used to make simple structures rather on the lines of 'Meccano', the children's construction kit. Its success has been phenomenal, very largely through first-class management and enterprise. Owing to its rapidity of growth, one of the major problems of the Dexion Company was to train efficient managers fast enough to take over its growing number of foreign businesses.

Dexion is only one of a considerable number of small businesses which have flourished during the last twenty-five years or so and become of world-wide significance. The reason for its success is two-fold; first, it hit on a new and valuable idea for which a potential demand existed and second, it applied highly efficient principles of management control to the development and marketing of that idea.

There is plenty of room for the small business today (see Chapter 8, pp. 113–14). Changes are taking place hourly, the potential demands of the consuming public are almost infinite. Moreover the facilities for starting new businesses and stimulating new markets have increased enormously and are still increasing rapidly. A man with imagination and drive, with a sound knowledge of management techniques and a determination to succeed, has just as much chance today as had Ford or Morris half a century ago or Crompton nearly 150 years earlier. Crompton missed his opportunity because he lacked managerial qualities and managerial skills – knowledge of which has now been enormously developed.

If anyone thinks that all the good ideas have been thought of he is wrong. Good ideas need not necessarily lie in the field of new products. They also lie in better methods of production of existing products, in better methods of distribution, marketing, transport, financial management and consumer finance. For example, it is not so long since hire-purchase was unthought of. Its effect on industrial and commercial trade has been enormous, and those who originally developed it have made vast fortunes. Millions of consumers may be grateful for the amenities it has brought to them and thousands of manufacturers must be grateful for the markets it has opened up to them. It has brought with it new problems of management which require more rigid controls, but management on the whole has been able to cope with them by the development of new techniques and new methods. Who knows what the future will bring forth?

CHAPTER 2

The functions of management

Management breakdown

In the last chapter we saw how business control is the responsibility of management. Management can be used both as a collective noun for managers, or for the function which managers perform. In the last chapter the word management was used somewhat loosely. In this chapter we shall try to break it down into more detail.

In the smallest firms, management can of course be concentrated in the hands of one person who may act as general manager, accountant, buyer, salesman and possible machine operative, as, for instance in the case of a small village shoe-maker and shoe-repairer or the now nearly obsolete village blacksmith. However, the principles of good management or efficient control operate equally in a small business as in a large one. Some years ago Tube Investments Limited, the owners of some of the largest tube manufacturing companies in the world and also a number of other ancillary companies, wished to make a film explaining balance sheets and profit and loss accounts to their employees. They took as a basis a small village blacksmith's shop and showed how all the same principles operated there as in such a vast business as their own.

As a business grows, however, it is necessary to introduce division of labour; not only in the manufacturing operations, as in Adam Smith's classic example of the pin-making industry, but also in management itself. The village grocer, for instance, who may have started by serving behind the counter and doing his accounts in the evening after shop-hours will find it necessary to employ a shop assistant and later a full-time accountant who may also be a cashier. Later he may employ a delivery van which will require a driver. If he thrives he may open a second shop and possibly a third or fourth, and gradually he will have to divide his business into departments dealing with the purchasing and supervision of stocks, the control of personnel, the supervision of transport and the careful control of cash and accounting transactions.

The grocer himself will have to divest himself of his original day-to-day functions in the shop in order to devote more and more of his time to general management of the enterprise. As his business grows, he will have to set up a central office staffed by people who are experts in functions which may have nothing to do with actually selling groceries.

A visit to the central office of any of the great chain stores such as Boots, Sainsbury's or Marks & Spencer reveals the tremendous ramifications which arise when a small company starts to grow. All these ramifications demand rigid and intelligent control. When one is buying stocks valued at millions of pounds, a mistake may cost the company many thousands. There must therefore be careful checks at every point to ensure the maximum of efficiency and the minimum of waste. Every department must be under the control of an expert in his particular line whether it be accountancy, marketing, advertising, purchasing, stores control, personnel management or transport.

Management objectives

Today there is a lot of talk about 'management by objective'. To return to our earlier metaphor, a company, like a military formation, must be moving towards some objective. In most cases, however, it cannot achieve this objective in one operation. An army's objective may be to defeat the enemy, but in order to achieve this it has to set subsidiary objectives or targets and embody them into a programme. The same applies to industry or commerce.

To say that a company's objective is to make a profit is much the same as to say that an army's objective is to win a war. Obviously if the army loses a war its efforts will have been in vain, and the same applies to a company if it fails to make a profit, since it can only go into bankruptcy. The important question is how it proposes to achieve its objective, and the only sensible answer must be: by providing goods or services which fulfil a need of the community at a price which consumers are willing to pay. This is no altruistic idealism but a matter of pure common sense. If an enterprise does not supply goods or services to satisfy consumer needs, at prices which people are willing to pay, it cannot possibly make a profit or remain in business.

Definition of 'need'

The author of *The Practice of Management*, Professor Drucker, has defined the object of business as 'the creation of a customer'. I find this slightly unsatisfactory because it implies that a customer can be created against his will, so to speak. Before a man becomes a customer he must have a genuine need for something. This need cannot be created, it already exists, though possibly he may not be conscious of it. The legitimate role of modern marketing and advertising methods is to draw the attention of potential customers to needs of which they may not be aware, and to means of satisfying those unknown needs.

The need may be for an existing product at a lower price than that at which it is available; or it may be for a higher-quality product at that price. It is an axiom of the advertising trade that however good the advertising it can never, for long, sell a bad product; and no self-respecting agency would accept the advertising of a product in which it did not have confidence. I, personally, would amend Drucker's definition to 'the creation and retention of a customer'. This definition was admirably illustrated by the case of Sears, Roebuck, which Drucker quotes at some length.

Towards the end of the last century Richard Sears's idea of a business was buying up distress merchandise cheap and selling it dear through spectacular advertising. He made a lot of money in the process but each transaction was a separate speculation and was in no sense building up a business.

In 1895 Julius Rosenwald took over and completely reorganized the business on a basis of careful market analysis and methodical organization to satisfy that market. His market consisted of the middle-western farming community who, though growing in wealth, had no means at that time of getting to the shops to spend it. Rosenwald provided this community with an access to distribution centres hitherto unavailable to it. He brought out the famous Sears Roebuck Mail Order catalogue and made certain, by highly successful management, that all needs within their means could be satisfied. It created a revolution in business and brought in fantastic profits.

The same definition could be applied to Henry Ford or William Morris. Mobility was no new need, but it was one which had only been partly satisfied. The motor car answered the need, and Ford and Morris put it within the grasp, not merely of the wealthy eccentric, but of the middle- to lower-income group. A need existed and was satisfied and both men made enormous profits. Later, by failing (unlike Sears Roebuck) to adjust to changing conditions, the Ford business nearly destroyed itself; but fortunately Henry Ford's grandson was a better business man than his grandfather and took the necessary steps to stave off disaster by complete reorganization of the business on modern lines. This task had already been accomplished for Sears Roebuck by General Robert Wood who, realizing that the original need which put Sears Roebuck on the map had now been satisfied, set about satisfying further needs. (For the whole story of Sears Roebuck, see Peter Drucker's *Practice of Management*, Chapter 4.)

The role of profits

It may be said that my definition of an objective is unnecessary and platitudinous. It is, I believe, very important. We live in an age of Marxism, whether we like it or not, and Marx saw profits as unethical. If profits were the sole end of business there might be justification for this view, and if Richard Sears was a typical business man Marx would be right to consign him to the guillotine. But fortunately he is not. Whether he likes it or not the business man has to consider the community. The community is his customer. He cannot ignore its needs. On the contrary, however anti-social he may feel about it, he must consider its needs very carefully.

There is no evidence that Julius Rosenwald was a philanthropist, but there is abundant evidence that he was a good business man and that he made remarkable profits. He made these profits because he studied the needs of the middle-western farming community of his day and did everything possible to satisfy them. This is not a question of values but of ordinary business common-sense. We must get our priorities right. The reason Marx and his followers hated profits was because they identified them with exploitation. In fact they need not be anything of the sort. They are a legitimate reward for a valuable service to the community; a reward for enabling its members to live richer, fuller, more civilized and more comfortable lives.

Theoretically, in a competitive, free-enterprise system, exploitation becomes impossible because as soon as profits rise beyond a certain height, competition steps in to lower them. If supply exceeds demand the price automatically falls. It is only under monopoly that exploitation is possible, and monopoly, strangely enough, is one of the inevitable results of state control of industry. If upholders of free enterprise and competitive economy had understood this clearly and made it more widely known they would have had little to fear from Marxism or leftist agitation and obstruction. The trouble is that many business men are lamentably bad at public relations and are often extremely poor economists.

There is however, another reason why my definition should be accepted by management; it is the only definition of an objective which leads to profitability. To tell a worker or a manager that his objective is to make profits for the shareholders leaves him either cold or resentful. To tell him that he will only make his business a success by providing a service to the community is to give him a legitimate incentive and a realistic aim. After all, what is quality control? It is a means of ensuring that the customer gets adequate value for his money. What again, is market analysis? It is a means of discovering the needs of the consuming public in order to satisfy them at a price they can pay. Unless the eyes of the business man are constantly focused on the consuming public, their needs, their habits and their way of life, he cannot possibly succeed in business. He may create the most perfect product using all the latest techniques, but unless it satisfies a desire within the means available for purchasing it, all his efforts will be fruitless. His market may be a limited one as was that of Rolls and Royce, but first a need or desire must be identified, and secondly it must be satisfied.

In a competitive economy as we have seen, the need may be for an existing product at a lower price, or a better product at the same price. It may also be an entirely new product or service. The growth of the launderette, for instance, is the result of satisfying the need for cheaper laundry service without the expense of buying a washing machine or the labour of doing one's own washing. The idea was a stroke of genius, but until the invention of the washing machine itself it could not have been developed. This also met a need of the housewife like so many other labour-saving devices.

Secondary objectives

Having fixed our first objective, we may now pass on to the secondary ones. As in a military operation we have to move step by step and consolidate our forces at every point. This is how a business is built up. Few businesses, if any, have sprung fully armed like Minerva from the head of Jove; most businesses have started from small beginnings and built up slowly and gradually. Consolidation is essential at every point. Without it there is danger of being overwhelmed by the 'enemy' before one has established a footing – and business is beset by many enemies, some of which exist within itself. Having achieved a small success, a business too often becomes over-confident and launches into ambitious projects which only end in disaster. One has seen this happen so often, and here control is vital, including control of ambition. Ambition is an excellent thing provided it is leavened with discretion. Without it there would be no progress; but it must be realistic, based on facts, and not merely fantasies or wishful thinking. We have all seen many examples of businessmen biting off more than they can chew and ending in dismal failure.

It is necessary to plan our secondary objectives carefully and approach them one at a time. One is reminded of the story of the young bull who, seeing a field full of cows, said to the old bull at his side: 'Come on, let's charge in and have the lot.' 'No, my boy', said the old bull sagely, 'we will walk in very slowly and have them one by one.' It is easy to be impetuous, more difficult to plan progress wisely. Planning must not be too rigid, but always sufficiently flexible to allow for possible variations and emergencies. The essence of planning is setting objectives and deciding on their priorities.

Marketing Concept

In starting a new business the first step is not, as might be thought, to raise capital. The first is to analyse the market. If the market does not exist no amount of capital will create it, however brilliant the advertising. The first thing is to find a need which is not being fully satisfied. The next is to work out how that need can be satisfied at a price which is acceptable to the consumer and which yet leaves a profit to the business. This means an analysis of costs, of sources of raw material, of availability of labour, of equipment, of channels of distribution of management ability and technical know-how. Many people go into a business because they think they know its technicalities. They have worked for a firm in the same line and want to be on their own. They may be production experts but what do they know of marketing – or vice versa? What do they know about finance? – of accounting? – or budgetary and stock control? One can always hire a good accountant, they may say. But can they? And how are they able to judge who is a good accountant?

Far be it from me to discourage any enterprising person from setting up on his own, but let him consider carefully just what it must entail. It can still be done successfully, but it isn't as easy as it used to be. Business is more complicated now than it was in Samuel Crompton's day, and even he was a tragic failure. One has to know more about business. One cannot afford to be illiterate, in spite of Somerset Maugham's story of the illiterate verger who was sacked for being unable to read or write and became a millionaire. Even barrow boys have to fill up forms today and they must learn how to bank their takings. Life is more complex now for the average businessman, and he must understand accounting even though he employs an accountant. How else is he to know whether he is being cheated?

Having decided that a market exists and that means are available to satisfy it and develop it, the next objective is to raise capital. Perhaps one has one's own supply, one's savings or an inheritance. Fine. But by putting it into this business, is one going to get a greater reward than if one invested it wisely, or put it aside for one's children? If an idea is good and a plan is worked out sensibly, capital should be obtainable without encroaching on one's savings. There are plenty of means of raising it.

Business structures

A business can take one of four main forms today; the one-man business, the partnership, the private limited company, or the public limited company.

The word 'limited' means that if the business goes bankrupt the owners, namely the shareholders, cannot be held liable for the company's debts beyond the amount of their shareholding in the company. A one-man company or a partnership is liable for the whole of the company's debts to their full amount and the owner or owners can be called upon to forfeit their own personal property to pay these debts if necessary. The reason the word 'limited' has to be incorporated in the title of the company by law is so that potential creditors will be aware of the limitations of the company's liability. The original legislation establishing limitation of liability was a great incentive to capital development, because it freed potential investors from the risk of having to forfeit their own personal possessions if the enterprise to which they gave financial support went bankrupt.

The private limited liability company does not offer its shares for sale in the public share market or 'stock exchange'. There are also limitations regarding the amount of information it is legally obliged to reveal to the Registrar of Companies concerning such matters as the salaries paid to directors. It is in fact, virtually a private partnership with limited liability regarding payment of debts. It generally restricts the sale of shares to those originally within the company. An outsider can only buy shares in it provided the directors agree. If an original shareholder dies, the shares remain within his family.

Many private companies fall by the wayside, often through lack of sufficient initial capital or lack of managerial ability. A large number of successful private limited companies eventually turn themselves into public companies: that is to say they offer their shares to the public with the object of raising further capital for expansion.

One of the legal obligations of a public limited company is that it must disclose its annual profit and loss account and balance sheet to the public. It must hold at least one general meeting a year, which all its shareholders are invited to attend. The shareholders have to approve the profit and loss account and balance sheet, and appoint directors and auditors to ensure the efficient running of the company. They also have the right to call an extraordinary general meeting of shareholders if they wish to do so. In fact the shareholders are the legal owners of the company and they have a right to vote at meetings in accordance with the number of shares they hold.[1] Certain changes in the constitution of the company can only be made if approved by a 75 per cent majority of the shareholders, others by a 51 per cent majority. Directors, having been elected by the shareholders, hold office for a limited period, after which they have to retire and may be re-elected. Directors, like the auditors, are servants of the shareholders whose interests, as owners of the company, they represent.

Thus shareholders exercise control of their company through the board of directors, which is responsible for running the company efficiently and profitably. In most cases today the majority of directors are also executive managers of the company itself. The so-called 'guinea-pig' director, like the one-time 'sleeping partner', who is only associated with the company for show or prestige, is rapidly becoming rare. A director is expected to work for the company in one way or another, though possibly he may be elected for his influence in high places, his experience in public service or his standing in public esteem. Nevertheless a man may be, and often is, a director of several companies. He is generally expected himself to own a shareholding in the company of which he is a director and he generally receives a fee for his services as a director.

Holding companies

Many successful companies today are financed by what are called 'holding companies', whose main business is to supply finance and financial control to smaller companies within the group. With increased diversification in industry and commerce, one large company, such as Unilever, for instance, may embrace a large number of industrial and commercial activities spread throughout the world. The holding company owns shares in these subsidiary companies and keeps an overall controlling eye on them. They supply those services which are more economically provided centrally, such as advertising, managerial recruitment, supply of

---

[1] Certain shares may not entitle the holder to a vote. They are generally preference shares, carrying a fixed rate of interest.

raw material and financial management, while leaving the separate companies a good deal of leeway in the day-to-day management. They act mainly as advisers, and because they are generally majority shareholders in the subsidiary, they can exercise a final control and act as arbiters where necessary.

Provided a subsidiary company is managed efficiently and profitably, the holding company seldom has to interfere beyond laying down broad lines of policy. It is only when local management fails that the holding company has to intervene. The same applies to the shareholders of any company. Provided the company is operating smoothly, the shareholders do not need to exercise their powers. It is only when things go wrong or when some major decision has to be taken, such as one concerning an amalgamation or a 'take-over', that special general meetings are held or shareholders become galvanized into action.

Functions of directors

In the smaller or medium-sized company the directors are generally *all* executive managers; they have to wear 'two hats' in the current phrase. They are responsible for an active department as well as for managing the company as a whole. As directors they are the servants of the shareholders while as managers they are the servants of the board of which they are members. There should be no conflict, but conflicts do sometimes arise, and these it is the chairman's business to resolve, both as a servant of the shareholders and of the company as a corporate entity. Though a company belongs to the shareholders it also has a corporate existence in which the shareholders are only one contributor.

Just as the company is dependent on the shareholders, so the shareholders are dependent on the company, and the company is a social organization in relation to which all members have certain rights and obligations. A shareholder contributes capital, but the members of the company contribute work and managerial ability and are dependent on it for their livelihood. It is therefore unrealistic to identify a company solely with its owners. It would be equally unrealistic to identify a man solely with his stomach; just as a man is very much more than his stomach so is a company very much more than its shareholders, or even its board of directors.

THE FUNCTIONS OF MANAGEMENT

An overseas example

Let us take as an example of cigarette-manufacturing company employing about four thousand people in a country overseas. The company consists of three main divisions: production, sales and tobacco leaf-buying. It has four factories at various distances from each other and generally divided by several hundred miles. It also has four sales branches and nine leaf-buying depots. All these are controlled from the head office in the main commercial town in the country. At Head Office is located the chairman and his board of directors. Each director is responsible for one of the divisions of the company, as for instance Production, Sales or Leaf. Another director is responsible for finance and another acts as secretary of the company. In most companies there is also a personnel director, or a personnel manager who reports directly to the board or possibly to the company secretary.

The sources of tobacco leaf are two-fold. Some tobacco is imported from overseas, mainly America, the rest is grown in the country itself. It is the Leaf Director's responsibility to ensure that there is always enough for each type of tobacco to supply the cigarette factories with raw material for their total production programme, which probably runs into several millions a day and hundreds of millions a year. To help him, the company has set up nine leaf-buying depots for the purchase of local tobacco in the various tobacco growing areas.

Each depot is under a depot manager, whose job is to buy a scheduled amount of tobacco as each buying season comes round, at a price which leaves a margin of profit to the company after processing and manufacture. His responsibilities are quite considerable, particularly when he is competing against buyers from other cigarette-making companies. He must ensure that the quality of tobacco is consistent with the company's requirements and that the price is such that the price of the cigarettes made from it is not above what people are prepared to pay, while yielding the company a reasonable profit. He will be guided by his Leaf Director on quantity, price and quality, but he still has to use his own discretion; costly mistakes can easily result if care and judgment are not exercised. Buying leaf is a gruelling job in a hot country and it is easy to be misled about quality. The leaf buyer also has to grade the leaf. He may easily make a mistake in grading which may cost the company a large sum of money.

Production department

Before the leaf buyers get to work however, a great many calculations have to be made in which other departments are closely involved. The Leaf Director can only give his instructions to the depot managers when he in turn has received his instructions from the production department. If he buys more tobacco than is needed, money will be tied up unnecessarily. If he buys too little, factories will be unable to meet their quotas and valuable profit opportunities will be missed. His purchases of tobacco, both local and imported, will depend on the production programme, and this has to be worked out by the Production Director in consultation with his factory managers and in accordance with the productive capacity of their factories. The number of machines available, the speed of production and the output and skill of machine operators are obviously relevant factors. Each factory consists of three departments: Leaf Conditioning, Cigarette Making, and Cigarette Packing.

When leaf is brought into the factory it has most of the moisture taken out of it because duty is paid on weight and there is no point in paying duty on moisture. Once duty has been paid the leaf has to be 'conditioned', which entails greatly increasing its moisture content and making it pliable and soft. The next process is to blend the various leaves in accordance with each brand to be made. They then have to be shredded and cut. The stems have to be removed and fed back again after being separately treated. All this is done by machinery requiring certain degrees of skill in its operation. The moisture has to be removed again to make the tobacco suitable for feeding into the cigarette-making machines. The cigarettes are then stored for a short period before being put through machines which automatically feed them into packets. They are sealed and packed into cartons ready to be despatched to the distributors.

It is the Factory Manager's duty to see that all there operations are harmonized so that a continuous flow is maintained of each brand of cigarette required. If several brands are being made, then he has to allocate different machines to each brand and make sure that the correct blend of tobacco is put into each brand. Each department – conditioning, making and packing – is under the control of a senior supervisor, who is in control of several junior supervisors. Below them are section supervisors each of whom controls a group of machines.

Sales department

How does the Production Director work out his production programme? Like the Leaf Director, he too must have information, and the information must come from the Sales Director. It is no use making cigarettes unless there is a reasonable chance of selling them, and it is the Sales Director's job to provide the production department with estimates of output figures of each brand of cigarettes, over given periods, to meet sales estimates.

For accurate information the Sales Director has to rely on his sales branch managers, who in turn rely for information on their sales supervisors, one of whose duties is to report regularly on market changes within their areas. It is on the reports of these sales supervisors, whose job of reporting back is just as important as that of selling cigarettes, that the success or failure of the company may well depend. It is the sales supervisor's job to keep his finger constantly on the pulse of the market in his area and to report on all relevant developments which may affect the sale of particular brands and also of competitive products. On their reports are built up, at the end of each year, a sales forecast for the following year, and on this is based the production programme.

On the production programme in turn is built up the leaf-buying programme, but here there is an added complication, because leaf which is bought in one year is often not used until several years later. Thus the Leaf Director always has to be looking ahead. He has to plan his programme on something like a five-year basis and he has to ensure that in each year there is enough tobacco of all grades, whether imported or local, to meet the future production programme.

Fortunately no duty has to be paid on tobacco until it is actually used in the factory, when the excise representative watches the weighing out of tobacco and assesses the duty payable. Imported tobacco is bonded in the warehouse and duty only paid when it is released. It represents a large capital investment which it is the

Financial Director's job to minimize while ensuring that production needs are met. In the buying season vast sums of money are paid out to the tobacco growers in cash, which can only be recovered from future sales over a period of two or three years. Conversely, the revenue from one year's sales represents a recovery of cash paid out two or three years before. As revenue from sales does not always coincide with large cash payments for leaf, however, it is the Financial Director's job to arrange that sufficient cash is available at the time it is needed for purchases. This is why the overdraft figure in the balance sheet often appears somewhat higher than might be expected. But overdrafts cost money in interest, and careful control has to be exercised to ensure that borrowing is kept to a minimum. Thus the Leaf Director, the Production Director, the Sales Director and the Finance Director and their respective departments are mutually dependent on each other, and each has to exercise controls at all levels to ensure the maximum efficiency and the smoothest possible flow of operations.

Supply department

Most production companies have much the same problems as the one I have described, though the products may be different. In some cases all raw materials may have to be imported. Even in the cigarette making industry there are other raw materials besides tobacco, all of which have to be made available at the right time and in sufficient quantities. One of these is cigarette paper, another is paper board for packages, another is cellophane and foil, another is wrapping paper. Some of these can be obtained locally, others have to be imported. To ensure their constant supply at the time and in the quantities needed is the responsibility of the Supply Manager, who is not only responsible for purchasing of supplies at economic prices but also for their storage and maintenance. This entails a large number of controls and also considerable decentralization. Stocks have to be at the right place, at the right time, in quantities which are required. This may involve serious transport problems as for instance in a country like Pakistan where the Head Office supply department, located near the port of entry of most imports, is separated from important factories by 1,000 miles of alien territory entailing a sea journey of two or three weeks.

Such contingencies have to be allowed for and calculations adjusted.

I remember visiting a soap factory abroad, belonging to a well-known international company, where productive capacity has been down to 20 per cent for six months owing to government restrictions on the import of certain essential raw materials. Problems of management often arise in overseas countries which require the greatest ingenuity and management skill to solve. This may explain why at least one great international company invariably sends its promising young men abroad to manage one of their overseas branches or subsidiaries before promoting them to higher responsibility at home. As a training ground for resourcefulness and initiative, experience in overseas countries is most valuable.

Decentralization

We have sketched the responsibilities of a board of directors in a fairly typical overseas company and described the duties of their subordinates, each of whom has a certain degree of responsibility and authority. Owing to the wide spread of operations in the company I have described, branch managers have to exercise a good deal of discretion and initiative in dealing with problems as they arise. Head Office is sufficiently far away for them to be able to exercise a fairly free hand and they do so. A branch manager at a factory some 800 miles from Head Office cannot keep referring back to the Production Director or the Personnel Manager. Very often he has to take quick action on his own responsibility. Sometimes he makes a mistake, but mistakes are to be expected. On the whole they are relatively infrequent. Responsibility is graded in accordance with authority. Decentralization is essential within reasonable bounds of supervision. A regular system of reporting ensures that communication is kept open. Disagreements may arise, and often do, between senior and less senior executives but they can usually be solved by sensible consultation. The junior manager has a duty to keep his superiors informed not only of all relevant facts but of ideas he may have for improvement. A junior should never be afraid to voice a genuine opinion and if necessary to stand by it. If he is finally over-ruled he must accept the fact with grace and not bear resentment against his seniors who over-ruled him. He must remember that he is part of a team, all of whom must have the same objective, to make the company successful in achieving its aims. These objectives must be made clear at the outset.

CHAPTER 3

Human relations in management

Business as an organism

A business is not just a collection of people any more than a house is a collection of bricks. A house, like a business, has to be planned with certain objectives in view. A house has to withstand the weather as a business has to withstand competition – that it so say it has to make a profit. But a house has many subsidiary objectives just as a business has. Unlike a house, a business is a dynamic entity, not a static. In this respect a business is like a machine. But unlike a machine it has the capacity for growth and development, and is therefore more like an organism which is always developing and changing and adapting itself to its environment. A business is a living thing and it is composed of living people, and no two people are alike though they may have common characteristics. The science of psychology is an attempt to analyse human motivations and reactions and draw universal conclusions from them. It can probably never be an exact science but it can teach us something about how human beings, or at least the majority of them, may react to given sets of circumstances.

Incentives

It used to be thought that the only effective motivation of human beings was money. This has been proved a fallacy. Nobody wants money for its own sake and most people want it for different reasons. Once the basic needs of existence have been met (that is food, clothing and shelter), people differ greatly as to why they need more money, if, in fact, they need it at all. Some people are quite content to earn merely sufficient to keep them from want and starvation, others are more ambitious: they want may money for power, for indulgence of certain interests, to achieve a certain social status, to protect them from future hardship or to broaden their range of possessions. Others are less concerned with money than with prestige and status; they like authority over others; some enjoy responsibility. In a well-run business these factors have to be considered.

Human variations

The first thing to realize is that each person requires the appropriate kind of stimulation to make their maximum contribution. The old idea that management's job was simply to tell people what to do has now given way to the realization that some people resent being told what to do, while others insist on being guided and are lost without positive direction. Both can contribute to a business if handled tactfully and sympathetically. The main object of a manager is to engender maximum co-operation in achieving a given objective, not merely to be an autocrat whose subordinates act as automata. A man who is promoted from the shop floor to the ranks of supervisory management often believes that in order to carry out his new duties he must change his personality and 'boss his men around'. The results are often disastrous. From being a popular worker he becomes an unpopular foreman and is unable to get the co-operation which, as a worker, he might have commanded.

Leadership

A foreman, on the other hand, has to exercise some control, and a weak foreman commands no more respect than an autocratic one. The answer does not lie in compromise; it lies in qualities of leadership. A leader is very different from a driver. Men follow a leader because they want to, not because they are afraid of the consequences of disagreeing with him. These qualities may be inherent or they may have to be developed. Hence the emphasis today on supervisory training.

The foreman/supervisor

The supervisor is part of management, and to shop floor workers he is the embodiment of management because he is most closely associated with it. 'Management' to many is merely a remote body of people who make the ultimate decisions. The man who interprets management decisions on the shop floor is the foreman or supervisor. He is, in fact, the first line of control and, as such, needs to be carefully considered as a key man in the management hierarchy. In the past he received too little consideration and was often not only confused himself, but also a source of confusion to others.

Today the foreman/supervisor is being recognized as an important link in the management chain without whom control, however good it may be at the top, breaks down at the very point where it is needed most, in actual control of the work force.

Today he needs to know a great deal more than he did in the past. He has to understand certain techniques such as quality control, cost control, safety control, waste control, personnel control, incentives, method study, planning control, and operational control. Even if he does not operate these controls himself he has to understand their purpose and how they work and contribute to success. Many supervisors complain bitterly that so much of their time is taken up with paper work and returns that they have not time to supervise. This complaint may be legitimate and it is management's job to regulate the supervisor's work so that he is not snowed under with such details that he cannot exercise proper control over his workers. Nevertheless he must know what is happening and see why such controls are necessary and why his cooperation is essential. In the long run these controls are there to help him, to enable him to do his work more efficiently, but if nobody has explained their purpose, how is he to know this? To him they merely represent so many more extra chores to interfere with his 'legitimate' duties which are to get, as he believes, the maximum work from his men.

Method study

For instance, the object of method study and work measurement is to analyse a job in such a way as to eliminate waste of effort, waste of time and material. In its early days it met with considerable resentment from workers who saw it as a means of getting more work out of them without more pay. Today it is becoming recognized as a means of increasing productivity by reducing effort and eliminating unnecessary fatigue. If the supervisor can show this to the worker and co-operate with management in its analyses, he can do a great service to the business; but if he himself is ignorant of the objects and methods it employs, he is helpless in face of labour resentment and may only make matters worse.

Group psychology

The foreman is the leader of a group and as such must know something about group psychology. He must be able to recognize the differences both between each individual in a group and between a group and a mere collection of people. He must recognize that a group is a team which is actuated by a common objective. It is his job to ensure that it is positive and constructive. He may know these things instinctively, he may have to learn them by painful and often costly experience, or he may learn them from others. The sooner he learns them the better.

A foreman must know the rudiments of costing and probably something more than the rudiments. He need not be an accountant but he should appreciate the common sense of accountancy. He must be supremely waste-conscious and be always on the alert to discover and reduce waste. He must also be safety-conscious not only in the interests of his men, for whose well-being he is responsible, but also for the sake of the business whose productivity, and consequently whose profits, can be seriously affected by loss of time through accidents. Needless to say he must thoroughly understand the technicalities of the job he is supervising. If he does not he will not command respect. At the same time proficiency on the specific job is not necessarily a qualification for a good foreman. To promote a man solely because he is a proficient worker may merely be to lose a good worker and gain an indifferent supervisor.

Selection of supervisors

The selection of supervisors is a highly important function of management and is all too often neglected or conducted without proper consideration. A bad foreman can cause untold havoc in a factory or on a work site and cost a company a great deal of money in labour troubles, rejected work and general inefficiency. Something industry has sadly neglected is the adequate training of foremen, and it was only comparatively recently that the need for supervisory training was recognized at all. There are still many companies who believe that a foreman can pick up all he needs to know by experience. Possibly some may be able to, but it may be an expensive process in time lost through labour disputes and bad work. It is safer not to take chances, but to ensure that supervisory management is given as much knowledge as possible in the techniques required.

Graduate foremen

In the U.S.A. it has become the practice of some companies to recruit university graduates for supervisory jobs as a training for future management responsibility. Such a policy has its drawbacks in that it causes resentment among those supervisors who came up the hard way from the ranks. In England such a practice is rare and probably rightly so. It has been recognized that a university graduate has much to contribute to management; instead of making him a foreman he is usually taken on as a management trainee or graduate apprentice, which is generally considered a better method of training. For one thing a foreman needs actual experience of working conditions, which a graduate seldom possesses. The foreman's approach is strictly practical and down to earth, whereas a graduate's may be more theoretical. A foreman needs to know his men, and he should do, having worked with them. The graduate is more likely to be rather remote, having come from a different background or, if from the same one, may have arrived by a different process of conditioning. A man with a university education is not trained to be a good foreman, but he may have the qualities of leadership combined with certain mental qualities which are needed today by higher management but not essential to foremanship. Many foremen have risen to be managers and even to be heads of great businesses, but they are exceptions.

Until we get equal opportunities for all and a consequent classless society, the best foremen are likely to be those men who, recruited from the shop floor, show qualities of leadership and intelligence beyond those of the majority of their fellow workmen. They have a right to look forward to supervision as a natural reward for their abilities and, if they can, to rise higher. To frustrate their chances of promotion by filling their places with graduates seems to me unfair and unpractical as experience in the United States has frequently shown, in spite of the far wider opportunity for a university education which prevails there.

Span of control

One word is perhaps necessary here about the supervisor's span of control. Obviously this will depend to some extent on the type of business, but it is a mistake to narrow it excessively. If the span of control is too small, the foreman may well feel frustrated; if it is too big he may find it unmanageable. It used to be the fashion to lay down definite limits to the number of people over whom a man could exercise direct supervision. In practice a foreman may find himself responsible for a group of anything from 10 to 100 people, sometimes even more. Beneath him he may have assistants or charge-hands responsible for smaller groups.

One rule which can be laid down is that a supervisor should never be in control of so large a group that he does not know each member of it fairly well. The size of his group is nevertheless to some extent a symbol of his status. A good foreman would rather be stretched to his full capacity than feel his powers are only half utilized. As a part of management he likes to feel that he is managing something significant and the size of the group of which he is in charge may well stimulate him. Moreover, the channel should always be open to further promotion if he can earn it. This however raises certain questions of recruitment for management which will be dealt with below.

Junior management

We have mentioned at some length the foreman or supervisor because his position is a key one. We must now turn to his immediate superior in the management hierarchy, namely the junior manager. The junior manager must never be looked upon as static; he must be seen as a potential senior manager and possibly a potential director. Like the junior officer in one of the services, the junior manager is useless if he remains a junior manager for long. In the services it is a very good rule that if a man has not achieved a certain rank by a certain age he is judged redundant and compulsorily retired. To some this may seem rather ruthless, but it is a wise rule making for efficiency. No job should be looked upon as an end in itself but only as a stepping stone or training ground for the next job higher up.

Management development

Since a business is a dynamic entity, a stream of activity and not a stagnant pool, senior management must always be planning ahead and this applies particularly to recruitment for the management team. The modern phrase 'management development' does not only mean developing individual managers, it also means developing the management team in such a way that it will be adequate and effective to meet all future contingencies, including expansion of the business and inevitable vacancies in future years due to retirement or resignation.

A wise management development policy should be looking at least ten years ahead in planning for future requirements. Wise selection for management is essential to the progress of a business, and a haphazard hope that the right people will be there to take over responsibilities, when they are needed, is likely to be disastrous. In fact it has often proved so, and many highly successful businesses have eventually fallen behind or even packed up completely because of lack of management development planning. A business cannot be built on chance or pious hopes. It must be planned progressively, yet in such a way as to remain flexible and able to react to current changes. Such planning and flexibility must be built into its structure, and in no department are they needed more than in the planning of management development.

Management recruitment

The first stage, of course, is recruitment. We are now talking of the established business – the new business is rather different. How do we find and develop the material for future effective management?

A number of sources of recruitment for managers are available. One, as we have seen, is existing supervisory staff. A manager is more than a supervisor, though a supervisor is a manager. Has the average supervisor the qualities of a senior manager? If not we cannot make him a junior manager knowing he will always remain one. If we believe he has the qualifications to become a senior manager then we should promote him, while realizing that he may lack some of the educational background which we require in such a manager. It will then be the company's business to help him to acquire that background if it thinks him capable of doing so. If not, then he should not be promoted.

I have seen many painful cases of men with excellent supervisory qualities floundering hopelessly as managers because they could not acquire the background necessary to the task of management. It requires a high order of intelligence, of capacity for adaptation, to develop one's habits of thought and behaviour into those required by senior management. The older the man the more difficult this often is. If I were asked to define intelligence I would say it is the power to keep the mind open, to avoid falling into habits of conventional and second-hand thinking: to be constantly able and prepared to adapt oneself afresh to new ideas and to new ways of looking at things; to be capable of taking a realistic and objective view of things, to be critical and alert, and to be *aware* in the widest sense. Not many people have this capacity, but those who do are likely to make good managers. They are creative and constructive thinkers and generally wise in action because they can see the logical consequences of their decisions and the factors involved in any given situation. Intelligence includes imagination but not mere wishful thinking. For a good manager, it must also be accompanied by a degree of emotional stability that enables him to judge clearly without prejudice or passion.

Such qualities may be discerned by tests or they may only emerge in experience. In selection one can only use all possible means to eliminate those who manifestly do not possess them, bearing in mind that such qualities may lie hidden beneath the surface.

It used to be believed that these qualities were developed by the public school system of education which gave a man self-confidence and self-reliance and taught him to think independently. It could on the other hand also have the opposite effect and make men into slaves of convention and stamp out all initiative. It was thought to be, in other words, a testing ground from which those with strength of character and courage emerged all the better, while the weak and the timorous went to the wall. The process was somewhat ruthless and far from the bed of roses some left-wing politicians have tried to paint it! It certainly developed leaders of the type needed to build an empire and it is probably still developing men fit for leadership in business. But of course it was not the only such breeding ground, and many leaders have emerged from very different environments. In the old days many public school men inevitably went on to universities; today far more young men are going to universities by right of academic merit who never went to public schools.

At universities it is generally believed that people are taught to think critically, objectively and analytically. If so it would appear that universities are the best recruiting grounds for management. One large company I know believes this. It argues that since universities are now far more selective than they used to be and hold out far wider opportunities, only the best pass through them. The argument may be sound, but one has to bear in mind that the basis of selection for a university is academic, and character is not necessarily a qualification. In management, character is necessary as well as intelligence, and even intelligence can manifest itself outside academic circles. This leads us to an examination of exactly what we mean by character.

Character

We have already thrown out some hints regarding the qualities which go to make up character such as integrity, courage, emotional stability and so on, but as character is such an essential requirement of managers (that is to say of those who will be or are in control of business) it is worth examining these qualities in rather more detail.

Character is not quite the same as what is often called 'personality'. A man may have a 'charming personality' and be generally acceptable to all kinds of people but he may often, in times of crisis, show signs of weakness or cowardice, of unreliability or even dishonesty. Character is something deeper than personality, that enables a man to weather all storms and remain steady and effective under the most extreme strains and stresses.

Hackneyed though it may be, and often derided as it is, it is possible that in his well-known poem 'If', Rudyard Kipling described as well as anybody has yet done the qualities which go to make up what we call 'character'.

Character is the result of a certain innate attitude to life, an attitude guided by certain fundamental principles and not by mere conformity to convention or custom. It includes being able to stand by one's principles even when they are unpopular or even harmful to one's own immediate personal interest.

An illustration is shown in a recent American training film. A man who has been out of work for many months comes home to his wife laden with purchases made out of his first day's pay in a job he has just landed. The job is selling a cleaning fluid from door to door. This fluid is supposed to remove all stains, including ink stains, on immediate application. To demonstrate it he pours ink from a bottle supplied by the manufacturers on to a piece of material and then cleans it off with the product. He has made a considerable number of sales and demonstrates the product to his wife. Finding the ink supplied by the manufacturers has run out he uses a bottle from his house only to find, to his dismay, that the stain remains exactly as it was after application of the cleaning fluid. The 'ink' supplied by the manufacturer is obviously a phoney chemical resembling ink in order to deceive the customer. He realized that he had been selling the product under false pretences and that his customers have been cheated.

Instead of blaming his employers, he shoulders the responsibility of his actions and decides to pay back the money he has been paid for the product, in spite of the sacrifice involved. He realizes that his judgment was at fault and that he allowed himself to be influenced, by his own distress and humility at being unemployed, to accept a job which was questionable. His inborn integrity prevented him from profiting, as he could have done, by something he recognized as dishonest.

This is one illustration of character. A man with character does not blame others for his own mistakes whether they be his superiors or his inferiors in status. He takes full responsibility for his actions and those of others. If he disagrees with the orders given him he says so, and if his subordinates disobey him he recognizes that it is his fault for being a bad leader. Only thus will he gain respect either from his superiors or his subordinates. This calls for a certain degree of courage and also of emotional stability. A man of character does not allow himself to be carried away, or his judgment to be distorted by emotional considerations, by prejudice, favouritism or personal dislike of individuals.

Above all, a man of character is a man who can keep his head and remain calm in times of crisis, who, when everything seems to be going wrong, can yet exercise his intelligence and such wisdom as he may possess to find a way of putting things right. A man of character is also a man of sympathy and consideration for others, who does not put himself and his own advantage first but who recognizes the rights and needs of others and does his best to satisfy them, in so far as he can, within the achievement of the objective in view. He is a man who gives his best to the job he is doing, who does not skimp his work or try to evade responsibility. He faces problems squarely and carries assignments through to their conclusion instead of leaving jobs half done, even if it means sacrificing his leisure to do so. He is a man who can be relied on, respected and trusted.

The 'Management Grid' as an assessment of character

How does one recognize character? The main method is by analysis and observation of performance by those who are in a position to observe a man's work closely. A method much in use today is what is known as the 'Management Grid', originally worked out by an American consultant, Robert R. Blake. According to this system a manager is assessed under eighty-one headings set out in the form of a nine-by-nine square. Each square represents a quality of management and the degree to which the manager possesses that quality. A main distinction is whether the individual is people-orientated or production-orientated.

The nine horizontal ordinates are graded as 'Concern for Production', the nine vertical ordinates are graded as 'Concern for People'. A grading of 1·1 is described as follows: 'Exertion of minimum effort to get required work done appropriate to retain organization membership'. At the other end of the scale a 9·9 grading reads: 'Work accomplishment is from committed people: interdependence through a "common stake" in organization purpose leads to relationship of trust and respect'. On the other hand a 1·9 grading described as 'maximal concern for people with minimal concern for production' reads: 'Thoughtful attention to needs of people for satisfying relationships leads to a comfortable friendly organization atmosphere and work tempo', while 9·1 at the bottom right-hand corner of the grid, described as 'maximal concern for production and minimal concern for human relationships' reads: 'Efficiency in operations results from arranging conditions or work in such a way that human elements interfere to a minimum degree'. The 5·5 rating described as 'the middle of the road in both areas of concern' reads: 'Adequate organization performance is possible through balancing the necessity to get out work while maintaining morale of people at a satisfactory level'. First of all a manager is asked to assess himself according to the 81 classifications of 'managerial style'. He is then assessed by the group of which he is a member. Some managers are reported to have broken down and wept on learning how their colleagues rated them in comparison to their own rating. Others are reported to have become changed men overnight.

Dynamic group

The Management Grid is a development of what has been called 'the dynamic group' in which each member of a group tells the others, in turn, exactly what he thinks of them with 'no holds barred'. This too is said to have had certain drastic consequences. Both methods have been called forms of psychoanalysis. Whatever the merits or dangers of these methods, there is no doubt that both self-analysis and objective assessment by others are necessary parts of management development. A manager should not only be able to analyse his weaknesses and shortcomings, as well as his positive qualities, objectively, but should also know how he is rated by the company for whom he works. He should bear in mind that all judgments are subject to human error including his own, and, in fact, particularly his own, since it is extremely difficult to be objective about oneself.

Most firms, if they employ any form of management assessment, use a rather more simplified form; but the principle is roughly the same, though self-assessment is not so common in the U.K. as in the U.S.A.

Value of 'Grid' assessment

The value of the Management Grid appears to be that it is more than an assessment of an individual's personality and character, in that it considers the individual throughout in his relationship to the organization of which he is a part. It can therefore be most successfully applied to a particular work situation, as for instance a company reorganization plan or the setting up of a new department. It can also throw considerable light on why things have gone wrong in a department or a company and how they can be put right. Inevitably it has met with a good deal of opposition from management personnel, probably from those members of it who are least confident of their own ability and possible rating, and resent what they may describe as 'inquisitorial methods'. Rightly used, however, it can probably be of great value, as is suggested by an article by Robert R. Blake, Jane S. Mouton, Louis B. Barnes and Larry E. Greiner in the *Harvard Business Review*, based on research into its application in a practical business situation. (See the *Harvard Business Review* November–December 1964.)

Personnel control

Such forms of managerial assessment come under the general heading of personnel control, which of course includes a number of other factors and situations such as wages and salaries, bonuses, incentives, promotion policy, merit rating, welfare amenities, selection, training, redundancy and retirement and trade union negotiation.

All these problems exist in embryo in the smaller company, but as the company grows, the task of dealing with them needs to be put on a methodical basis and to be carried out in accordance with a policy laid down by higher management. In the small business the owner or general manager is personally in touch with all his employees and can probably be his own personnel manager. He carries out his own assessments of management ability. As the business grows he has to delegate some of these functions and will probably have to appoint someone whose sole responsibility it is to look after personnel matters.

Hence the growth of the art or science of personnel management. This may lead to certain dangers which have recently been considerably publicized. It has been said that personnel management is being used as an excuse for departmental managers to shift their responsibilities, as managers of men, to the personnel department.

This may be partly true. At the same time many departmental managers resent what they look upon as the interference of the personnel department in matters of their own prerogative, such as 'hiring and firing' workers.

Line and staff

This raises the question of the relationship of what is generally known as 'line' and 'staff' management. Theoretically 'line' management is concerned with the direct production of goods and services while 'staff' management acts in an advisory capacity in such matters as accounting, personnel, work measurement, engineering or supply. In fact it is difficult to draw a distinction between the two and this leads to conflict. The object of staff should be to relieve line management of certain ancillary activities which, though necessary, are not its main concern. It would, for instance, be unpractical to expect every departmental manager to keep detailed accounts or detailed records of his departmental personnel. He could also hardly be expected to be an expert in method study, work measurement, welfare facilities, statistical quality control, training methods or network and critical path planning. At the same time he cannot ignore these things because they all impinge on his work.

The ideal situation is that, while handing over these techniques to specialists, he nevertheless has sufficient general knowledge of their uses to be able to see why they are necessary and how they can help him make his department more efficient. Valuable productive time might well be lost if the Departmental Manager became constantly involved in trade union negotiation regarding wages, but at the same time he is bound to be concerned with the feelings of his workers about their pay and conditions, which may ultimately affect his production. He should therefore be consulted at all points that concern him and be glad to be able to leave the detailed work to others more experienced in the actual negotiating machinery. In matters of hiring he should also be consulted but the initial screening process of applicants for work in his department should be done by the personnel department. As far as costs are concerned he is vitally interested, because if his department is making a loss, his will be the responsibility for increasing its efficiency. He will have to tolerate interference from the accounting department and co-operate with it by seeing that all relevant information is supplied.

Discipline

In the question of discipline the Departmental Manager will have to realize that the company has to conform to certain government and trade union regulations and that arbitrary sacking of a man, for example, may lead to serious repercussions having far-reaching consequences on the profitability of the company. In the matter of discipline, therefore, he is no longer his own master and has to abide by the rules of procedure laid down by company policy and administered by the personnel department. He has to accept these limitations in the interests of the smooth working of the company.

Importance of human relations

On the other hand there is undoubtedly a tendency of 'staff management' to usurp authority which is not theirs by right and so cause unnecessary resentment. A zealous personnel department may often appear to the line manager to be telling him his own business and dictating lines of action which he does not agree with. Such clashes are often clashes of personality, but they can be very important and also remarkably costly in time and wasted effort. It is for this reason that the frequent attempts to dismiss the study of 'human relations' in industry as 'poppycock' and 'high-falutin' nonsense' is unrealistic. Ultimately human relations are the bedrock on which all business is built and a failure in human relations may well lead to a failure of the business itself. Through failure to get its human relations on to the right basis, a company could well find itself faced with a serious dispute costing thousands of pounds in lost production, and which could have been avoided by the devotion of a few hundreds of pounds in an effort to eliminate, in advance, causes of discord.

Such efforts might take the form, for instance, of an opinion survey conducted by an impartial observer. It might take the form of installing a 'Management Grid' (see pp. 44–6) investigation, or even the simple action of installing an effective grievance procedure. The basis of all such prophylactic action is first the collection of accurate information and second the provision of means to act on it. Information is often available but action may not be taken, if at all, until too late.

Opinion surveys

I once conducted an opinion survey in a company, after reluctant agreement to such a course had been obtained from higher management. No positive action was taken on it and six months later the company was faced with a strike lasting several months, which lost them thousands of pounds. Had realistic action been taken at the right time the strike would probably have been avoided.

The same applies to management and supervisory training. Unless management insists on such training, even at the cost of a temporary reorganization of production, the ultimate loss due to bad human relations, flowing from uninformed and untrained supervision and management may be enormous.

New methods in human relations

Management today cannot afford to ignore the growing amount of information available as a result of research and experience of better methods of handling human and technical situations. In the U.S.A., whose productivity is about double that of the U.K. and whose standard of living is over 40 per cent higher, the tendency has possibly been too far in the opposite direction and numerous gimmicks have been put forward to increase profitability, some of them highly suspect. But at least the Americans have had the courage to try experiments and generally sooner or later to act on them, though even in the U.S.A. the findings of the Hawthorne Experiment (conducted in the Western Electric Company by Mayo and Roethlisburger), available in 1928, were not fully applied until Roosevelt introduced his New Deal programme several years later. (For a more detailed description of this experiment, see Chapter 4.) British managers on the whole are very conservative people, and tend to be timorous in trying out new ideas. Conservatism and hesitation can be expensive luxuries in running a business.

CHAPTER 4

The control of people

Treating people as human beings

In our last chapter I mentioned the Hawthorne Experiment and the fact that its lessons were not fully applied until many years after its findings. The main lesson of the Hawthorne Experiment is that, if people are treated as people and not mere appendages to machines, their output will increase considerably. For those who may not know the story I will recapitulate it briefly.

In the Western Electric Company in the late 1920's it was found that output was declining and human relations were deteriorating. Higher wages did not solve the problem and investigators were called in from Harvard University. Various control groups were selected and subjected to changes in working conditions such as better lighting, better ventilation and more rest breaks. Output went up remarkably. Then the improvements were withdrawn but output still remained as high as it had been after the introduction of the improvements.

The conclusion eventually drawn was that the mere fact that somebody had taken the trouble to treat the group as human beings and give them some human attention and consideration had stimulated them into higher productivity. Hitherto they had seen themselves as mere mechanisms engaged in a dreary repetitive job; then suddenly they were made to realize that they were part of a productive organism and that their performance was important. This may seem common-sense today but in 1928 this discovery was revolutionary, so revolutionary in fact that the majority of industrial managers refused to recognize its significance. It has been said that common-sense is the most uncommon thing in the world, and there are many people in the industrial field who, either through ignorance or deliberate policy, refuse to apply the lessons of the Hawthorne Experiment – as it has come to be called after the name of the factory where it was conducted. Those firms who have applied the lesson have reaped considerable rewards in increased productivity and comparative freedom from industrial unrest.

This lesson is a very simple one. As the personnel manager of a large British corporation once said to me: 'After all, personnel management is only a new name for what we used to call good manners and courtesy; consideration for the feelings of others.' How true that is, but how few people actually practise it.

On the other hand there is a justifiable suspicion today of what has been called 'paternalism'. Employees have now come to regard consideration as their right, not merely as a patronizing gesture of condescension on the part of management. This is also a matter of good manners. If one does a good turn to someone one does not draw attention to it and ask for gratitude. One does it because one feels it the right thing to do. With the strengthening of trade unionism and its focus on the rights of the workers, management has been forced, often against its will, to recognize that good pay and conditions of work are the only conditions under which it will gain freedom from industrial unrest. But grudging consideration is not enough today, and the worker rightly claims to be treated as a human being, not a mere cypher on the pay-roll or a piece of human furniture.

Living with trade unionism

Today it is necessary to realize that organized labour is in a far stronger position than it has ever been and that its power is growing and is likely to grow even further. It is also realized that unless management can devise a formula to live and work with trade unionism it is in for a very rough time. Trade unionism was brought into being in the past by bad management, and the only answer to trade unionism today is good management. Nor does good management consist in merely pandering to trade unionism, in appeasement or rearguard action. The attitude of management to trade unionism must be a positive one; it must be constructive and co-operative, not merely negative and defensive.

Conflict or identity of objects?

In theory the objectives of management and labour are the same:

namely to provide goods and services to the consuming public at prices which they can pay. Both are performing a public service and this objective should be realized and acknowledged. Management has been at fault in not making this clear at the outset. It has talked too much about profits and not enough about service. It has been suggested that for management to talk about service to the community is hypocritical, because the average businessman is not interested in service but only in making profits. My answer is that if he is not interested in service to the community then he is a remarkably poor businessman and more likely to make losses than profits.

Yet even in spite of management's bad public relations and lack of ability to define its real objective, the trade union movement as a whole has accepted the fact that, at least in the national interest, it should try to raise productivity. The support given by the T.U.C. to the Anglo-American Productivity Council and subsequent productivity effort is ample evidence of this. Trade unionism is not fighting against productivity, it is fighting against exploitation and unfair distribution of profits. The fact that certain trade union action appears to be against the interests of the country is no argument against this fact. The reason for apparently anti-social behaviour on the part of the trade unions is the actual or supposed anti-social behaviour of management. Management has never proved conclusively to labour that its ultimate objectives are not profit for the minority, but benefit for the community as a whole; and the reason it has never proved it conclusively is that it does not, generally speaking, believe it! The result is that though in fact management and labour have basically the same objective, namely to serve the community, neither is capable of realizing it to the full.

Labour management relations

I am stressing this point because I do not believe that management relations with labour, which are vital to progressive industrial development, can ever be put on an effective footing until these basic facts are understood. It is now recognized that a psychological attitude is the most important factor in successful business relations. How can there be a satisfactory and co-operative psychological attitude between two men, when one of them believes he is being exploited by the other and cheated of his rightful dues, and the other not only does nothing to disillusion him but persists in bolstering up his argument?

The T.U.C. has accepted the necessity for management and labour to work together in the common interest of increased productivity, but many of its rank and file still persist in following Marx's doctrine that in fact management is exploiting labour by trying to maximize profits at labour's expense. Is it not time that both Capital, represented by management, and Labour, represented by trade unionism, examined the premises of their arguments and realized they are both wrong? For wrong they undoubtedly are. Only when capital and labour understand that they are both working for the satisfaction of the community, and take steps to work effectively for that objective, will they cease to haggle over the 'nicely calculated less or more' of legitimate profit. Both sides must change their psychological attitudes and accept that management and labour are both composed of human beings with certain fundamental human needs and motivations and qualifications; that the skill of a manager is just as important as the skill of a craftsman and that both command a certain market value, depending to some extent on supply and demand, which cannot be exceeded without serious economic consequences.

Communication in industry

A lot is talked today about bad communication in industry and it certainly is a field in which communication is lamentable. Not only are channels of communication blocked but the material to be communicated is often fallacious. Psychological attitudes have been built up which it may take generations to break down, but broken down they must be if industry is to be fully productive. As long as mutual suspicion, distrust and sense of grievance and resentment persist, management will be unable to exercise effective control and labour to give its best to the community.

Much can be done, however, even by the individual manager, with proper information and training. In the first place he must himself be aware of the lack of any fundamental distinction between himself and those he manages. He must cease to take the view that because he has had certain advantages, or is more intelligent or knowledgeable, he is a better man than those he manages. Differences are only superficial; they may be due to a number of factors over which the individual himself has had little or no control and for which he can therefore take no credit or blame. A manager's job is to manage, not to dictate to people. His job is to get people to work with him to gain a given objective. He is the leader of a team, not a despot. If he does not command respect and obedience it is probably his fault and there is something inherently wrong with him, not with his subordinates. He must ensure maximum, clear communication at all levels, both with his subordinates and his superiors. His means of communication consist very largely of words and he must therefore know how to use words to communicate effectively. The inarticulate manager is of little use today. But if he is to use words to communicate he must also know their meanings and, more important, he *must have something significant to communicate*. He must be capable of clear thought and critical analysis. If not he will only confuse people and block channels of communication.

Self-control

If a manager is going to control others, the first person he must learn to control is himself, not only in the sense of governing his passions and emotions but also in the sense of directing his activities effectively towards the objectives he has set himself. He must always be capable of seeing himself and his activities objectively and realistically, untrammelled by wishful thinking, prejudice or confusion of thought.

It has been said that there are times when a manager has to act autocratically. It would perhaps be truer to say that there are times when a manager has to make unpopular decisions and stand by them. The degree to which he obtains co-operation in carrying out such decisions will depend on the respect for his judgment which he has been able to engender previously. No autocrat in recent history has ever been ultimately successful, as the lives of Napoleon, Mussolini and Hitler amply demonstrate. The political history of England is the history of a struggle against autocracy; it is not a struggle towards democracy because democracy has not been achieved and possibly never will be; all we have been able to do is to put certain curbs on autocracy and to establish certain freedoms. The same process has been going on in business since the early days of the industrial revolution. Management by autocracy is now giving place to management by consent or management through co-operation. The role of labour based on the old master-servant relationship is now giving place to a new role based on collaboration. Wise management has already realized this and is adjusting itself accordingly. It is no use trying to put the clock back. We have to face realities.

The Glacier experiment

An interesting experiment in management was carried out some years ago by the Glacier Metal Company, where production was being seriously affected by constant labour disputes. The managing director, Mr Wilfred Brown (now Lord Brown) decided that action must be taken, and called in the Tavistock Institute of Human Relations and the National Institute of Industrial Psychology to help him devise a method of management which would avoid constant conflict with labour. The result was the establishment of a system of joint consultation which in those days – the 1930's – was somewhat revolutionary.

Hitherto joint consultation between management and labour had only been used to discuss problems connected with welfare, fringe benefits and other such matters. The idea of applying it to major management decisions was unheard of. At the same time matters of wage negotiation had been left severely alone as being within the sphere of trade unions and management only, not of joint consultative committees.

With considerable courage, Wilfred Brown decided to set up joint consultative committees to advise on actual management decisions of the type which, in most companies, would be left to management alone. His justification was that a business is a co-operative venture in which management and labour have an equal interest in making it a success, it was therefore right that all decisions concerned with the success of the company should be discussed with representative bodies of the workers. The effect on production was phenomenal. In the first place it ensured maximum communication on vital topics between management and labour; in the second place it gave labour a sense of participation in the day-to-day affairs of the business so that they felt a sense of commitment to all decisions made and were prepared to do everything they could to make them a success. For further particulars of this experiment the reader is referred to two books: *The Changing Culture of a Factory* by Elliott Jaques and *Glacier Project Papers* by Wilfred Brown and Elliott Jaques.

Labour participation

A number of experiments have been made in labour participation in management, with varying success, since the first world war. In the U.S.A. in the 1920s cases are on record of trade unions actually taking over businesses and running them with great success. In others trade unions have put in consultants to prove to management that they were failing in efficient control, (See *America the Golden* by Ramsay Muir (Williams and Norgate 1927).) Since the second world war, a strong movement has been on foot in Germany to promote trade union participation in management. In England such schemes, like those concerned with profit-sharing, have met with some opposition from management with a few notable exceptions.

The usual argument against them is that it is the business of management to manage and of workers to work, and that the skills and experience of each make them unfit to shoulder the others' responsibilities. The assumption is that any worker who possesses management qualities will, through the ordinary channels of promotion, eventually achieve management status. This assumption is not always justified, for reasons which we have seen. Apart from class background and educational difficulties the line of promotion is frequently blocked by the fact that people are taken direct into management above the heads of potential managers from the shop floor. How far this is so depends on the promotion policy of the company and the manner in which it is carried out.

Joint consultation

Most companies today have some form of joint consultative machinery, and in some cases it is compulsory. The most important factor in its success is whether it is the intention of management and labour to make it successful. Trade unionism is often against it, since a certain body of opinion sees it as a means of bypassing the established role of the trade union as the representative body of the workers, and as their protective shield. Supervisory staff are often critical of it because they see it as a way of cutting out one of their essential functions as a link in communication between workers and management. One has often heard the complaint from a foreman that the workers seem to know more about management decisions than he does and that they get their information quicker. Management is often antagonistic to joint consultation, seeing it as an interference with its prerogative.

The result is that often, though consultative machinery is established, it becomes largely ineffective and deals only with trivialities. Another complaint from the workers is that they lack the necessary educational qualifications to put their case effectively to management, and frequently get shot down by superior management's verbal ability. It is in an attempt to meet this complaint that classes have been set up for joint consultative representatives in the use of words and argument, in chairmanship, and in general meeting procedure. If either or both sides are suspicious of the value of joint consultation it can easily be shown as a failure. Where one side ardently believes in it and is determined to make it a success – or preferably both sides, as in the Glacier experiment – it can be a valuable aid in management. It can however only be based on the premise that in the long run the objective of both management and worker is the same, that is the success of the business by the maximum service to the community. It is also based on the premise that members of management and the work force are fundamentally equal and deserving of equal consideration as human beings. In fact by the mere act of bringing members of both sides together face to face, round a table, it can do much to break down the mutual suspicions and prejudices each may harbour regarding the other. Once more we come back to the human element in business, and the necessity to avoid identifying people solely with their functions, as we do a machine.

The new Industrial Revolution

Today, it has been said, we are going through the third Industrial Revolution. The first was the application of mechanical power to production, on which Britain's economic dominance was built. This led naturally to the second revolution inaugurated by such men as Henry Ford in which the potentiality of the machine for mass production was exploited. This involved new organizational problems which brought forth a new type of manager, whose advent has produced what is called the Managerial Revolution. This in turn is rapidly giving birth to a new revolution: automation.

Each revolution has been a stage in the development of the relationship between men and machinery. In the first industrial revolution, men were displaced by machinery but soon absorbed again into industry by the tremendous growth of business made possible by the machine. The second revolution was based on the adaptation of production to mass, uniform markets. 'A customer may have a car any colour he likes', said Henry Ford, 'provided it is black.' The demand for black Model T Fords showed that standardization in design and even colour can satisfy a vast market. But mass production itself called forth new managerial techniques of planning, supply and mass marketing. It also brought forth labour problems which some employers in America sought to solve by mounting machine guns at their gates to shoot down strikers.

This was obviously a return to barbarism, and a few far-sighted employers including John D. Rockefeller, Junior, of the Standard Oil Company of America, where labour unrest had been most acute, decided it was time to overhaul the whole management-labour relationship. This meant the development of new managers who were concerned as much with human elements as they were with mechanical processes. Today Henry Ford, Junior, the grandson of the first Henry Ford, is on record as saying that the major contribution of our time will be the solution of the human relations problem in industry.

But a further problem awaits us with the progress of technology. In the easily foreseeable future, we may find once again that machines are replacing men in a new and unprecedented way. It was stated recently that before the end of the century computers will have developed to such a high degree of efficiency that they will virtually be running businesses, and human working hours will be reduced to 15 or 10 per week. Already computers can be used in planning business operations through their application to network analysis and critical path priorities. The demand, it is said, will increasingly be for highly skilled technicians and top decision-makers only. The majority of manual operations are gradually becoming mechanized.

Even in 1951 I remember visiting a vast sparking-plug factory in the U.S.A. and being shown an enormous hall containing some dozen machines each about the size of a steam railway locomotive. The only human beings present were less than half a dozen mechanics. In another room I saw a line of women fitting parts on to plugs on a moving belt which could easily have been done mechanically and no doubt is today. Not only has the machine taken over manual work but mental work as well. This will soon raise a major social problem with which, fortunately, this book is not concerned. I merely use it as an example to show how management is constantly changing and having to adapt itself to new conditions both technical and human, and that the manager who is not alert and aware of human and social trends is rapidly becoming obsolete.

Changing role of management

Politically, socially and psychologically a manager must always remain open-minded. The die-hard conservative and the red revolutionary marxist are equally hide-bound and inflexible. They have no place in modern management, any more than has the man who refuses to face the social obligations of business or who sees it as nothing more than a means of making profits for himself and his shareholders. The manager must be an idealist in the best sense of that much misused word: not in the sense of an idle dreamer or wishful thinker, but in the sense in which Ford and Morris or Bill Lever and Alfred Mond were idealists: looking not only to the present but also to the future – and an idealist also in the sense that he will not be content with second best but insist on the best possible whether his product be mousetraps or mountain borers, gloves or giant jet air-liners.

The manager must be capable of injecting his idealism into those who work for him, of vitalizing them with his own enthusiasm and integrity. We cannot afford second-rate managers, or managers who, in Drucker's words, are illiterate. They must know the world in which they are living not only through academic studies but through intelligent observation and analysis. They must know how to make use of all the techniques available to them, whether they be cost control or job analysis, critical path analysis or operational research. They must not be put off by the high-sounding names of certain techniques that can assist them. Management is largely common-sense, but common-sense scientifically applied, as for instance network analysis and critical path, both of which are components of each other (see Appendix B).

Role of consultants

Managers should beware of those who try to persuade them that techniques of management are more complicated than they really are. The 'mystique' of the Management Consultant may often be daunting to the manager. The consultant undoubtedly has a useful role to play but his role is that of a doctor who is called in in case of illness but can never be a substitute for health. A healthy and well-managed company should not require a consultant. In fact the success of the consultant is a measure of the inefficiency of management. It is due to the fact that management is ill-informed and often illiterate, that it is lacking in intelligence and foresight and too often downright lazy.

It is better, however, to call in a consultant than to go muddling on into bankruptcy. A management that calls in a consultant has at least the merit of humility in recognizing its own inability to cope with the forces of disruption which beset it, and consultants can do much to inform management of methods of which it may be ignorant and factors which it may have overlooked. A consultant can see a business objectively while a manager, being in the thick of it, often cannot. He may have allowed himself to become bogged down with detail to the extent that he is unable to see the picture as a whole. Alternatively the management may have stretched its resources too far and neglected important factors to which a consultant can draw attention. If every man and women were healthy, doctors would be unnecessary. If every business were healthy, consultants would be redundant. Unfortunately, since the world is imperfect, we need both doctors and consultants and the best thing is to learn from them the best way to avoid the pitfalls which first made it necessary to consult them. Many consultants are now setting up training centres where principles of good management are being taught, generally at somewhat expensive fees. The consultant, being more of an observer than a participant, is often, as in the case of Robert Blake (already mentioned as the inventor of the Management Grid), able to devise new techniques for dealing with management problems which might not occur to the manager, burdened as he is with the day-to-day running of a business.

In the United States it is common practice for university professors in business and management subjects to be called in as consultants. This is an admirable system because it prevents them becoming too academic by keeping them in close touch with business, while it also maintains a constant stream of objective observation which can be of value to firms themselves. Robert Blake and Jane Moulton of the Management Grid were former members of the faculty of Texas University. When I visited Chicago University some years ago I found it in the middle of an important research project being undertaken for the International Harvester Company. It was the Harvard Business School that was responsible for the already mentioned investigation at the Western Electric Company which became known as the Hawthorne Experiment.

The management team

The consultant certainly has a role to play, but, because he is a professional expert he may well blind his clients with science and overwhelm them with unfamiliar jargon. Since science is largely the codification of common sense, every manager should make it his business to understand new management techniques and see how they can be applied. Ideally, in fact, he should be capable of being his own consultant and not have to rely on outside help.

The trouble is that, as we have seen, too few managers are able, for various reasons, to stand back and view their businesses objectively, to see where savings can be made or useful developments started. But this is an essential function of management and the manager has to face it.

Much depends on sound delegation. One man cannot handle everything. He must rely on his subordinates, and if he is going to rely on them he must have subordinates he can trust. The autocratic one-man business is a menace when it gets beyond a certain size. It is well known that the first Henry Ford nearly wrecked his own business through autocracy, and, that had it not been for the decentralization introduced into the company by his grandson the business might well have packed up. The Ford case is far from unique. Delegation is essential to management, and management must be a team. Through wise consultation with its management group, top management can often work out solutions to problems as well as, if not better than, a consultant. But there must be mutual trust at all levels so that vital information is not withheld or important danger points concealed.

It is here that courage and integrity are among the more important qualities in the management team. A manager who is merely a 'yes-man' is useless, however much his boss may wish him to be one. A man must have the courage of his convictions in management as in any other walk of life, even at the risk of jeopardizing his job. In fact his job is worth nothing in an autocratic organization where he has no chance to make decisions or constructive suggestions, because such an organization is moribund and cannot make any progress beyond the limitations of the boss, which even in a genius like Ford may prove to be considerable. Unless the boss can trust his management, and the management can trust the boss, there can be no business progress, and sooner or later the business will die. It may die either when the boss dies or before, or if not at least soon after, because if all decisions are taken by the boss, the management personnel will have no experience in making decisions or in shouldering responsibility. A 'yes-man' is not a leader but a follower, and when he has no one to follow he is helpless.

The manager as consultant

Every good manager, as we have seen, should be his own consultant but he should also be capable of acting as consultant to his board. Conversely, the board should look upon the management team and every member of it as a potential consultant, not only in their own specialist field, but on the activities of the company as a whole. To carry out consultancy functions is an excellent training for increasing future responsibility. It is a means of keeping top management informed of management attitudes and ideas and of new and potential developments. In smaller firms the board will probably consist of executive managers, who should be encouraged to view their own functions and those of their colleagues objectively and to make constructive suggestions. In some companies, a 'junior board' is appointed as an advisory body to the board itself and as a training ground for future directors. Because it is closer to the day-to-day problems of the business the junior board is often in a better position than the main board to suggest ideas and improvements which may be of practical value.

Management training

A young man recruited as a junior manager in a business may at first feel that he is only a cypher with restricted functions and responsibilities. But once he has had time to study the business and its various ramifications, and once he has gathered sufficient experience in his own restricted sphere of influence, he should if he possesses the necessary qualities of management, be able to make useful suggestions and to use his own initiative. The more opportunities he is given to learn about the business as a whole, the more use he will eventually be to it, and many firms have introduced job rotation as a means of widening the experience, knowledge, and outlook of their young managers.

Most progressive firms run management trainee courses lasting possibly three months, in which a young manager is given the opportunity to become familiar with the company's background and its various often scattered, activities. Later he may be sent on an intermediate management course where he will be exposed to further knowledge of management techniques and a deeper insight into the business. Such a course may consist of case studies, group discussions, projects, role-playing and other exercises designed to stretch the manager's imagination and give him practice in analysing problems and making decisions.

At the Administrative Staff College at Henley, founded by Sir Noel Hall, more senior managers, being groomed for top management, are exposed to broader exercises in problem solving, involving such questions as the relationship between government and industry, or the reorganization of a business. In America, the Harvard Business School and the Massachusetts Institute of Technology were pioneers in running courses for senior managers, designed to broaden and deepen their outlook and stimulate constructive thinking about management problems. Now a large number of American universities run courses for junior and senior managers, and, in England, Business Schools have been started at Manchester and London under the sponsorship of the Management Education Foundation. Courses in management studies are also being run by other universities and by a number of technical colleges and colleges of advanced technology. Many of these courses lead to a diploma in management studies, originally established by the British Institute of Management.

Role of the B.I.M.

The B.I.M. itself was set up in 1947 with a seven years' government grant as a step towards raising the standard of management throughout Britain. Today it is self-supporting with a membership of over 10,000 collective subscribers and some 22,000 individuals. Its main function is to supply information and guidance on management problems, to organize seminars and conferences, 'presentations' and lectures on management techniques and practices. It has a large range of publications and one of the best management libraries in the world.

Many other countries have similar management institutes and associations, of which the American Management Association, the U.S. National Industrial Conference Board, and the All-India Management Association are well-known examples. In Great Britain there are many other bodies devoted to various aspects of management. These include the Institute of Personnel Management, the Institute of Works Managers, the Institute of Production Engineers, the Institute of Marketing and Sales Management, and the Industrial Society. The main objects of all these associations is to improve knowledge among managers concerning specialist techniques of management by means of courses, seminars and conferences. There is in fact no lack of courses on which managers may be sent to broaden their knowledge of management and study its various techniques. Some of these courses include temporary attachments to business organizations where techniques may be seen in practice and actual experience gained. 'Simulation' and business games are often included in the curricula. These games simulate the actual conditions of business, thus adding a realistic touch to the instruction.

Internal training centres

Many of the larger firms such as Shell, British American Tobacco Company and Imperial Chemical Industries run their own management training centres where executives from all over the world are drawn from their overseas branches, associates and subsidiaries and may attend junior and more senior management courses. In these courses senior managers and directors from Head Office often act as instructors and discussion leaders.

Management: a science and an art

All this goes to show that management today has been accepted as a science as well as an art, which can be developed not only by experience but also by greater knowledge and by broadening the processes of thinking.

One criticism – a common one – by those who participate in such courses is that when they return to their companies they often find themselves frustrated if they try to apply the principles they have learnt to actual situations. They complain they are met with the attitude expressed in such word as: 'All right, now you can forget all that and carry on as you did before. We have no time for theory here, we are too concerned with practice.'

This is an attitude of which top management should beware and should be on the alert to remedy, if it really believes in training and education. If it does not believe in them it should not send managers on courses; but if it does not do so it is heading for disaster, because it is mainly through such courses and conferences that management can keep abreast of new developments and techniques which could, if properly understood, be of considerable value. One compensation is that in the process of time the new generation of managers, who believe in what is taught in such courses, will themselves be in positions of authority, where what they have learnt can be of use to them, and where they can exercise a healthy influence on management attitudes in general.

CHAPTER 5

Motivation and communication

Authority and interdependence

In his book *The Human Side of Enterprise* Douglas McGregor suggests that our ideas of authority are wrongly derived from the Church and the armed forces, both of which are based on a system of leaders and followers, in which arbitrary authority is backed by ultimate sanctions of excommunication in the one case and death (in extreme cases) on the other. 'Theirs not to reason why, theirs but to do and die', as Tennyson wrote of the Light Brigade.

But even in war a leader is as dependant on those who are led as the latter are dependant on their leader. In extreme cases, as is well known, men have not only shot their leaders but have preferred death to following them. Unless a platoon commander, a brigadier or a general can get the wholehearted support of the unit he commands he cannot achieve his objective. The same applies to leadership in industry. As Professor John McMurray, the philosopher, has said: 'fear can never be a motive for constructive action'. Coercion can never achieve creative results.

In the Church, interdependence is constantly stressed. 'Ye are members one of another', said St Paul, and the most superficial analysis of our economic life bears out this dictum. As is forcefully demonstrated by a strike in any essential industry, the whole fabric of our complicated social and economic life today depends on a vast network of co-operation. A breakdown in even one small section of the economic community can cause havoc in the whole economic structure. Voluntary co-operation is the foundation of our entire economic system, and leadership or 'management' is the art of obtaining voluntary co-operation in the achievement of carefully planned objectives. The only discipline which is worth anything, as Peter Drucker has said, is self-discipline.[1]

[1] See also McGregor *Human Side of Enterprise* p. 152. 'Human beings

MOTIVATION AND COMMUNICATION

Multiple roles

Douglas McGregor points out the common error of seeing a man's role as constant, unchanging and absolute. We tend to forget that though man may be a boss to his subordinates, he is also a subordinate to *his* boss. He will also be a colleague to his equals. So a man may be a father, a son and a brother. People play a triple role in their own everyday lives. To play this triple or even more multiple role is not always easy. The answer is to tackle the problem as one of co-operation: co-operation not only with one's superiors and equals but also with one's subordinates. They need a leader and expect his guidance and encouragement. He can supply the co-ordination of their effort in the achievement of their group objectives, without which they are merely a purposeless rabble. Left to itself a group will naturally throw up its own leaders, and the object of the manager is to demonstrate to the group that he is the leader they need. To do this, he has to understand them as people and not merely as instruments of his will or cogwheels in a machine.

Work or drudgery

One of the assumptions which has been made for generations, and is still being made, is that most human beings dislike work and work because they have to. This is a false assumption and one which has disrupted work relations to a dangerous degree. It is natural for people to want to work provided they can see some object in the work apart from merely earning a living. Work is an extension of the instinct of play and it is significant that a child's play very often spontaneously takes the form of imitating the work of its elders. Rightly directed the play instinct can be used to make not only learning but work itself a form of considerable satisfaction.

'Happy is the man', says Professor Higgins in Shaw's *Pygmalion* 'who can make a living by his hobby'; and many of the most successful business and professional men have been those who were merely extending their hobbies to make a living by them. No man can force himself successfully to do what he hates – at least

possess an internal "control mechanism" which can largely render ineffective any form of external control...even physical coercion under certain conditions.'

not continuously. His performance is bound to suffer from his innate sense of resentment against doing what he would rather not be doing and so being prevented from doing what he would much rather do. The idler, the waster and the bungler are people whose natural bent for work has been thwarted and distorted. On the other hand the tycoons and the pundits, who like to claim in public that they only got to their position of eminence by sheer hard work, are leaving out an important factor in their success. They worked hard because they enjoyed their work, not because they had to force themselves to work. It is the enjoyment of work which we need to bring back into industry; and productivity will only rise as industrial psychologists, economists and managers devise means whereby men and women can once more take a pride and a joy in their work and feel satisfaction in doing it.

Work can be fun

I am not suggesting that we should go back to mediaeval craftwork. That would be impossible. On the contrary we should make the best use possible of the inventions which science has given us to relieve people of purely repetitive and uncreative work. We must however organize work in such a way that it provides satisfactions other than merely economic ones: that it provides, in fact, psychological satisfactions and yields a sense of achievement and enjoyment of the same nature as that achieved by the craftsman or the golfer or the tennis player or even perhaps the bridge player.

The businessman and the industrialist are pitting their wits against material and psychological forces in order to provide for the enrichment and enlargement of economic life both for themselves and the community. The degree of satisfaction this can give is shown by the reluctance of many men to retire from business once their economic needs have been satisfied and they have reached an age when retirement would seem appropriate. To many such men it seems as illogical to retire from active business life just because they have reached a certain age, as it would seem absurd to a keen golfer, still active and healthy, suddenly to stop playing golf for the same reason.

Misconceptions about incentives

These factors need to be taken into consideration by management

MOTIVATION AND COMMUNICATION

today in their general study of motivation in industry, one of the most vital aspects in achieving higher productivity. Motivation is not something which can be imposed from outside. It is something that needs stimulation in a man or a woman from within. The manager's business, with the help of the industrial psychologist, is to find out what motivates people and to harness that motivation to constructive and fruitful ends. The failure of many incentive schemes is due to the belief that people can be motivated from outside by sticks or carrots, as if, in fact, they were donkeys. Events have shown that if we treat people like donkeys they will behave like donkeys. But people are organisms not only physically highly complex but also mentally and psychologically, and it is high time that industry realized this and ceased treating its employees like beasts of burden. Old ideas, prejudices and misconceptions die hard, partly because the majority of people are too lazy or too stupid to examine them objectively and take steps to reconsider them. They are, however, highly expensive and have cost and are still costing this country a great deal in time and money lost through bad work, strikes, lockouts, go-slow tactics, sabotage and general industrial unrest.

Participation

We have said that unless work is felt to be interesting and worthwhile it probably will not be done well; but how, in a highly mechanized age, can work be made interesting and worthwhile? To discover this is the job of the manager. By means of mechanization he can eliminate a great part of purely repetitive work and hand it over to machines. Other work can be organized in such a way that it has a creative content, that it leaves room for initiative, imagination, creativity and the exercise of ingenuity.

Workers themselves must be given more chance to express their own individuality and creativity, not only by formal suggestion schemes but also by less formal consultation and discussion. The worker must be allowed to feel that he is not merely a dogsbody or a mechanism, or worse still an appendage to a mechanism, but that he is an active member of a team contributing to the achievement of an objective, not only with his hands but also his brain, his experience and his personality.

A large number of firms today all over the world, and not least in England, have some sort of co-partnership scheme whereby every employee of the firm can share in its increased profitability. This is good so far as it goes, but it does not go far enough. It is not merely an increase in his pay packet which gives satisfaction to a worker. It is a feeling that he is personally responsible, an active contributor to his own and his company's prosperity; and history has shown that where such is the case a worker is far more prepared, when things go wrong, and profits fall, to accept necessary sacrifices and give his best in an emergency. This was particularly demonstrated in the case of the Glacier Metal Company as described by Wilfred Brown and Elliott Jaques. (See p. 55.)

Centralization and decentralization

One of the obvious factors which has, to some extent, destroyed this sense of personal pride and responsibility for a company a man works for, is the growth in size and hence in impersonality of many large companies. It has been said of some of the larger companies today, that they are like a branch of the Civil Service rather than an industrial concern. The wise ones however have deliberately made efforts to overcome the impersonality which results from size, by taking drastic steps to decentralize and to split up the total concern into as many small components as possible, without detracting from the obvious advantages which can be obtained from some measure of centralization. In fact, one of the organizational problems of modern business is how to combine the advantages of centralization with the advantages of smaller units, with their greater opportunities for close personal relations and freedom of expression.

Many of the components of the larger combines such as Unilever or I.C.I. started as small family businesses – like Kynoch, the cartridge makers – and an attempt has been made in many cases to preserve some of the characteristics of the original units without destroying the value of centralized services. In these days of extensive take-overs, not only of smaller firms by larger ones but even of large firms by other large firms, this problem is a very real one. One of the most alarming tendencies is, in fact, the taking over of British firms by American ones with resulting removal of higher control from Britain to America. This often engenders a feeling of remote and impersonal control which is resented by

British employees, not only on the shop floor but even in the higher ranks of management. In certain cases however American management has proved itself more aware of the dangers of such impersonality than British management, and, by giving greater freedom and scope for initiative, has more than made up for the apparent remoteness of control.

Attitude surveys

As with all such problems, the place to start is with the employee himself, viewed as a human being. Attitude surveys can do much. So can joint discussion and consultation at all levels. American business is, on the whole, more conscious of the value of the opinion survey than are firms in England. One large American firm, Sears Roebuck, has built a periodical opinion survey into its overall personnel management structure, with excellent results. This survey keeps higher management in close touch with what its employees are thinking and feeling about many critical factors in the day-to-day running of the business. The results of such surveys need to be carefully handled and checked, while appropriate action must not only be taken, but *seen* to be taken, by all.

The technical organization of an opinion survey is comparatively simple. A questionnaire is drawn up asking a number of relevant questions about the employee's attitude to his work, the company, his supervisor, his co-workers, his terms of service, rates of pay etc. Questions are carefully worded to avoid ambiguity or irresponsibility in their answers. They are then circulated to the group or groups concerned and each individual is asked to fill up the questionnaire anonymously and put his answer in a box. It is important that, in order to get purely unbiassed answers, nobody should have any fear of being identified.

An alternative method is to have the survey done by an outside firm of consultants. Questionnaires are circulated confidentially, but employees are also interviewed anonymously. One large firm which I have in mind had been going through a period of crippling labour troubles, and had obtained valuable information in this way on which it was able to build a realistic and effective labour policy. It must always be borne in mind that, however misguided, misinformed or distorted an opinion may be, a man acts on opinion rather than facts. But until one can find out what opinions people hold it is impossible to correct false ideas and substitute facts for fiction.

Danger of false opinions

People often hold false opinions because they have never been told the real facts. This indicates failure in communication. It is always the duty of management to keep every employee informed about everything and anything which concerns his work. There is sometimes difference of opinion as to what does concern a worker. The phrase 'It's none of your business' is often used to save the trouble of keeping people properly informed about what is going on around them. The first thing a worker is concerned with is obviously his job, but his job is also part of the total activity of his company and he naturally wants to know something about the company as a whole: about its management, its policies, its financial status, its progress, its failure and successes. How can a man – or woman – feel *esprit de corps* for something of which he or she is largely ignorant? Where people are ignorant of fact they will be only too quick to invent distortions, and these distortions can be dangerous.

A company which takes its employees into its confidence, not only about its successes but also about its failures, will do far more to build up respect and morale than one which keeps them in ignorance and treats them as mere cogs in the machine or beasts of burden. Moreover, a company which takes its employees into its confidence has much more chance of getting their co-operation and support in difficult times. Loyalty and sentiment can be tangible assets in times of stress and can show a credit on the balance sheet which may make all the difference between financial success and failure.

Management must never forget that a business is a community of people: a group of human beings whose voluntary co-operation is necessary if objects are going to be achieved. The same applies to an army, as Field-Marshal Montgomery realized in the last war, when he insisted on the maximum information being passed down to the humblest private so that he was fully 'in the picture' regarding every battle in which he participated. There is a lot, today, which industry can learn from the armed forces, particularly in the field of man management, and not least is the lesson that subordinates must be treated as thinking human beings and taken into the confidence of their leaders if the best is to be got out of them. A man must know what he is working for, just as he must know what he is fighting for. He must know what part he plays in the overall enterprise and how his contribution relates to the total achievement expected. There are many methods of improving communications; it is the manager's job to find the combination of methods best suited to his company. Many firms, for instance, find that house magazines make a useful instrument both for dissemination of information and building up *esprit de corps*.

Importance of individuality

But to return to the question of incentives, Douglas McGregor makes an interesting and valuable point in his book *The Human Side of Enterprise*: this is that once a need is satisfied it no longer acts as an incentive. To a man living at subsistence level a few extra shillings a week may be an incentive, but to a man whose basic needs are satisfied, who is already earning a fair wage, other incentives than purely monetary ones are necessary. But different people may react differently to different incentives. One man may crave for responsibility and power over others, another man may shrink from it, and only desire more freedom or leisure. One man may want prestige or social standing, another may want security. To assume that every man is actuated by the same motives is a dangerous generalization. There is room in an industrial enterprise for all types, and one of the tasks of good management is to see that every man is suited to the job to which he is best fitted by temperament, outlook, knowledge, experience and character.

In making a personality assessment, which is a valuable method of analysing the abilities and potentialities of one's staff, the object should not be to criticize or praise so much as to assess a man's capabilities and individual characteristics. Because one man is cautious and dislikes making decisions hastily, whereas another may show initiative and be prepared to take risks and even be reckless, this does not mean one is better or worse than the other; it merely means that each should be given a job where his particular characteristics can best be utilized. Sometimes two men can work together in a team with excellent results, though their characteristics may be quite different. One can act as a steadying influence on the other and supply those characteristics which may be missing in the other. Recklessness can be as dangerous as over-caution. Harnessed together in a team they may each have a modifying influence on the other.

Building a team

The manager should never try to impose his personality on his subordinates or judge them by his own characteristics. He should aim at building up a well-balanced team, not a body of 'Yes men' or a group of people who think and feel as he does. He should be prepared to listen to other views and to weigh them against each other and against his own. At the same time a subordinate must be led to feel that he should have opinions and be allowed to express them freely. A man should have the courage of his convictions and be prepared to express them effectively and convincingly; but he must also have the grace to respect the opinions of others and bow if necessary to the majority opinion. If he cannot do this he should get out, and many people have done so, with excellent results both for themselves and the company. A man must have courage in business if he is to get on. But if he is content to stay where he is then nobody need blame him, and his services may also be useful to the company, though possibly not spectacular. The important thing is that top management should recognize the temperamental differences of those who work for it and give due credit to all of them.

Business, as I have suggested, should be fun, not drudgery. But it should not only be fun for the boss, but for everyone who works in it. But now can it be fun to the man who only sees its results in a pay packet? The intangibles are more important than the tangibles, and if a man's only interest in his work is what he takes home at the end of the month, then there is either something wrong with him or with his company. Most likely it is with his company, because he has never been allowed to feel part of a creative enterprise, of a worthwhile undertaking.

Communication and management

We have already touched on the need for effective communication as a basis of good management, but a manager needs to communicate more than mere facts and instructions: he must communicate less concrete things, and persuade people as to *why* certain things should be done and *how* they can best be done. He can communicate emotions such as enthusiasm, loyalty and comradeship.

It is what lies behind words that matters: the feelings, the attitudes, the meanings. A foreman may say: 'I'm telling you, Jack. Do it this way, or else!' or he can say: 'The best way to do this, Jack, is like this.' There is a world of difference between the two communications though they may both refer to the same thing. One indicates domination, the other co-operation. Even the sentence: 'I suggest you do it this way', can be used either as a menace or as friendly advice according to the inflection. The way a man uses words can indicate his character. If a man is a bully, he will find it difficult to conceal the fact, however much soft soap he uses or however mealy-mouthed he is. An honest man uses words honestly and straightforwardly. An equivocator used words equivocally. He indulges in what is known as 'double talk'.

The average worker can usually judge a man pretty shrewdly, whatever sort of language he uses; but this is not to say that the use of language isn't important. 'The object of speech', as Confucius said, 'is to be understood.' Some people use speech deliberately to conceal what they mean. This has been said to be the object of diplomacy. On the other hand bluntness is not necessarily sincerity. A friend of mine was once a member of a board of directors of a Yorkshire firm. It was a habit for a certain member of the board to say: 'We're blunt here in Yorkshire. We say what we mean.' 'No you're not blunt,' said my friend one day in exasperation 'you're just bloody rude.' Rudeness does not help communication because it sets up emotional reactions and creates barriers to real understanding. Courtesy and politeness cost nothing and can often help to make communication more effective. A man is not only an intellectual animal but also an emotional one and a man who is working with others whether as equal, subordinate or boss, must realize this, and must respect other people's feelings. He does not have to crawl to people – in fact most people hate a sycophant. He can however, exercise courtesy and *have* the courtesy to express himself clearly and intelligibly. If we hate a man's guts we don't have to tell him so but we don't have to pretend to admire him. What we want to ask ourselves is whether we have a valid reason, and if we have what can we do about it. Many people hate others without any valid reason and this corrodes relationships.

Human relations and communication

Human relations are bound up with communication because it is mainly through communication that we establish relations with people. Most of the human-relations problems in industry arise through lack of effective communication, not merely at the intellectual level, but more often at the emotional level. Most people are, in fact, emotionally immature. We may be educated intellectually but emotionally we are too often just children. Many people are dominated by fear, anxiety, ignorance and suspicion. Anything unusual frightens us and makes us feel insecure.

In management-labour relations, barriers are deliberately built up. Managers tend to see labour as illiterate scallywags whose only aim in life is to do as little work as possible and get as much money as they can. Labour sees management as bloodsuckers, out for the last ounce of work and reluctant to pay more than can be forced out of them. Both are the victims of a myth, deliberately encouraged by those who believe it is in their interest to foster it. The same sort of misunderstanding, often deliberately fostered, leads to wars between nations. In all these cases communication has broken down, not so much at the intellectual level but at the emotional level. Until managers realize that men are emotional as well as thinking beings, labour unrest will continue. An attempt to face this problem has been made by industrial psychology, but progress in this is as yet elementary.

It is no use for managers to tell workers that all they want is their welfare when actually all they want is profit. Workers can see through this and label it as insincere 'paternalism'. No doubt Cadbury and Lever were sincere and genuine when they introduced better working conditions in their factories and no doubt it paid them handsomely to do so, as Robert Owen, the socialist millowner at New Lanark, had already proved it would do. These were steps in the right direction; but today workers take 'welfare' measures as a matter of right, not condescension by employers; and strikes and unrest persist in spite of these measures.

A more advanced step was joint consultation as practised by Vauxhall Motors at Luton and Glacier Metal at Perivale. This was an experiment in better communication which, under Sir Charles Bartlett at Vauxhall's and Wilfred Brown at Glacier, kept both companies relatively strike-free for a considerable number of years. Why labour relations have deteriorated at Vauxhall's since Bartlett left would make an interesting case study. It may be that joint consultation is no longer the answer to the problem, or it may be that under new management, its nature has changed. Vauxhall's, it must be remembered, is a subsidiary of General Motors. Possibly since Bartlett left there may have been greater Americanization, and this may have caused resentment.

These problems are not insoluble. They require a careful analysis as to why communication has broken down, if it ever really existed. A considerable amount of research is being done at present in the U.S.A. about human motivation; but all at a rather academic level. I personally suspect that the answers may be simpler than we think and merely entail a deeper understanding of people's feelings: of people as human beings, not as instruments of someone's will. The dangers of looking upon people as instruments was pointed out some years ago by John Macmurray, a former Professor of Philosophy at London University, in his book *Reason and Emotion*. (Faber & Faber 1935). Once people are looked upon as instruments they cease to be looked upon as humans, and all our attitudes get distorted.

Dangers of obsolete thinking

There are many so-called 'hard-headed businessmen' who may look upon what I have said in this chapter as misguided idealism. I am, however, no stranger to the realities of business and have had to live and work among strikes and lockouts, sabotage and even violence in the industrial scene. I know something about the costs in terms of man-hours and cash of ignoring the human solutions to these human problems. When John D. Rockefeller, Junior, saw strikers being shot down at the gates of the Standard Oil Company's plant in New Jersey he determined to find a way of stopping such things happening again. The result of his efforts was a new, human understanding of people, embodied in a revolutionary personnel policy. Standard's record since those days has been remarkable. You cannot control people by fear. The consequences are too expensive.

MOTIVATION AND COMMUNICATION

It is often said that in the old family business, as Lever's, Cadbury's and Brunner Mond's were once, the employer knew each of his employees personally and had no personnel problems. This is probably an oversimplification. There are still small family businesses and not all are without labour problems. The human touch is certainly valuable, provided that it is genuine and sincere. If not it will merely engender contempt. But times have changed, and the conditions of the nineteenth century no longer operate in the twentieth. An important factor is trade unionism, and trade unionism has come to stay. It is the price we have had to pay for past bad management. Today we have to re-create an atmosphere in which people can work freely without anxiety or fear, with a sense of purpose and achievement.

To do this will not be easy, but unless we do it labour relations will get worse and not better. The solution lies, as I have suggested, in understanding and better communication at all levels, not in domination of one group by another.

The operational group

Management today as we have suggested is no longer carried out by arbitrary decisions of the 'boss'. Management is done by groups – the board of directors being the final controlling group. But under the board are a number of operational groups who have to arrive at decisions by consultation. Such groups should consist of all those who are involved in carrying out a decision and making it effective. Each member of the group has something useful to contribute from his own particular knowledge and experience. The senior manager in the group, who has to act as its chairman, must take responsibility for the decisions and must ensure that they are the right ones in the circumstances. He must make certain that all relevant facts are presented and that all useful opinions are obtained. The hunch of a single individual is not a good basis for a decision. It should be tested against other opinions, even if they do not agree with it. The leader may have overlooked certain important factors which the group can bring to his notice. If he then decides to go ahead in face of opposition he at least does so with his eyes open.

To handle a group effectively requires a certain skill, which is why of late years a number of courses have been developed in 'chairmanship', 'running a meeting', 'discussion leading' and 'conference technique'. A great deal of time can be wasted if meetings are not properly handled and irrelevances allowed to creep in. Certain people try to dominate groups by thrusting their own opinions forward too forcefully, others tend to be diffident though they may have useful views to offer. A wise chairman will see that everyone gets a chance to contribute but that nobody monopolizes the meeting. He will also avoid getting into personal arguments or allowing others to do so. He will use the group as a means to keep the balance of discussion even, using judicious questioning to elucidate relevant facts. As a means of keeping the discussion under control he will first state clearly the objective of the meeting and sum up each stage of the argument, making notes of decisions and trying to work towards unanimity. To achieve this will thus not only strengthen his own confidence when putting decisions into practice but will ensure the co-operation of those who helped to formulate them and hence are committed to them.

Delegation and development

Once a decision has been made, its implementation must be delegated to those who will have to put it into operation, and each man must be left to use his own discretion in its implementation. A manager should not interfere with his subordinates unless they ask for his help. If he does so too readily, he will leave no room for initiative, self-reliance, or self-control.

One of the functions of a manager, as I have said, is to develop the management team and train for succession. He should be on the look out always for men qualifying for promotion and should do all he can to develop their talents and abilities. A manager who is continually 'spoon-feeding' his subordinates gives them little scope for development.

Delegation entails taking risks: but the risks are worth taking in the long run. Business, by its very nature, is full of risks. That is what makes it interesting. The risk taken in delegation depends on the accuracy, of the judgment exercised in choosing and training subordinates. If one cannot trust a subordinate to carry out an assignment successfully without one constantly 'breathing down his neck' then he should not have been given the job. Mistakes, will, of course, be made, but as it has been wisely said: 'a man who never makes a mistake will never make anything'. The important thing in a man is that he should learn to profit by his mistakes – and also by the mistakes of others.

Communication and delegation

Good delegation cannot work without good communication. If a man is left on his own to do a job, as he should be, he should know exactly what he is supposed to be doing and what his objectives are. Otherwise he may well make a mess of it. This is the value of the management or operational group which is in itself an instrument of communication, since it not only gives adequate opportunity for clarification of tasks and objectives but also for discussion of methods.

Management by integration

Since Douglas McGregor's book[1] *The Human Side of Enterprise* (McGraw Hill 1960) has had a considerable impact on management on both sides of the Atlantic, it might as be well to examine his main conclusions.

According to McGregor there are fundamentally two schools of management theory, resulting in two forms of management practice and attitude. He calls them Theory X and Theory Y.

Theory X is the old authoritative idea of 'traditional view' as McGregor calls it. The inherent implications of this theory are:

1. The average human being has an inherent dislike of work and will avoid it if he can.
2. Most people have to be coerced, controlled, directed and threatened to get them to put forth adequate effort towards organizational achievement.
3. The average human being prefers to be directed, wishes to avoid responsibility, has relatively little ambition, wants security above all.

McGregor claims that 'the principles of organization which comprise the bulk of the literature of management could only have

[1] Douglas McGregor is a Professor at the School of Industrial Management, Massachusetts Institute of Technology.

been derived from assumptions such as those of Theory X'. He also believes that Theory X must provide explanations of *some* human behaviour in industry, otherwise its assumptions could not have persisted. He believes, however, that recent behavioural research now makes it necessary to revise drastically the principal assumptions behind Theory X.

As an alternative to Theory X, McGregor puts forward Theory Y, based on the following assumptions:

1. The expenditure of physical and mental effort in work is as natural as play or rest. The average human being does not inherently dislike work. Depending upon controllable conditions, work may be a source of satisfaction (and will be voluntarily performed) or a source of punishment (and will be avoided if possible).
2. External control and threat of punishment are not the only means for bringing about efforts towards organization objectives. Man will exercise self-discretion and self-control in the service of objectives to which he is committed.
3. Commitment to objectives is a function of the rewards associated with achievement.
4. The average human being learns, under proper conditions, not only to accept but to seek responsibility.
5. The capacity to exercise a relatively high degree of imagination, ingenuity, and creativity in the solution of organizational problems is widely, not narrowly, distributed in the population.
6. Under the conditions of modern industrial life, the intellectual potentialities of the average human being are only partially utilized.

Among the conclusions which McGregor draws from these assumptions are the following:

1. They are dynamic rather than static.
2. Human collaboration in the organizational setting is not limited by human nature but by management's ingenuity in discovering how to realize the potential represented by its human resources.
3. If employees are lazy, indifferent, unwilling to take responsibility, intransigent, uncreative, unco-operative, the causes lie in management's methods of organization and control.

4. These assumptions are consistent with existing knowledge in the social sciences and are unlikely to be contradicted by further research.
5. They challenge many deeply ingrained managerial habits of thought and action and may therefore be difficult to implement in practice.
6. They imply the principle of integration: the creation of conditions in which members of an organization can achieve their own goals, and can best be directing their efforts towards the success of the enterprise.
7. The organization will be more effective in achieving its economic objectives if adjustments are made, in significant ways, to meet the needs, and promote the goals, of its members.
8. Acceptance of responsibility is correlated with commitment to objectives. Genuine commitment is seldom achieved when objectives are externally imposed.

Target setting

An important feature of what McGregor calls 'management by integration and self control' is that each man should set his own targets – in consultation with those concerned. People should not have targets imposed upon them from without. Targets should be the result of joint consultation. Only in this way can each man be fully committed to the achievement of clearly defined goals. This is the essence of the Y theory as compared with the X theory. He insists that this form of management is a strategical exercise from which the appropriate tactics naturally emerge after consideration of the circumstances.

Self-assessment

The basis of McGregor's method of self-assessment is the encouragement of individuals to see themselves objectively in relation to their jobs, to their objectives and the objectives of the company they work for. In this respect Blake's Management Grid (see pp. 44–6) is a natural development from McGregor's theories and it is interesting that one large international company with which I have been intimately connected was naturally led on from McGregor to Blake and has based its management policy, covering a large number of companies spread throughout the world, on their work. McGregor's book also acknowledges his debt to Peter Drucker, author of *The Practice of Management* and various other studies of management.

Theory and practice

The importance of these theories is that they are revolutionizing our entire attitude to management and particularly to the psychology of organization. They are the result of practical analysis of actual situations by men who have been actively engaged in business and who have applied intelligent observation of its problems. Some people have an instinctive suspicion of theory, but a little thought will show that without some degree of theory, no practical objectives can be achieved. If the Wright Brothers had not worked out a theory of flight they would never have discovered aviation. If Marconi had not worked out the theory of wireless telegraphy – using the theories of numerous other scientists – we should not today have radio, television and the radio control of space vehicles. If Pasteur and Lister had not had theories of infection we should never have developed the science of antisepsis with its enormous benefits to humanity. It is to the theoreticians that we owe all the benefits of civilization. But theories have to be proved in practical application, and management has been a valuable testing ground for theories which may at first, like the theories of Pasteur and Lister, have appeared revolutionary and even fantastic.

Some of the greatest advances today have been made in the social and behavioural sciences. These advances may well prove to have been the most important advances of this era: more important than space-travel or supersonic aviation, though possibly less spectacular. That this will be so is the opinion of, among others, Henry Ford II, grandson of the founder of the Ford Company, who saved his grandfather's vast business from disaster and adapted it to modern conditions.

There are still many managers who say: 'These new-fangled theories are all nonsense. We have got on all right without them so far and there is no need to change our ideas!' I have worked with such managers and listened to their arguments and have seen the results in strikes, lockouts and monstrous losses of revenue, all of which could have been avoided by forethought and understanding.

Such ideas are often unpopular because they entail time and effort in mental and organizational readjustment. Many managers are too busy getting out products even to spare time for essential training. But sooner or later the crunch comes and much time is wasted through industrial battles that could have been more usefully employed in working to achieve constructive attitudes, developing integration, and fostering self-motivation and self-control.

CHAPTER 6

Commonsense of management

Dangers of mystiques

As has been said before, management is largely common sense, but common sense is not always as common as we should like it, and many people who pride themselves on their common sense and 'down-to-earth' attitude are actually more hidebound by prejudice, ignorance and conventional thinking than they know. The so-called practical man tends to despise theory as high-falutin' and academic. He believes in such catch-phrases as: 'a penny-worth of experience is worth a pound of theory'. He may forget that experience may merely mean constantly repeating the same mistakes! He may, like the Bourbons, have forgotten nothing, but like them he may also have learnt nothing. And we all know the fate of the Bourbons.

His suspicion of new ideas may not be entirely his fault. As we have seen they are sometimes presented as some sort of obscure 'mystique', which only the initiated can understand – such as consultants, who have a vested interest. In fact the details of most modern management techniques are readily available, and to understand them a manager does not need to be a higher mathematician or a highly trained scientist. Obviously every manager may not have the time or possibly the ability to be an expert in all these techniques, and it may save him time and trouble to employ a specialist practitioner whether in such specialisms as work study, cost-accounting, quality control or operational research. What he does need to know and must know is how these techniques can help him to make his business more efficient.

The basis of most techniques is the breaking down of a task into its component parts, which can then be examined and handled conveniently. This was the basis of the famous T.W.I. (Training

Within Industry) 'Job' Programmes,[1] used with astonishing success to train supervisors during World War I; when supervisors were in short supply owing to many of them having joined the Forces, new ones had to be trained up quickly. It is also the basis of critical path analysis, of operational research and all production planning. There is nothing magic or mysterious about such techniques any more than there is about cost accounting or work study. They merely consist of breaking down operations into their components and tackling each in turn. They do, however, involve some disciplines and these may sometimes be irksome. It is no use working out a plan and then acting according to rule of thumb. Things have to be done in sequences, as every engineer is aware. In assembling a car, for instance, parts have to be put on in the right order, otherwise one part may have to be taken off again in order to fit the other part. Instructions have to be laid down on a practical and logical basis and followed carefully, otherwise time will be wasted.

Operational research

Operational research is concerned with profitability. It determines which operations are profitable and which are not and how operations can be combined to make the maximum use of common resources. It can apply, as we have seen, equally to a grocer's store as to Unilever. A grocer does not want his shelves cluttered up with goods which he cannot sell or can only sell slowly, while fast-moving goods are cramped for space and display. He also has to work out priorities and reckon what each line is costing him in storage and deterioration. A village blacksmith may have to decide whether it is more profitable to continue shoeing horses or to go in for repairing farm machinery or starting a service garage. He wants to know what the latter is going to cost him and how profitable is it likely to be; what equipment he will need and what capital

[1] At one time 'T.W.I.' was a well-known technique of training, consisting of four one-week programmes of instruction called 'Job Instruction', 'Job Relations', 'Job Methods' and 'Job Safety'. The last was added later. They reduced training in instruction methods, human relations, method study and safety precautions to a simple, fool-proof drill which could be mastered simply and effectively in the shortest possible time.

will be sunk in buying it. Can he borrow money for its purchase and if so what will it cost him? Must he hire mechanics and if so what should he pay them? All this is involved in operational research. With the village blacksmith, however, it is probably a one – or two – man task – he may talk it over with his wife or his bank manager or a friend or a partner if he has one – but in a business the size of I.C.I. or Unilever it becomes a major operation in which a computer is probably necessary to work out the various alternatives. The principle however is the same.

Management assessment

The same applies to the Management Grid. (see pp. 44–6). It is merely a form of assessment of management ability (a) in relation to the business and (b) in relation to people. Both are obviously important, since, if a man cannot get on with people he is useless, and if he is not concerned about the business itself he will certainly not put his best into his work. Even the method of self- and group-assessment is not so revolutionary. It is not unusual for two or three junior managers in a small business to discuss their relative merits with each other and for home truths to emerge which may well cause a change of attitude and more effective co-operation. The only difference is that the Grid makes a system of such discussions, instead of leaving them to chance.

Bases of new techniques

As we have seen cost-accounting is nothing new, nor is budgetary control. Method study is as old as the hills and was described by Adam Smith in *The Wealth of the Nations* nearly two hundred years ago in his observations of pin-making. It is merely an extension of the division of labour into the simplification of labour. Taylor, Gantt and Gilbreth, the fathers of 'scientific' management, merely codified common sense and raised it to a scientific level. It may be asked why, if scientific management is so simple, we need to teach it? The answer is that scientific management today is the application of old principles to new circumstances. Men have not changed appreciably but machines and production methods have changed incalculably in the last two hundred years.

Nevertheless machines were invented by men and must therefore be comprehensible at least as to what they do, if not always how they do it. A manager does not have to understand how a computer works to be able to assess whether it can help him to solve his management problem. What he wants to know about a computer is the kind of problem it can solve and the kind of problems it cannot solve. A computer is a machine for giving information quickly. The information it gives is based on the information it receives. If the information fed in is inadequate then the information it gives cannot help. It speeds up the process of 'thinking' and though it does not make decisions it can indicate which, of a number of decisions, is most appropriate to the objective in mind, Take for instance profitability and operational research. A computer can work out accurately, if given the right information, which operation is most likely out of a number to be most profitable.

As we have seen profitability in the long run depends on whether goods or services satisfy a need of the consumer at a price he is willing to pay. This involves market research and market research is based on statistics gained from 'sample' surveys. These are meat and drink to a computer. It can also work out probabilities based on statistical laws. So, of course, can human beings, but a problem which might take a man a couple of months to work out can be worked out by a computer in a matter of seconds. Then we come to relative costs, manpower availability, sources of raw materials, machine capacity and power supply. All these the computer can take care of, if given the right material. Instead of employing an army of clerks and accountants we merely hand the lot to the computer (in the right form, of course), and it gives us the answer immediately. But the data has first to be programmed and this is a highly skilled job. Any one, however, who wants to use a computer must know at least something about programming and this is something which can be learnt at a short appreciation course.

Human and electronic mind

A manager's mind performs four main functions. One is identifying and analysing problems. The second is marshalling the relevant facts, the third is drawing conclusions from them and the fourth is taking decisions in the light of those conclusions. If he draws the wrong conclusions he may make the wrong decisions. The computer can help him in two ways: it can help him to marshal the facts and it can indicate the right conclusions, and in indicating the right conclusions it can indicate the right decisions. It is obvious that if a computer can indicate the right decisions it can eventually be so geared as to control certain operations and even to control men. There is nothing very new in this. When we drive our car up to a traffic light we obey its signal to stop or go on without any sense of loss of dignity. Many human activities have been controlled by bells and clocks from time immemorial. The computer is merely an electronic device to tell us what to do next. What neither the bell, nor the clock, nor even the computer can do is to take appropriate action if we do not obey its signal. The same applies to the traffic light. The degree to which future management will be superseded by the computer is therefore going to be determined by the degree to which men are prepared to obey machines, and the degree to which they find it more convenient and beneficial to do so. But as actual manual work is becoming increasingly mechanized by automation, it may well be that men will only be of minor importance, because the number of men who will be expected to obey computers will be negligible and in fact computers will be merely controlling machines. The possibility that men can be landed on the moon is no longer in the realm of science fiction, nor is the possibility that before very long factories, devoid of human beings, will be started and stopped at the press of a switch. Nor would it be a difficult operation to automate rail transport, loading and delivery. In an age which is changing technologically as rapidly as ours is, such speculations no longer lie outside the bounds of practical possibility and, as far as management is concerned, they cannot be ignored. The trend must be recognized and exploited to the full, and the manager who does so first will have an advantage over his competitors. Meanwhile the manager has to use whatever means are at his disposal, and in the most effective way. Computer techniques are among these means and should be understood by managers as a possible aid to management. It is not even necessary for management to invest in a computer. There are many firms prepared to hire out the services of computers to those who are willing and able to make use of them. The cost of such services is comparatively small, the advantages can be considerable.

Use of statistics in business

Statistics is another science which may appear to some to be an unfathomable mystery. But statistics are only numbers, and conclusions drawn from numbers. Managers of every productive organization like to know how many units of a product it produces over a given period such as a week, or a year. Not only do they want to know, they must know. Moreover they must also know the amount of raw materials used, manpower involved, power consumed and numerous other factors. All these are statistics and they have to be carefully recorded. They are in fact a form of 'control' like the pilot's altimeter or a motorist's fuel indicator.

Statistics must be accurate to be of any use: they must be constantly checked. In a progressive business, statistics must be the basis of all forward planning, of budgetary control, of forecasting, of cost accounting and productivity assessment. The grocer has to use statistics to determine what stocks he has to hold, the blacksmith has to use them to determine whether his business is profitable.

Laws of probability

Experience has shown that statistics can be representative as well as actual; that is to say that they can indicate trends and suggest possibilities as well as actualities. They can be linked with the known laws of probability to produce estimates which are correct within minor margins of error. If a large enough sample of people is taken, for instance, it will be found that their characteristics conform to what is known as the Gaussian Probability Curve, in which the average always preponderates and exceptions are in two minorities. This curve, if plotted on a piece of graph paper always has the same shape, rather like a pixie's hat. If the horizontal ordinate shows heights or weights of people, and the vertical ordinate numbers, it will be found that the hump in the middle shows the average, while those of less than average slope down steeply at first and then less steeply on the left, while those which are above average slope down in a roughly balancing shape on the right (see figure 1, p. 91). This fact is of considerable significance in conducting, say, a consumer survey. If the total consuming public in a country is, say, 20 million, it is possible to deduce that a sample of perhaps not more than 2,000 will, if chosen representatively from appropriate income groups, conform to much the same buying habits as the total. This is also the basis of opinion polls now widely used for forecasting election results. Thus if we can determine the buying or voting habits of 2,000 people, we will have a reasonably similar picture of the buying or voting habits of 20 millions.

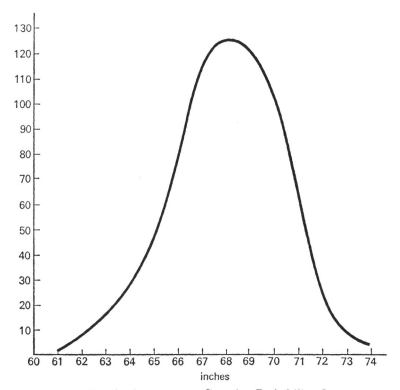

Normal distribution curve or Gaussian Probability Curve

Figure 1. Based on an examination of 730 male adults in respect of height. This curve will be roughly the same shape for 7,300 or 7,300,000.

Statistical sampling theory is also widely used in quality control. Instead of examining every unit in a batch of say 20,000, if we examine one in 20 we may deduce from the laws of probability that our check will apply within certain calculated margins of error to the whole batch. Such sample checking can only be used where 100 per cent reliability is not required and where any defective unit which may get as far as the customer is replaceable under a guarantee. In the components of, say, an aircraft, such sample checking is inadmissable since people's lives may depend on a comparatively minor component.

Ratios and units

Statistics consist of numbers of units: units of a product, units of money, units of weight or any other unit of convenience. They may consist of people, of electrical power, of thermal heat, of atmospheric pressure. Their value is as a measure of comparison and relationship or ratio, as for instance of man-hours worked to the units of output over a given period, which measures productivity. If the ratio of man-hours in relation to the same output drops, in February, below that of January, productivity has increased and vice versa. Cost is also expressed as a ratio of money spent in relation to units produced. These ratios are important as indications of trends. A downward trend in productivity or an upward trend of cost per unit obviously calls for action. Unless statistics are available to indicate these trends, management will be ignorant of them and the correct action may not be taken.

In helping to supply this constant flow of accurate statistics management and supervisory co-operation is essential. The collection, maintenance and analysis of statistics may seem a tedious chore to the superintendant of a department, particularly if that superintendant has not been informed of their purpose and how they cannot only help higher management but also himself to control and improve performance. A bad superintendent may resent the demand for statistics because he fears they will show up the inefficiency of his department. This is a matter for discipline and all discipline in the long run has got to be self-discipline. But generally speaking a man is more likely to co-operate in providing necessary information if he knows what it is going to be used for and how he can himself use it to advantage too. It is higher management's job not only to explain the need for correct information, but also to see that the supervisor concerned is given the results of his own returns of figures and shown how to use them effectively. This, again, is a matter of good communication.

Information passing

Good communication should be in all directions: up, down, and sideways. Information should be passed clearly from top management via middle management to supervision and from supervision down to the shop floor. It should also be passed from the shop floor via supervision up to middle management and from middle management to the top. It should also pass horizontally from one supervisor to another and from one manager to another at every level. Obviously it will get sifted as it goes along but nothing that is relevant should be allowed to get blocked. The important thing is that everyone should be fully informed about everything affecting his work and his responsibilities. Too often we hear the complaint: 'But nobody told me,' or 'How was I to know?' Too often the complaint is justified; if nobody told him how *was* he to know? Some people are more alert than others in finding out information. But nobody can be blamed for not knowing something if, in fact, nobody told him. It is management's job to see that everyone knows as much as possible about everything which concerns him.

There are many forms of communication such as notice boards, public address systems, circulars, verbal communication and joint consultative committees. They all have their part to play if used correctly. A firm overseas I once knew used to complain that the trade union leaders were spreading all sorts of rumours about management and that the men believed them. What steps, I asked, were management taking to communicate the truth? The union called frequent meetings attended by all the workers, with the management's full permission. Why, I asked, did not management also call meetings and put their point of view? The management protested that this would be beneath their dignity. In this case, the management deliberately put themselves at a disadvantage. The union leaders met the workers face to face. Management remained in the background clinging grimly to their dignity. What chance had the workers of learning the true facts or hearing management's case? Management's case went by default and eventually unrest became so bad that the factory had to close for a time until the trouble could be sorted out and remedies found. Here, in fact, was a serious breakdown in communication. Such breakdowns are not uncommon.

Language and communication

The main instrument of communication is obviously language, but language can be used to inhibit communication as well as to enhance it. Silence can also be a means of communication, so can gesture and intonation. Change of stress on certain words can alter the meaning of a sentence. But to confine communication to language alone, how many people have been trained or know how to use language effectively? In his book *The Practice of Management*, Peter Drucker has suggested that the best university vocational courses for managers are those on poetry and short story writing. Some may think this is a frivolous suggestion: but the reason is obvious. In writing poetry or short stories a man has to learn to use words in such a way as to stimulate the maximum response. He cannot afford to be sloppy or inexact; he must learn the precise meaning of words and use them to convey meaning as accurately as possible. In fact, as exponents of semantics have pointed out, few words have precise meanings, but are only approximations, mere symbols of ideas. Their meaning depends on experience and unless the user and the hearer or reader has the same or at least similar experiences, communication may fail.

Take the simple example of the word 'dog'. To a child who has a pet dog of whom it is fond, the word will call up a sense of affection. To a child who may have been attacked by a savage dog the word will call up associations of fear, horror and antagonism. The meaning of words also depends on associations, as for example such words as 'capital', 'labour', 'trade union', 'socialist', 'fascism' or 'communism'.

Stuart Chase records in his book, *The Tyranny of Words*, the result of a survey taken in America on what a list of words meant to different people. The results are most enlightening. Out of a hundred or so people very few attached the same meaning to the same word. The more abstract the words the more diverse the meanings attributed to them: such words as 'loyalty', 'patriotism', 'idealism' and 'industry' can vary enormously in their meanings according to the upbringing, social environment and experience of the person asked to define them. Chase's advice to those using words is to stick as far as possible to concrete words, but even these, as we have seen in the case of 'dog', can have different associations and therefore different meanings.

This is one of the factors which makes communication difficult, but a lot can be done to overcome this difficulty if the inexact use of words is realized and steps taken to define them precisely in using them. English is a particularly difficult language because so many words have different superficial meanings to say nothing of the more profound ones – as for instance 'fire' or 'industry' or even the word 'control' which is the subject of this book. Discussing the word 'control' with a friend from a developing country recently his immediate reaction was: 'But there should be no control in industry'. He was thinking of control in the sense of arbitrary dictatorship, but this, as I hope I have shown, is not the only meaning of 'control'.

The effective use of words is a study in itself and this is why members of management today do well to attend courses in communication, and why these courses contain an examination of language. There are no doubt those who think that such a suggestion is merely pedantic, but serious crises have been precipitated, not only in national and international affairs but also in industrial and commercial ones, by misunderstandings due to lack of care in the use of language. Most people believe optimistically that when they use words their meaning will be instantly apparent. Unfortunately they are usually not.

Language of mathematics

Mathematics is a language which only mathematicians can understand, but within its limitations it is a very much more exact language than that of ordinary speech. Today, in business, mathematics is coming to be increasingly used in such fields as operational research, network and critical path analysis, programme evaluation, manpower allocation, statistical decision theory and the host of new techniques which have grown up in recent years to assist management in decision making. To the ordinary manager, who is not a mathematician, these techniques may seem somewhat bewildering. They may be based on common sense but once they come to be expressed in mathematical language they plunge into depths beyond his comprehension. In most of them, computers have to be used to work out the calculations, and computers require programming, an art of which most run of the mill managers are generally ignorant.

There are now, fortunately, a growing number of 'computer appreciation' courses available where managers may learn, without being mathematicians themselves, how computers can help to make short cuts in planning future operations. Most of these techniques are based on weighing probabilities, that is to say, deciding which line of action is most probably to be more profitable than the others, in view of existing resources or in view of possible variations such as taking on fresh manpower, building new factories or installing new equipment. Formerly decisions on such matters were largely based on guesswork, reinforced by experience, but now the probabilities of success or failure can be calculated, provided the relevant data can be supplied and the programmer does his work correctly. The main point of using a computer is that it saves an enormous amount of time and effort all of which cost money. The computer can accomplish in a few minutes what it might take an army of clerks months or even years to achieve. It works by electronic impulses, and though it is in fact a calculating machine it no longer involves machinery. It is also self-correcting so that if it makes an error it can put it right itself. It is also self-proliferating in that computers can be used in the design of new and more complicated computers capable of dealing with more complex situations and sets of data.

Computer application

The trouble is that most of the books and pamphlets on computerized planning are written in mathematical language which is a bar to its understanding by non-mathematicians, but is a simplification to those who *are* mathematicians. Does this suggest that the manager of future has got to be a higher mathematician? I do not think so. It may however mean that he is more dependent on consultants and experts, and that every manager, even in the smaller firm, would do well to try to understand, at least, how computers can be used and what operational research consists of. Computer time can now be hired and for a smaller firm this is obviously the most economical way of using computers if and when the value of doing so can be assessed. There is little doubt, however, that the manager of the future cannot afford to be ignorant of what computers can do for him in helping him to run his business. There must be many managers who have said: 'If only I had the time and the resources to carry out research on such and such, it would be of the greatest value to me.' With the advent of the computer such a research may now well be possible, as for instance in market analysis, in man-power allocation, in capital utilization, in personnel assessment, in materials availability.

Basically we come back to the original theme of this book, that a business can only be run effectively when maximum information is available, and presented in such a form that it can be used for rapid decision making. By putting data through a computer it can be made available in such a form; moreover a computer has the great advantage that it can be used for the storage of information for future use. It has a built-in memory which may eliminate acres of filing.

Management and the computer

The microfilm is another method of storage of information which in recent years has become popular because of its saving in space. Important documents are photographed in miniature and the originals destroyed. But for use in a computer this information has to be translated into symbols on a tape which can be processed and stored and re-translated when required. The computer thus takes over two functions of the human brain: memory and calculation.

Those who wish to study the implication of the computer's impact on industrial Britain are referred to an article by Mr John Davies, formerly Director General of the Confederation of British Industry and previously Vice-Chairman and Managing Director of Shell-Mex and BP, in *The Manager* of December 1965. The article is called 'By the End of this Century' and is a supplement to a series of articles entitled 'Management in the Year 2000' by three Professors and a consultant. I take the following quotation from the article by Mr Davies:

> Design, research and marketing will have become the primary activities of management. With so much transformed by computer from conjecture to certainty, the range of problems on which

management skill can be exercised will be much reduced. The reduced range will be more searching and more critical of competence . . .

The computer can simplify the manager's job in some directions but will complicate it in others. In Mr Davies's view, for instance, 'human relationships in industry will become more formal and much less contentious' and 'the number of independent industrial units will become greatly reduced. . . . It is difficult to see how such a situation is compatible with the idea of intense competitive effort save in the field of the unquantifiable design, research and customer relations'. According to Mr Davies: 'All will tend to have access by means of simulation studies to knowledge of the main conditions within which others are working'. Just as an architect or a ship-designer makes a model of a building or a ship before he builds it, so a business man can construct a model – on paper – of a project before he puts it into action, and he can, if he knows the main circumstances facing his competitors, do it equally for them as for his own business and thus forecast in what direction they are likely to develop.

Management and design

It is interesting to note the three directions in which the future manager, according to Mr Davies, will have to exercise initiative – design, research and customer relations – because even today, when computerization is in its comparative infancy and competition is still operative, though possibly to a diminishing extent, these are the main concerns of management.

So far we have not considered design as one of the main preoccupations of management, but if we go back to our original premises we can see that this must be so.

Our main premise, it will be remembered, is that the function of management is to organize resources in such a way as to satisfy the needs of the consuming public at prices within its capacity to pay, or to put it another way, to identify and satisfy a market. Anyone who has studied industrial development over the last half-century will recognize the importance of design in meeting the needs of the public, particularly in household equipment, where convenience and labour saving are of paramount importance to the housewife. But the same applies to any product, as for instance the motor car.

When cars first came into production they were designed as imitation horse carriages, and were called horseless carriages. In the same way, the early railway 'carriages' as they were (and still are) called, were designed as strings of stage coaches. As railways and motorcars developed it was realized that design could be altered from slavish imitation of the past to meet the requirements of the present; 'streamlining' became possible with actual economies in production. A study of the design of ships and houses shows how design has been modified by two factors, convenience of use, and change in basic materials. The change from wood to steel in ships, as also from wind to steam or oil have profoundly modified design. In buildings, the change from timber to brick and from brick to reinforced concrete and steel frame building has revolutionized architecture.

Technological development has accelerated changes of design, particularly in the field of machinery, where function is all important. But 'functional' design is not confined to machines, and Le Corbusier's claim that a house is 'a machine for living in' had a profound effect on modern architecture. Unnecessary ornamentation so beloved of our Victorian ancestors has now been largely abandoned and design and function are inextricably interwoven, as they were in the Middle Ages before sentimentality and snobbery distorted the purpose of design. Today design has come into its own again as a primary function of industry, and every good manager must recognize its importance. It is recognized that design is not something which concerns only the artist, nor is it something in which tradition has to be adhered to. When Gilbert Scott designed St Pancras Station in London, design was looked upon as something needed to conceal the starkness of purely functional building. Today it is realized that the real beauty of St Pancras is not Scott's bogus façade but the functional simplicity and efficiency of the steel and glass station itself. The Gothic façade is not only unnecessary but, as Ruskin pointed out, completely inappropriate. The Gothic style was evolved to perform an entirely different function from that of disguising commercial activities to look like religious sanctuaries. One of the pioneers of modern design was the Duke of Devonshire's gardener, William Paxton, who, faced with the problem of running up a gigantic building at short notice to house the Great Exhibition of 1851, designed the Crystal Palace as a prefabricated structure of inter-changeable steel girders and sheets of glass, which could not only be rapidly erected but equally rapidly dismantled and re-erected elsewhere. Ironically enough the Crystal Palace was built to house an exhibition of the worst specimens of design which the world has ever seen.

Design and research

Today design is inextricably bound up with research, and this research takes many forms. Market research is necessary to determine the type of product which is needed. Coupled with it is consumer research, to investigate the uses of the product and the practical needs of each individual consumer. From this information a prototype can be created to perform the maximum number of functions required. The next stage in research is concerned with the actual materials to be used and their current availability. Later research is required into the best possible methods of assembly and manufacture. In course of these various researches modifications of design may be made as well as other modifications due to the needs of profitability. Materials may be found to be too expensive to market the product at a profit, or operational research may reveal that additional equipment may be required which will make the development uneconomical. Continual adjustments may have to be made before the product is launched on the market, all arising from research into various factors involved. To overcome these obstacles and make the necessary adjustments is the function of the management. In doing so management must draw on the expert knowledge of specialists either within its organization or outside it. It may in fact employ a firm of consultants to conduct a 'feasibility' study.[1]

[1] A 'feasibility' study is an investigation into whether a project is 'feasible' or 'viable', whether in fact it is likely to be successful and to continue to be so. It will include research into profitability, existing competition, markets, capital requirements, availability of manpower etc. Finally must come a continuous process of value analysis in which each product and process is periodically reviewed in relation to use, cost, materials, profitability and effectiveness.

Packaging and design

Bound up with design is packaging, the presentation of the product. This applies mainly to consumer products and is also involved with display, which in turn is concerned with advertising. Packaging is a science in itself which is partly concerned with consumer psychology. When Rowntree's brought out 'Black Magic' Chocolates, they spent £10,000 on consumer research to discover what kind of container they should use. The research revealed that a simple unadorned black box was the most acceptable container to the consuming public for this particular product, and its success has been phenomenal. Obviously other factors were involved in this success, but the package was undoubtedly an important one. It set a new, distinctive tone and is as popular today as it was when the product was launched some 30-odd years ago. In our highly competitive economy, in which actual standard and quality of product are difficult to differentiate, apparently trivial details like design of containers and advertisements have become of considerable importance. The consuming public are very vulnerable both to suggestion and association and, while good packaging can never mask a bad product, it can often ensure continuation of consumer loyalty to a good one as Rowntree's black box has demonstrated. A more detailed discussion of packaging and brand loyalty will be found in Chapter 9.

CHAPTER 7

Customer relations and advertising

Hypnotism and advertising

We have already referred to the considerable nonsense talked and to the amount of opinion which has recently found expression concerning the sinister role played by advertising in our modern industrial economy. Among those who have contributed to this opinion have been Vance Packard in his book *The Hidden Persuaders* and Professor J. K. Galbraith in his book *The Affluent Society*. The main argument for these two writers is that society as a whole is being persuaded, by methods aimed at their unconscious rather than their conscious minds, to buy a lot of commodities which they neither need nor want, and that advertising is a form of hypnotism to influence people to waste their money in order to enhance the profits of manufacturers.

Not long ago it was claimed that an experiment was made in advertising whereby a slogan recommending ice-cream was flashed on to a cinema screen for such a short time that few people were actually aware of it. During the interval it was found that the sale of ice-cream greatly increased. It was suggested that in fact this message had penetrated to the unconscious minds of the audience, without them being consciously aware of it, and that their unconscious minds had induced them to demand ice-cream as the result. So seriously was this threat to human free will taken that such advertising was made illegal. It is now believed that this experiment in what came to be called subliminal advertising was a hoax. It does however raise an interesting point in psychology. Where in fact do our needs and desires originate, and how far can people be hypnotized to take action against their conscious wills?

CUSTOMER RELATIONS AND ADVERTISING

Informative advertising

Such methods are only an extension of a process which has been known for centuries as education and training. The unconscious mind can certainly be a potent force and no doubt unconscious influence is a factor used by advertisers to persuade people to buy consumer goods. Nevertheless it is an axiom in the advertising business that no amount of persuasion can induce a consumer to buy a bad product more than once. Most people are attracted by novelty and a new product invariably attracts customers – for a time. Frank Harris is supposed to have boasted to Bernard Shaw that he had been invited to all the great houses of England. 'Yes,' answered Shaw, 'once.'

The main function of advertising today is to persuade customers to buy one of a number of products of similar quality and price, and the only advertising which is useful and justifiable is that which informs people (a) of the existence of a product and (b) what it can do. As we have seen, Emerson's mousetrap maker would have had to make his mousetrap known in the first place and he would also have had to inform potential customers in what way it was better than any other mousetrap, before anyone would even think of beating a path to his door to buy it. Crompton's form of advertising was to take his yarn to the market so that people could see its excellence for themselves, and this in fact is the soundest form of advertising. It is not until the customer has seen and sampled the product that he or she can fully appreciate its qualities. Advertising is merely a means of conveying some knowledge of these qualities by various forms of media. If its claims are spurious it will soon be found out; if true it will satisfy a legitimate need.

What advertising can and does do is to make people aware of a need or a desire of which they were previously unconscious. The average intelligent person's reaction to good advertising is to say: 'Yes. That is just what I want but I never realized it before' or, 'I've always wanted one of those but the price has been more than I could afford before'. Most of us want far more than we can afford to possess and have to exercise careful choice in relation to the extent of our incomes.

Advertising can help us to choose by informing us of what is available. The Sears Roebuck catalogue, one of the most monumental pieces of advertising ever produced, could not force people

CUSTOMER RELATIONS AND ADVERTISING

to buy what they did not want. What it did do was to put within their grasp the purchase of satisfactions they craved for. There is no doubt that advertising exploits the baser characteristics such as snobbery, greed, acquisitiveness, sentimentality and a desire to keep up with the Joneses, but it does not create these characteristics, which existed long before advertising. In presenting products to the public, it is the business of advertising to use every possible legal means of attracting attention to them. If it exaggerates and misleads it merely cheapens its own currency and makes itself suspect. Extravagant claims eventually rebound on those who make them.

But an advertising agency is bound to use all possible methods to sell its client's products: in a competitive economy, advertising is the means by which competition is fostered.

The functions of advertising

It is said that advertising is wasteful and that the cost of it raises prices. It can be argued that advertising lowers prices by expanding consumption sufficiently to enable manufacturers to employ mass production methods, which greatly decrease cost of production. In fact, mass production would be impossible unless its results were 'pre-sold' to the public through the mass media of advertising.

Advertising has three main functions:

1. To draw the customer's attention to the product.
2. To give information to the consumer as to how the product can satisfy his needs.
3. To persuade the customer to buy the product, rather than any other similar product on the market.

Advertising media

There has been, in the last half-century, a considerable increase in advertising media such as the daily and weekly press, magazines, posters, films, radio and television. It is the manager's job, with the advice of his advertising agent, if he has one, to judge which of these media are most appropriate to sell his product. He must also know how to use his advertising agent as a consultant and how to judge the advertising he produces. Many sales managers believe they know more about advertising than their agents who are, after all, the experts. Nevertheless great discretion is needed in choosing an advertising agent, particularly today when the number of agents is increasing rapidly. Managers who are concerned with marketing and sales would be wise to study advertising and its principles more deeply, so that they can use wise judgment in choosing their advertising agent. Advertising is a specialized art, and few businesses are equipped to handle their own advertising; though some of the larger firms, such as Unilever, have set up their own internal agencies which may also undertake outside work.

A good agency should not only have a first-class art department and media manager but also a market research section and a section for advertising research, by which it can test the effect of its advertising. This is usually done on a sample basis in the same way as market research. Random samples of the consumer public are asked various questions regarding the impact of advertising upon them. They are asked what advertisements they remember, what they associate with brand-names, what they associate with various products, and, most important, what effect advertisements have had on their buying habits. Such researches are most revealing and are of great help both to the advertising agent and his client. Many agencies also have their own film production units for making advertising films for cinema and television.

The account executive

The key man in an advertising agency is the 'account executive'. A client's business is known as an 'account' and the executive may look after several accounts provided they do not compete with each other. His job is to act as liaison between the client and the agency. The client must give the executive as much information as possible about the product he is advertising. One of the features of a product which an agency has to look for is its 'unique selling proposition' or U.S.P. The U.S.P. is that feature or combination of features which distinguishes the product from similar products. Unless a unique selling proposition can be found, the agency may be merely repeating the same sales points as are used for competitive products. In his *Confessions of an Advertising Man* David Ogilvy quotes his slogan: 'The loudest thing in this car is the clock' as a means of advertising the noiselessness of the Rolls Royce. This of course was an easy one because a Rolls Royce is unique anyway.

It becomes more difficult with a highly competitive product like a washing soap or a detergent. The first thing an agency has to do is to direct public attention to its advertising. This it must do by surprise or novelty of approach, as for instance Ogilvy's man with the black patch over one eye, in selling shirts, or Schweppes' use of the somewhat striking appearance of the red-bearded Commander Whitehead.

But this is only the beginning. Nobody is going to buy a product continuously merely for the sake of a black-patched man or a bearded naval commander. Nor is he going to buy it because of an attractive slogan. All these tricks can do is to draw attention to the product and make the reader notice the advertising. This is where the 'copy' becomes important. The copy may be written or spoken or it may be embodied in a picture or the action of a film; it may be long or short. Ogilvy favours long copy, while other advertising men disagree on the grounds that people have no time to read or listen to a lot of words. The length and presentation of the copy depends very largely on the product and the medium used – and its cost.

The object of advertising is to sell, and this is the ultimate criterion by which it must be judged. The cleverest and most spectacular advertisements do not necessarily sell the product, when sometimes the simplest do. While the business manager does not need to know all the techniques of advertising, he must know enough about them to be able to judge the effectiveness of the job his agents are doing for him. Having entrusted his agent with the job he should leave him to get on with it and not interfere on the technical side. Having given him all relevant information and clearly stated and discussed his marketing objectives, he should then sit back and watch. It is not a wise policy to change one's advertising agency frequently. Advertising must be an integral part of the business and the agent a trusted servant, like a consultant or a family doctor. Only if his work is demonstrably ineffective should an advertising agent be sacked. He must be given a fair chance to prove his effectiveness.

Public relations

Bound up closely with advertising is public relations and the building of the 'company image'. This 'image' is an important entity. It is, in fact, the impression existing in the public mind of the company and its product. It can be created in a number of ways. Advertising does much to create it but it is subject to other influences. A company with a bad labour relations record will acquire a bad public image. Involvement in lawsuits can also affect a company's image adversely. Every individual within a company helps to make or mar its public image. A chain store whose sales assistants are rude or offhand to its customers is doing harm to its public image. Some companies go out of their way to give benevolent donations to public charities with the object of building up a favourable public image. Some firms still invite well-known public figures to sit on the board in order to improve their image.

Public relations can take a number of forms and is now becoming a specialist function conducted by professional experts. It is one of their jobs to see that as much favourable publicity appears in the press and other media as possible about the company's activities, and that all notable achievements are duly publicized. Dinners, cocktail parties and press conferences are among their methods of publicity and large sums of money are spent on them. Press hand-outs are sent to the newspapers when any signal events take place such as the appointment of a new director or the launching of a new product. Motor car firms employ well-known racing drivers to drive their cars in races; aircraft firms see that new developments are duly publicized. All these things help to build up the public image. On the other hand such events as air-crashes, accidents to buildings, or cases of food poisoning greatly injure the public images of air-lines, firms of contractors and restaurants. The public image is important and cannot be neglected. It is merely a new phrase for the old word, 'reputation'; and reputation, in business, has always been a vital asset.

Product and consumer relations

However much a company may spend on advertising and public relations the main link between producer and consumer will inevitably be the product. If the product is not up to the standard expected and required by the consumer, no amount of public relations or advertising will make up for it. Thus the key word to consumer relations must be 'quality'. If quality is sacrificed or allowed to deteriorate no amount of publicity can restore the damage done to the public image of the product. This is why quality control is of such vital importance today in this age of mass production, mass consumption, and intense competition.

Protection of the consumer

Today there are a number of consumers' magazines, the best known being *Which?*. The object of these magazines, which flourish in many countries, is to protect the consumer from exploitation by giving a candid assessment of the quality of products available on the market. It is possible that the consumer is not always the best judge of quality and that he or she may be prepared to accept a product which is shoddy or second-rate through laziness, apathy or ignorance. Such magazines as *Which?* and various consumers' associations have been started to protect the consumer from accepting anything below the standard which is claimed for it and which he has a right to expect. Such bodies do a great service to the consuming public and also, incidentally, to producers themselves by ensuring that those who produce good quality products are not deprived of their rightful market by those who fail to do so. Quality, of course, must be judged in relation to price, and to what the consumer can afford. Too often, as we know, apparent cheapness is only a false economy.

In the United States (and elsewhere) there has grown up an attitude that believes that products should not be made to last because durability diminishes the market for new products, the objective of industry being to sell the maximum as quickly as possible. Thus shoes, motor cars, clothes and other products were deliberately made of poor material so that they could be thrown aside quickly and equally short-lasting replacements bought for them.

I remember once hearing the former professor of Economics at Cambridge, A. C. Pigou, point out that the only time our competitive economic system functioned effectively was in time of war, because war solved the problem of consumption by gearing the whole economy to make goods whose whole object was to be destroyed as soon as possible, thus requiring immediate replacements. This may sound a cynical comment, but it had a good deal of truth in it.

CUSTOMER RELATIONS AND ADVERTISING

Shortly after I left Cambridge the world was plunged into one of the worst economic depressions of all time due to what was then called 'over-production'. Of course this phrase is meaningless, because there can never be overproduction until all the inhabitants of the world have all they can possibly need. In those days the solution to the problem of 'over-production' was to burn wheat and coffee and other commodities while millions were starving and in need of them. In the end Pigou's solution to the problem came to pass and we found ourselves once more at war. We certainly heard no more about over-production then. Today we may have got things into better proportion. Consumers are now better organized and are developing means of insisting that their interests shall be observed.[1]

Quality control

Quality control goes through a number of stages. A new product starts as a prototype which is submitted to many stringent tests. These may lead to modifications and a further prototype. If this passes the requisite tests it is then put into production. But testing does not end there. It is submitted to sample testing which entails extracting units of the product at random from the production line and testing them against the standard. One sample is taken from each batch and if it does not pass all tests the whole batch may have to be tested or even withdrawn. A motor tyre for instance will be submitted to stringent tests, in some cases up to destruction. The tests will determine how long the tyre can be used safely and the mileage beyond which it would be dangerous. It can then be guaranteed for a mileage well within this figure The same can apply to many other products. Even a golfball is submitted to rigid distance tests to ensure that if properly hit it will travel a reasonable distance. Not only is it tested for resilience by being propelled at high speed from a compressed air gun but is actually hit by a mechanically operated driver travelling at the same speed as a human stroke might do. Chemical products are submitted to periodical analysis to ensure their correct chemical content. Materials such as cloth or carpeting are also tested for wear and tear. Components of a wireless or television set are carefully

[1] There is however such a thing as 'planned obsolescence' which will be discussed later. See pp. 177-8.

inspected for faults before assembly, when the final set is tested for performance.

As the intricacy of testing devices increases, so the human element is diminished and the chance of human error lessened. Where danger to health or life would be involved by a faulty product, the government has stepped in and insisted on certain standards which can only be ignored at the risk of serious penalties. The larger and better known a company, the less it can afford to fail in the quality or reliability of its product, and the more resources it will have available for effective quality and reliability control. On the other hand the smaller company struggling for recognition in face of competition will also have the strongest incentive to ensure the highest possible quality of its products. Quality is probably the most important factor in creating a good public image, whether it be quality of product or quality of service. This is why it is so important that every individual within a company should be aware of the meaning of the concept and should contribute in every way to seeing that it is not impaired.

Importance of the image

When we think of a person or a company we are aware of certain associations and these build up our image. It was the objective of the Guinness advertisements at one time to build up an association of strength. It did so with great ingenuity and a pleasant and whimsical humour which accentuated the association. Exaggeration is legitimate provided it is obvious; it is only when it attempts to be factual that it becomes untrustworthy.

But other associations creep in not only due to advertising. Marks and Spencer has come to have a reputation for training and looking after its work people. This reputation inspires confidence not only in the organization but also in what it has to sell.

Many years ago a cartoon appeared showing a squirrel running behind the old T-model Ford car. The implication was that it was hoping to pick up the nuts. The effect on Ford's public image can hardly have been beneficial. In Singapore after the war, Lufthansa was becoming a popular air-line making serious inroads on BOAC's business. One day somebody casually dropped a remark that Lufthansa pilots had learnt to fly by carrying out bombing raids over England. From then on their British customers started

CUSTOMER RELATIONS AND ADVERTISING

to fall off considerably. Such is the power of the public image.

A large part of public relations is aimed at counteracting false impressions, as for instance the rumour that BOAC, in Pakistan, catered only for European passengers and not for Pakistanis. The result was an intensive campaign to prove that not only were Pakistanis welcome on BOAC flights, but would receive special treatment in regard to food requirements and other amenities. British firms abroad have serious public relations problems to contend with due to prejudice against 'imperialism'. Propaganda is a form of public relations and frequently involves considerable image-building, as for instance in Nazi Germany where it became public policy to create an image of the Jewish race as sub-human monsters and traitors. During the first world war an attempt was made by his opponents to build up an image of Mr Asquith as being a teacherous pro-German. False images as well as favourable ones have played an important part in history and it is no good trying to ignore their significance. Even though an image we may have of someone may be a false one, we tend to act upon it rather than on the truth, which is often difficult to discern.

The object of public relations is to try to create a favourable image, and it is easier to create such an image if it is based on fact rather than fiction. If the facts are not consistent with the image, then either they must be altered to agree with it or else the image will be discredited – though it may be then be too late. The Swiss psychologist, Carl Gustav Jung, pointed out that the world is directed by myths, and myths are built out of images, some false and others true.

Opinion surveys and image analysis

The only way to find out what the average consumer thinks of a product or a producer is to ask him, and if you ask enough people in the right way you may get a reliable sample of public opinion. This is known as public opinion survey, or consumer research. It may reveal a public image somewhat different from that expected and it may help the public relations man to correct the image or change it. It is better to know the truth than to be misled by illusions, and there may be illusions on both sides – the consumer's and the producer's. This is a useful control which management can make use of in order to adjust its production and/or selling policy.

CHAPTER 8

Innovation and expansion

Varieties of business

Hitherto we have ranged over a fairly wide field of business activities and tried to establish certain basic principles of management control. The businessman reading this book may say: 'Yes. This is all very well, but how does it apply to *my* business?' One answer is: 'It all depends what your particular business is'. Is it, for instance, a small business or a large business? Is it a manufacturing business, a wholesale business or a retail business? Does it supply services, consumer products or manufacturing products? Business does, in fact, cover a very wide range of activities, and it would be impossible in a work of this kind to supply a handbook to which every business man could refer for a solution to his own particular problems. All one can do here is to indicate certain lines of policy which may help the small to medium-sized businessman to manage his affairs more effectively, and to avoid certain categories of more or less expensive mistakes.

One could, perhaps, take a typical business and examine the factors involved.

The typical business

Today we find ourselves surrounded by vast business combinations which appear to dominate the economic scene, such as I.C.I., Unilever, B.A.T., United Steel, General Motors, British Motor Holdings and Shell, among others, all with millions of pounds worth of capital and operating throughout the world. With these giants overshadowing him, the smaller businessman may well wonder whether there is room for him any longer. But of course there is, in fact, plenty of room.

INNOVATION AND EXPANSION

In the first place, as we have seen, these giants all began as small concerns which built themselves up gradually and amalgamated with others which enabled them to make large scale economies. Many of these big companies have only come to the fore comparatively recently, and largely because of good management. They studied their markets carefully and adapted their methods to meet them. There is always the danger in an old, established firm, however large and powerful it may be, that it will tend to become too conservative, to 'live on its fat' and become lethargic, even though when it started it was a pioneer in the business. This is the chance for the up-and-coming businessman who recognizes change and development and is prepared to meet their challenge.

Value of the smaller business

For those who may think that the role of the small business is played out let me quote from a recent article in *International Management Information* published in Zurich in 1966.

> It might be well to dispel a widely held notion that the small business is 'on the way out'. Quite contrary is the case... In the past ten years the number of small businesses (in the United States) has grown from 4,000,000 to 4,600,000 – an increase of 60,000 each year. Of firms with a net worth of $20,000 to $250,000[1] – relatively small – 90 per cent have been in business for 5 years.

Let me also quote from a publication called *Business and Society* published in the U.S.A. in 1966.

> Many important commercial inventions of the past half-century came not from the large companies but from independent inventors and from small business concerns. Among these are air-conditioning, automatic transmissions, the jet engine, continuous casting of steel, cellophane, magnetic recording, the gyro compass, the polaroid camera and the Xerox duplicating machine. A searching study of 61 twentieth century 'fundamental inventions' has indicated that more than half were individual inventions in the sense that much of the work was carried out by men working on their own behalf without the backing of any research institution.

[1] About £8,300 to £104,000.

INNOVATION AND EXPANSION

A former Vice-President of the General Electric Co. has said:

> In the electric appliance industry, the better clothes washing machines have not been produced by the monster companies specializing in one or two products. This is also true of ranges, vacuum cleaners, radios, toasters, air-conditioning units etc.
>
> Small business have been called millions of centres of initiative. They are a vast seed-bed for technological development and innovation.

There is no need therefore for the small businessman to despair. In view of the greater economies which the large scale operator is able to make, however, the small businessman has got to pay more attention to costs than in the past and to exercise greater control over details. Gone are the days when anyone could set up in business and expect to get by with slovenly and out-of-date methods. There are still great opportunities for the man with enterprise, initiative and industry to build up a successful business, even if in the end he gets bought up by a larger one. If so at least he will not have lost his capital, will more probably increased it, and can use it again in another activity.

Necessity for profit

Profit may be called a measure of public demand for a service or a commodity, it is also a measure of the efficiency of management. But no amount of good management can force the public to buy something which no longer fulfils a consumer need; and part of the function of management is to judge when and why demand falls off and to readapt the activities of a business to changed demand. This means that management has to be constantly prepared for innovation. In the clothing industry fashions change rapidly, particularly in women's clothing. Fashions change also in motor cars, furniture, house design, aircraft, household utensils, packaging. These changes are due to innovation caused by research into the needs of the consumer, particularly in the light of technical improvements and the use of new materials. The good businessman or manager does not wait for fashions to change before he makes a new move; he anticipates changes and even, if he can, contributes to them through new and commercially useful ideas.

INNOVATION AND EXPANSION

Relevant questions

The businessman or manager has to be continually asking questions not only about his own product or service but about those of others. He must ask such questions as: Why do we do this thing in this way? Why could we not do this another, more economical way? What is the object of this operation? Do people really want this thing we are making? – in this form, at this price? Why does it take so long for our products to get from A to B? What do we really know about our markets? Too many businesses, and particularly small businesses, tend to take too many of these aspects for granted without due examination. A common answer to queries is 'We've always done it that way'. Thousands of pounds of savings and new ideas have come simply from asking questions.

Brain storming

Some firms have what they call 'brain-storming sessions'. These consist of getting groups of people together and asking them to think of ideas on a particular problem. The more ideas the better, however crazy they may seem. Out of say a hundred ideas, however, five good ones may emerge which will lead to useful improvements and innovations. In a small firm every executive should be encouraged to think of at least one good idea every week. In large firms considerable sums are spent in the establishment of research and development departments, whose main function is to contribute new ideas for innovation and improvement of a product or a service. New ideas do not only come from executives, but many from the humbler ranks including shopfloor workers. For this reason many firms have suggestion schemes to stimulate the production of useful ideas, and reward them suitably. It is well worth paying a reward of £25 or £50 for an idea which may save the company many thousands, or immeasurably increase its profits and service to the public.

Organization and methods

The basis of such techniques as method study, work study and work simplification is constant questioning of methods from the viewpoint of effort and time spent. The 'job method' course in the U.K. Training Within Industry programme is designed to impart the elements of these techniques to the supervisor. Now work study has become a science of its own, resulting in considerable savings at all levels of business. In the office there has grown up a kindred science of organization-and-methods aimed at cutting down unnecessary activities, simplifying filing and correspondence and generally making administration more efficient – that is less costly in time, effort, materials and customer goodwill. Like most modern management techniques these sciences are largely built on common sense. Gilbreth, the originator of work study, is said to have started by watching a bricklayer at work and calculating the amount of wasted energy involved in building a wall. By eliminating a number of the movements involved, he not only increased the speed of the operation considerably but also saved the bricklayer some actual exertion. There is hardly a department of any business, large or small, where work simplification cannot be used effectively to reduce cost and effort and increase efficiency.

Innovation

We have seen that innovation is one of the principles of a healthy business and that a healthy business must be dynamic. But innovation costs money. In a motor manufacturing firm each new model requires an expensive set of new dies for making the parts and possibly a considerable amount of other changes in equipment. This represents a very large financial outlay. A comparatively small manufacturing company may not feel it can afford this expenditure and may only change its models every three or four years.

Now that the motor industry is gradually becoming concentrated into a few large combines, they are in a better position to incur such expenditure, and it is no doubt this fact which has operated as a spur to greater combination. A big combine can also afford to manufacture a far larger range of models to suit the requirements of a wider field of customers. Some people want small cars, some medium and others large; some people want fast sports cars, others want reliable family cars, others want luxury and prestige built into their cars. Some firms prefer to specialize in one type of car as have Rolls Royce; others wish to maximize their range. Some firms buy a large proportion of their components from outside and merely assemble them. Others, like Ford, produce the major proportion themselves, including the raw steel from which the parts are made and for which Henry Ford erected his own blast furnaces. In the past such decisions were dictated partly by prejudice and partly by economy. Kynoch, the cartridge maker, now absorbed into I.C.I., did not trust anyone to do his printing, just as Ford did not trust others to make his steel, so he set up his own printing works which is now part of I.C.I. Today a business man has to decide whether it is more economical and efficient to buy his components from outside and merely assemble them into his finished product, or to make the whole thing himself. In an age of specialization it is often better to trust the specialist, and a great number of smaller businesses exist today merely to make components for larger manufacturers.

Example of a small business

Before the war the writer started his own business to exploit an invention of his own for a new type of constructional toy. The main components were of wood, but the parts required careful machining which would have involved a considerable outlay in equipment. After a careful survey, in view of the limited capital available, it was decided to entrust the actual machining of the components to a firm of precision wood workers. The production manager's job was to work out the quantities of each part required to make up a given number of various sized sets. The size and components of these sets were worked out partly on the basis of a market research. As part of this research, sample sets were prepared and submitted to a selected group of retailers who arranged for them to be demonstrated to their customers. Catalogues of models to be made with each set had to be worked out and printed.

Having established a demand for the product, the question of price fixing arose. In the toy trade wholesalers demand 50 per cent discount, retailers 33⅓ per cent. Salesmen and demonstrators had to be hired. Expensive patents were taken out in a number of countries which involved a disproportionate outlay of capital. Sales however were encouraging but, owing to the imminence of war, the manufacturers of the components increased their prices to a point which, in view of the discounts demanded by the trade, made the retail cost prohibitive. Finally the war in 1939 forced the project to be abandoned.

Apart from the war the project would probably have been successful. Had I known as much about management as I do now it might well have made substantial profits. I learnt many useful lessons from my mistakes. One is that the mere possession of a new idea and a little capital are not a sufficient basis for building up a business. I was right in conducting a market research but it was not extensive enough. I was wrong in taking out expensive patents. All I needed to do was to register the name and take out a provisional patent which would have covered me for a year. In fact nobody has ever tried to imitate my invention which was patented on a mathematical formula, and not on the basic idea, which was really too simple to patent. These patents absorbed far too large a proportion of my limited capital.

I should also have investigated my costs of production more fully and related discounts to price more carefully. The margin of profit on my sales, after deducting cost and discount, left little over to meet my overheads, even though I kept them to a minimum. I employed an accountant and a production manager. The latter's job was to design the sets and catalogues and pack the components into sets. I employed one full-time salesman and a number of temporary sales-demonstrators whose work was mainly seasonal. I also rented a basement in London where the operations of packing and distribution were conducted. All this should have been costed at the outset and a 'break even' chart constructed based on graduated volumes of sales. Such a chart might take the form shown in figure 2, p. 119.

Break-even chart

The chart would be in the form of a graph in which the vertical axis represents costs and revenues and the horizontal axis represents sales. As we have seen earlier, costs are divided into fixed costs and variable costs. The fixed costs persist whether we sell any units or not. The variable costs vary with the amount sold. The fixed costs are therefore represented by a horizontal line parallel with the horizontal axis. They are made up of rent of premises, salaries of essential staff, light, heat etc. In the case of my business, to be strictly accurate, these should have included current interest on capital contributed, say £20,000 at 6 per cent or £1,200. Next my own salary at say £1,600 a year. Next we should include rent of premises at say £600 a year. Staff salaries

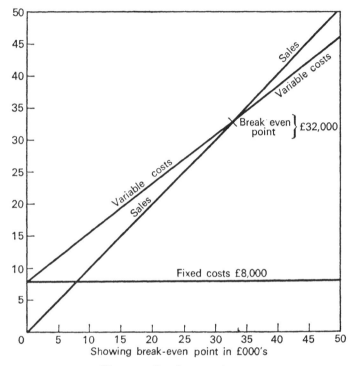

Figure 2. Break-even chart

might amount to £3,000, advertising to a further £1,000, and incidentals such as postage, stationery and lighting to £600. Total fixed costs thus amount to £8,000 per annum.

Let us say that we aim, in the first place, to sell 2,000 sets to the trade at a nett price (excluding discount) of say £2 each and a cost, in raw material, printing and other direct costs of 30s. each. Then for every thousand units sold our revenue will be £2,000 and our variable costs £1,500 leaving a gross profit (see footnote, p. 125) per 1,000 units of £500. Since the variable costs are additional to our fixed costs the line depicting them must start from where the fixed cost line meets the vertical ordinate, namely at £8,000. Our revenue line must start at zero so the picture presented will show that we must sell a minimum of £32,000 worth of sets per year before we can break even. After that figure has been reached we begin to make a profit. But meanwhile the question arises as to how we are to finance our operation before we start to make profits.

Cash position

Suppose that it take us three months before we can put our product on the market. This means that a tenth of our capital is already used up in meeting our fixed costs, leaving us £18,000 as working capital. Suppose however that our suppliers give us three months credit. We can now draw up another chart showing us what our target of sales must be in order to break even before the end of the second year. We already know that our break even point is £32,000 of sales. What we do not know is how long it will take up to reach this volume of sales. As our product becomes known and our advertising begins to take effect we may expect a rising figure of sales, though we also have to reckon with seasonal fluctuations including a peak period at christmas, with a falling off in January and February. Christmas stocks, however, are usually bought two or three months in advance so our peak sales will develop round about October or November.

Supposing that we started our operation in January and our sales commenced in April, we might set a series of progressive sales targets up to the end of the third year aiming at a total overall objective of £44,000. We might therefore fix our targets for the first year as follows: April to June: £4,000; July to September £5,000; October to December: £7,000. This means that our total costs for each quarter of our first year will be as follows: January/March: £2,000; April/June: £5,000; July/September: £5,750; October/December: £7,250.

This makes a total expenditure including overheads for the first year of £20,000. Revenue from sales amounts to £16,000 leaving a loss of some £4,000 to be made up during the second year. Given the fact that we shall probably have to give our customers three months credit before payment, can we finance our project so far? Is our cash position sound? Our total costs will have absorbed some £7,000 by the end of June leaving £13,000 in hand of our initial capital. Meanwhile by the end of September we should have received say £4,000 from our customers but by then we shall be faced with the raw material costs of £5,750 for the second quarter of the year. These, with our capital in hand we shall be able to pay. £4,000 plus £13,000 minus £5,750 leaves us with a capital balance of £11,250.

Thus at the end of the third quarter of the first year of our operation we have a balance of £11,750, and, in the following quarter, we shall be faced with a bill for materials of £5,250 plus overheads of £2,000 making £7,250. We shall however be able to collect £5,000 on sales from the preceding quarter. This will deplete our working capital by another £2,250 leaving us with £9,000 at the end of the third quarter. October/December is our peak period for sales which we hope will amount to £7,000 (hence our higher raw materials bill for the preceding quarter).

By the end of the year therefore we should be in a fairly good cash position, if we meet our sales target, with a credit owing to us of £7,000, bringing our assets up to £16,000. Our raw materials for the following quarter will be comparatively small, as January/March is a lean period for sales and will amount to only £3,750 on a sales target of £5,000. To this £3,750 we must add another £2,000 for overheads making £5,750 to be deducted from our £16,000 in hand and leaving us £10,250.

Our profit and loss account for the year meanwhile will be roughly as following:

Overheads	8000	Revenue	16000
Materials	12000	Loss on year	4000
	20000		20000

We have not yet reached our break-even point, but we hope to achieve this by the end of the second year, by which time our profit and loss account should be as follows:

Overheads	8000	Revenue from sales	32000
Raw materials	24000	Profit/Loss on year	Nil
	32000		32000

At the end of the second year we have £4,000 working capital still in hand and though our total trading losses of £4,000 still remain we have credits worth £12,000 due to us out of which to meet our raw materials bill and overheads for the first quarter of the third year amounting to £7,250. Our cash position drops to its lowest in the last quarter of the year with only £3,000 in hand but rises again to £8,000 at the beginning of the fourth year. Our profit and loss account for the third year shows a profit of £3,000 by which time our total loss on the three years trading has fallen to £1,000 – it would be hoped that this loss will eventually be wiped off and that a steady profit will continue out of which reserves can be built up to replace the initial capital of £20,000 and expand the business in various ways (see table 1b, p. 123).

It is clear from the summary of the above figures given in table 1a, p. 123, that a capital of £10,000 would have entailed constant borrowing from the bank and that by the end of the third year the company would have been £7,000 in the red. Although capital of £15,000 would not have been sufficient to cover cash liabilities completely and overdrafts would have been needed to ride over at least three difficult periods, a capital of £15,000 would have saved fixed capital charges of £300 a year whereas interest and temporary overdrafts would amount to only a small fraction of that figure. It would therefore appear that £15,000 to £17,000 would be a reasonable figure for capital required to tide the company over the break-even period and that this would give a slightly larger margin of profit due to savings on capital charges. One difficulty, as will be seen, is that we have to wait three months before collecting revenue to meet the bills for our manufactured goods, because we cannot collect our money until the goods are physically delivered. This time lag might, however, be reduced by favourable credit arrangements.

Once a reserve has been built up it can be used for a number of possible objects:

1. Increasing our sales force
2. Increasing our advertising
3. Increasing our salaries
4. Developing our product
5. Lowering the price of our product.

A wise choice would probably be towards (1) and (2) though the others must be borne in mind. We must also keep something in reserve for emergencies and cash requirements. As the business

TABLE I

A. *Cash position on capital of £20,000**

Year	Period	Fixed costs	Manu-facturing costs	Total costs	Revenue sales	Working capital in hand	On £10000	On £15000
1st	Jan/Mar	2000	nil	2000	nil	18000	8000	15000
	Apr/Jun	2000	3000	5000	nil	13000	3000	8000
	Jul/Sept	2000	3750	5750	4000	11250	1250	6250
	Oct/Dec	2000	5250	7250	5000	9000	−1000	4000
2nd	Jan/Mar	2000	3750	5750	7000	10250	250	5250
	Apr/Jun	2000	5250	7250	5000	8000	−2000	3000
	Jul/Sept	2000	6000	8000	7000	7000	−3000	2000
	Oct/Dec	2000	9000	11000	8000	4000	−6000	−1000
3rd	Jan/Mar	2000	5250	7250	12000	8750	−1250	4750
	Apr/Jun	2000	6750	8750	7000	7000	−3000	2000
	Jul/Sep	2000	9000	11000	9000	5000	−5000	nil
	Oct/Dec	2000	12000	14000	12000	3000	−7000	−2000
4th	Jan/Mar	2000	9000	11000	16000	8000	−2000	3000

B. *Profit and loss on three years*

Year	Total costs	Sales revenue	Profit/Loss
1st	20000	16000	−4000
2nd	32000	32000	nil
3rd	41000	44000	+3000

[1] A graphical representation of this table is given in figure 3, p. 124.

123

E*

INNOVATION AND EXPANSION

grows, consideration will have to be given to a number of points such as renting larger premises, taking on additional staff, taking out further patents, exploiting overseas markets, raising additional capital and so on.

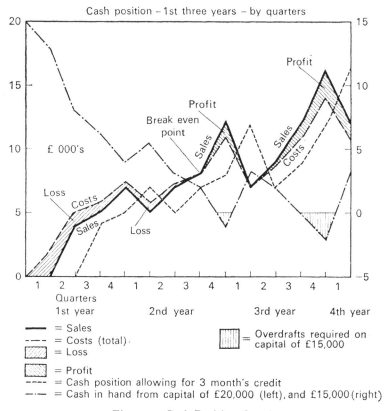

Figure 3. Cash Position Graph.

The picture has perhaps been over-simplified and the figures are not fully realistic. The ratio of capital to turnover may be open to criticism. But many businesses have started on less capital and turned out quite successfully. A great deal depends on management and careful attention to detail. Control, it will be seen, is necessary from the very outset.

I know of a publishing company which started shortly after the last war and now has an over £1,000,000 turnover. The firm supplied a need for high class illustrated books at a reasonable price and have now become specialists in prestige books costing anything up to 15 guineas, which they sell all over the world. Their original capital was small and their staff was less than half a dozen, all of whom have prospered exceedingly.

A simplification of the 'break-even' chart is merely to calculate your fixed costs, in my example £8,000 a year or £2,000 a quarter, and then reckon your gross profit per unit.[1] If the gross profit is 20 per cent then your sales must be five times the value of your fixed costs in order to cover them. That is if your fixed cost is £500 per month and your unit sells at £2 10s. 0d. you will have to sell 1,000 units at a total figure of £2,500 to reach your break-even point. A simple formula to calculate break-even point is: B.E.P. = Fixed costs × 100 divided by gross profit per unit. Whatever number you sell beyond the break-even figure will bring you in clear profit. The important thing is that a clear distinction must be made between fixed recurring costs and variable or direct costs, that is to say expenditure which varies in proportion to the number of units sold. One difficulty is that some costs cannot be fitted into either category with complete accuracy. Take for instance the salary of a salesman. Presumably the more salesmen we employ the greater will be our sales! Part of the salesman's pay may moreover be in the form of a commission. Clearly this is not a fixed cost since it varies with the amount of products sold. Neither is it a cost of production. Sales costs come into a category by themselves, though for break-even purposes they can be included in fixed costs since they have to be incurred whether sales result or not. A commission however is another thing and can be looked upon as a reduction of the gross profit. As an incentive, however, it is a useful means of sales promotion, but since it varies with the amount of sales it should be counted as a direct cost.

To simplify my picture I have left out the question of bulk order discounts and also discounts for quick payment. Ability to take advantage of these may be affected by, and also affect, the cash position. Cash costs money in terms of time, and if we wish to be

[1] Gross profit is generally taken to mean the profit made on each unit before deducting overheads. If it costs me 10s. to make a jack-knife and I sell it for 15s. my gross profit is 5s. The break-even point comes when gross profit per unit sold = fixed costs (i.e. overheads).

in a position to obtain cash discounts for prompt payment we may require more capital for which money has to be paid in terms of interest. It is reasonable to suppose that a loan could be obtained from the bank at a cost of about £17 10s. 0d. per quarter per £1,000. This is not an excessive amount to pay for temporary financial accommodation and most business firms make use of it fairly extensively if they can produce adequate security.

Overhead costs are seldom as rigidly fixed as I have shown them; they may in fact vary considerably for many reasons. It is always wise, even in a small business, to allow a margin or reserve for unforeseen contingencies. One contingency might be the payment of interest on a temporary overdraft. There may also be additional expenditure for payment of demonstrator-salesmen or saleswomen during the Christmas season. These would affect the total cost per unit but would also tend to increase sales. They would certainly affect the break-even point. In my example I also assumed that the sales targets were always met. It was assumed they were fixed with due regard to an estimate of the seasonal market. It will be noted that the break-even point was not reached until the enterprise had been established for two years. This on a capital of £10,000 caused a pile up of losses to a sum in excess of the original capital and this seriously affected the cash position. Higher targets might have been set but they might not have been achieved. On the 'production' side, consisting in this case mainly of packing and assembly of sets, there is always a limit to capacity which cannot be exceeded without incurring additional expense. As sales, and therefore profits, increased no doubt more staff and accommodation would have been hired thus increasing the fixed costs and reducing the profit per unit though probably increasing the total revenue from sales. The law of diminishing returns can only be offset by a considerable expansion in markets.

Diminishing returns

The law of diminishing returns is an economic concept which states that, after a certain point has been reached in an industrial enterprise, the more capital you put into it the less will be the percentage return, other things being equal. It was applied originally to agriculture owing to the fact that after a certain point of development of land for growing crops, the land eventually becomes worked out and will not produce more abundant crops without a rest. The use of manure and fertilizers will offset this to some extent, but these cost money, and a wise farmer will rotate his crops and introduce periods of fallow in such ways as to ensure that more is not taken out of the land than is put into it. Crops take certain chemicals out of the ground which have to be replaced. and different crops take different chemicals. Bean crops contain a lot of nitrogen which is partly absorbed from the air and can be ploughed back into the land to restore nitrogen taken by other crops. If land is allowed to lie fallow for a period and used perhaps for pasture, it will regain what it has lost.

The same principle applies to business. If we stretch our fixed costs too far the return per unit of capital diminishes, unless we take steps to counteract this diminution by greater economies which large-scale operation makes possible. We can spread our overheads more widely, centralize our buying and sales organization, make better use of our by-products. In this case we bring in the other economic concept, the law of increasing returns; this is the principle that the larger the unit involved, the greater will be the economies resulting from spreading the overheads. Economies of buying in bulk, fuller utilization of transport, greater mechanization, better utilization of manpower and supervision all come into operation.

One firm with a capital of £100,000 can produce and market a far larger number of a given unit at far less cost than can ten units with a capital of £10,000 each. Thus it should always be the objective of the small manufacturer to expand his business in order to be able to operate these economies. Such expansion is often by acquisition of other small businesses, but this requires capital resources which the small businessman may not possess. But a man who cannot run a small business successfully is not likely to run a large one any better. The key lies in efficient management and the fullest possible utilization of all economies and controls available. The two laws of diminishing and increasing returns are always struggling to gain mastery and it is the manager's job, by effective controls, to see that the law of increasing returns wins!

The mere increasing of capital does not automatically increase profits. For one thing, as we have seen, capital costs money. Even if it belongs to us, it might be earning a greater return on investment

INNOVATION AND EXPANSION

elsewhere; if it doesn't belong to us, its owner will expect a return on it either as fixed interest or a dividend.

We therefore have to be certain that our profits from employing new capital not only cover interest charges but also leave a wide margin over. Our object in employing new capital is not merely to extend our business and increase our turnover, but to increase the proportion of our profit to each individual unit of capital. A businessman will often say 'If I only had more capital I could double my sales.' Possibly he might, but would he increase his profitability? He might perhaps double his sales but actually decrease his profitability by incurring higher overhead expenses than were justified, even by increased sales. He might take on more expensive premises or erect more expensive machinery, he might take on more employees, or open another branch. Before going in for such expansion he must calculate what his returns would be, and this involves careful decision making, the first requisites of precisely-based calculation of prospects and risks and then of good management.

Discounted cash flow

As an aid to making decisions a technique has been developed called discounted cash flow, generally known as D.C.F.; this is based on the observation that a given sum of capital decreases in value every year by the amount which it could earn at compound interest if invested as a loan. Thus, if interest is calculated at 10 per cent, £100 this year is worth only £100 − £10 in the second year and £90 − $\frac{£110}{10}$ = £79 in the third year. This is called its discounted cash value. Thus if £100 is invested this year, the profit it brings over the years must be sufficient to offset its dwindling value each year.

In order to calculate the value of £100 in five years' time we must deduct from it the compound interest on the original sum at 10 per cent for five years which is some £75 5s. 0d. leaving only £22 5s. 0d. of the original capital. This sum of £75 5s. 0d. therefore represents the cash profits which will have to be accumulated over five years in order to justify its investment in the business. This means that cash profits would have to average about £15 5s. 0d. per year on the original capital over five years. On a new business it is unlikely that profits would be so high in the first two or three years, but certain investment allowances can be claimed from the tax authorities on new investment in productive enterprise, which may go some way towards offsetting the lower profits.

In calculating the D.C.F. on a 'takeover' of an already profitable business, no allowances would be claimed but profits would obviously be fairly high. D.C.F. is one of the many yardsticks by which to measure the feasibility of an enterprise. There are several other methods such as 'payback period' assessment. This merely calculates the number of years it would take to recover the capital outlay. It is inaccurate because, unlike D.C.F. it does not take into account the interest on the capital, which is obviously unrealistic. For a more detailed exposition of D.C.F. the reader is referred to the pamphlet by A. M. Alfred entitled *Discount Cash Flow and Corporate Planning* (*Woolwich Economic Papers*, Woolwich Polytechnic, London, 35s. 6d.).

Another method of determining investment decisions is known as the 'decision tree.'

Decision trees

Decisions can also be presented in the form of a tree with each branch representing alternative choices of action. Examples of these techniques are given in *Management Today* for July/August, 1966 in which reference is made to a book entitled *The Capital Budgeting Decision* by H. Bierman, Jr. and S. Schmidt (for a summary of this article, see Appendix B). The decision, in this case, involves a firm which is faced with the decision of whether to open an office in London or Manchester. Adequate office space in London would cost £30,000. The same space in Manchester would cost only £20,000. The effective life of the project for which the offices were needed, that of a consultancy firm, was ten years. Probabilities had to be worked out regarding the relative profitability of the two locations. There was also the possibility that a move might be made from one location to the other after three years. It was reckoned that the move would cost £5,000. It was then necessary to calculate the relative advantages and disadvantages of (a) setting up and staying in London (b) setting up and staying in Manchester (c) moving from London to Manchester, or vice versa, after three years. Obviously considerable research had to be done as to how much business could be obtained in each locality, the costs of obtaining it, etc. It showed that the firm should go to Manchester and remain there, wherever it won its major business throughout the ten year proposed life of the consultancy and that 'Reliance on the "decision trees" took account of quantified estimates of likelihood of events and led to a decision correct on facts, estimates and justments given'. This writer goes on to say: 'Trees do not replace manager's judgment. But they allow such judgment based on experience to be fully utilized rationally and consistently. Large and vital businesses must rely on formal procedures and systems for efficient organization and operation. The same is plainly true for decisions.' In other words a careful examination of the factors involved is essential rather than reliance on mere guesswork. Although probabilities may turn out to be wrong, they must be worked out even though a systematic approach to decision making has to be made to eliminate as many chance factors as possible. (See p. 143 as to how probabilities can be expressed mathematically.) Chance factors will always remain and it is on these that the manager has to exercise his judgment. The same applies to even such a comparatively simple decision as to whether to take on a management trainee or not. Modern selection methods can eliminate many doubtful points regarding character, intelligence, past performance etc., but they cannot foretell the future. Events may completely change one's view of the person. An element of risk thus resides in every business decision. All that a business man can do is to try to reduce the area of risk to a minimum. After that he must rely on his own judgment and experience. To many people it is precisely this element of risk in business which makes it interesting; it appeals to the gambling instinct. Yet even the gambler welcomes anything that diminishes his risk and is always in search of the cast-iron system of beating the bank or the bookmaker. In business the risks can be greatly diminished by knowledge and information, and the good business man will do his best to acquire the maximum of both.

CHAPTER 9

The marketing concept

Profitability and the market

The main object of a business is to satisfy a market, or in other words to satisfy the needs of consumers. If a business does not achieve this object it cannot make a profit.

Today we hear a lot about profitability as though profits were the main object of a business. We also hear a good deal about the share of the market. Reduced to commonsense these phrases merely indicate that in order to satisfy a market and command maximum sales in that market, a business must produce goods and services at the minimum cost, of the maximum quality, with the highest possible efficiency. If it is inefficient its costs will rise and it will have to raise its price to a point where its customers will no longer buy its products. In a free economy, its more efficient competitors will capture part of its market and eventually it will lose its profits. Thus profitability is essential if a business is to survive and the higher its efficiency the greater also will be its customer satisfaction. The process is a cumulative one because the larger share of a market a producer can satisfy, the greater, on the whole, will be the economies of production. His overheads will be shared between a larger number of units and all the economies of mass-production will come into force. This is the reason why the command of a large share of the market becomes a valuable objective.

Today there are a number of goods and services on the market which satisfy almost identical needs. These include soaps, toothpaste, detergents, cigarettes, shoes, clothing, washing machines, motor-cars, airline trips, coach tours, women's stockings, television sets, furniture and breakfast foods. A number of interested people appear to be fighting for a share of the same market and we measure their success by the proportion of the market they 'control'.

Brand availability

The question of availability is an important one. Most people though they ask for Brand X of a product are prepared to buy a substitute Y, if X is not available. Not many people are so particular that they would rather go without a product than not have the brand they ask for. In fact a larger number of people don't bother greatly about brands. They buy the brand which is offered to them. This raises two important questions, first, what is a 'brand'? Secondly the importance of availability in marketing.

Brands and brand names

A brand is a proprietary name given by a manufacturer to his product as for instance a toothpaste, a motor-car or a packet of cigarettes. Most brand names are registered, like a patent, so that other makers are prevented from using them. This means that the maker tries to build up an 'image' or association for the brand of constant quality, reasonable price and general consumer satisfaction. Having built up such an 'image' he obviously does not wish his hard work to be commercially exploited by someone else. He has to protect his 'image' and his 'good will', and once his name is registered, anyone who tries to steal his name is liable to legal action. In the old days such protection was gained through a 'trade mark' which acted as a guarantee that the article was a genuine product of the company it claimed association with. Today the registered 'brand name' has taken the place of the 'trade mark'.

An extension of the 'brand name' is the patent, which is a legal protective device for preventing a rival manufacturer from actually making a certain product. A patent however can only be granted where the manufacturer can claim that his product is new and contains ingredients or features not previously used in the same way. Many household devices are today sold under patent, as well as under registered brand names. A patent, in England, lasts for fourteen years, after which anyone can produce the commodity. But the brand name continues indefinitely. 'Meccano', though its patent has now expired, still sells under its brand name, though it now has many imitators. Its brand name alone, however, is now enough to enable it to command a good market and sell at a price higher than its rivals. A patent, in fact, confers a temporary monopoly, the brand name gives a legitimate protection and incentive to new inventions and ideas. To a lesser extent a 'brand name' gives protection and also acts as a guarantee that the product will be of the same standard as products bearing the same name. In many cases the name of an established manufacturer such as Cadbury's, Unilever, Boots, J & P Coats, I.C.I., Burroughs Wellcome is sufficient guarantee of quality. The object of a brand-name however is to make the product a 'household word' which automatically comes to mind when thinking of it: Cerebos salt, Kellogg's corn flakes, Singer sewing machines, Raleigh bicycles, Sunlight soap, Craven 'A' cigarettes, Swan Vesta matches, Double Diamond beer, Kia-Ora orange squash or Ronson lighters are all examples which use, in some cases, the name of the manufacturer as a registered brand name.

Brand loyalty

Marketing policy aims to build up first a 'brand image' and then 'brand loyalty'. For this purpose every possible means is brought to bear including, if available, sales force, advertising, public relations and promotion of every kind. The important thing is to try to ensure that when customers ask for a product they don't just ask for salt, soap, cigarettes, beer or squash but for the brand in question. 'Don't be vague, ask for Haig', announces a well-known whisky manufacturer. Some products are more often asked for under brand names than others. Whisky, cigarettes and beer are generally asked for by name, and so very often are toothpastes and ladies' toiletries. As the result of subtle marketing, branded goods are increasingly displayed and we now buy many things in branded packets which formerly we ordered indiscriminately. This is a protection for the customer who feels confidence in a brand name, particularly if it is associated with a well known supplier or manufacturer. It is often said that the name of a wine is less reliable than the name of the importer. The names of wines, in this country, are not protected, as they are in France, and 'Beaujolais' and 'Liebfraumilch', for example, may mean anything.

Availability and marketing

Let us now return to availability of a product. This is very important both from the makers' and the customers' point of view. In order to maximize his profits, one can broadly say that it is essential for the producer to sell as many units of his product as possible at a given price. In order to do this he must make it as widely available to the buying public as he can. Having established that there is a market for his product, he then has to establish channels of distribution. These may be of several types.

If he is aiming at the consumer market, that is at the buying public, and not at industry or commerce, he has many channels open to him. He can sell direct to wholesalers, who will sell in turn to retailers, or he can go to retailers direct. He may even, like some manufacturers, set up his own chain of retail stores, thus cutting out the 'middle-man' as he has been called.

The middle-man

In spite of the obloquy which has been heaped on him, the middle man has a useful function to perform in the economy of a country, and such profits as he may make are generally a measure of his usefulness. If he did not no doubt private enterprise would have seen to it that he vanished from the scene long ago. To the small manufacturer who cannot afford the high capital investment and elaborate organization of a complicated distribution system, a wholesaler or factor performs a very useful service: a service he has to pay for, of course, in discounts. In the toy trade for instance, wholesalers demanded a discount on the retail price of 50 per cent as against $33\frac{1}{3}$ per cent charged by retailers.

The advantage of a manufacturer dealing through wholesalers is that they generally provide the large bulk orders, whereas retailers involve greater expense and time in sales contacts and give very much smaller orders, until a brand is fully established. This is one of the decisions a small manufacturer has to make: whether to go for smaller margins of profit on larger orders, or larger margins on smaller orders, involving additional selling costs. In the field of mass consumer marketing, once a brand has been established, by advertising and sales promotion, the wholesaler can probably be dispensed with and probably, by that time, the manufacturer can afford to set up his own bulk distribution centres from which to feed supplies to the retail market.

On the other hand there are instances where the company prefers to maintain its own retail outlets which it supplies direct from its factories and so saves its retail discounts of $33\frac{1}{3}$ per cent. No doubt if its turnover is large enough this method may save money, but in fact the number of manufacturers who have their own retail outlets is small and some of these have been retailers first before they became manufacturers.

The tendency today is for retailers to control manufacturers – for the market to control production, through the large multiple stores and 'supermarkets' of which Marks & Spencer and Tesco are typical examples. But this only applies to certain types of consumer goods. As we have seen, a main object of marketing is to ensure maximum availability. This particularly applies to a commodity like cigarettes where failure in availability may involve a permanent loss in sales. A man who cannot buy a packet of cigarettes – or a boy who cannot buy a bar of chocolate – today may be able to buy one tomorrow, but the chances are that he would have bought one tomorrow anyway and today's loss of sale is thus *permanent*: whereas a day's difference in the purchase of a tube of toothpaste or a pair of shoes does not affect the total sales of the manufacturer to the same extent.

For quickly consumable goods, therefore, maximum availability is essential; it is also vital for all competitive commodities, for the obvious reason that if brand X is not available, the customer will probably buy brand Y and the X company will be the poorer. This principle of marketing is often too little appreciated. The *physical presence* of a product in a retail shop or store is often a powerful inducement to buy, and once customers start to buy a product, other retailers start to be interested in stocking it too.

Science of marketing

Marketing today has become a special branch of management: the modern business works from the market backwards, as it were. Marketing policy has become the directing force behind all production industry, because on marketing depends all the other functions of industry such as finance, forecasting, production planning, manpower planning, purchasing and material control, quality control, manufacture and distribution. This has become known as the *marketing concept*. The first thing to establish is whether a market exists and what that market consists of: what is the nature of the demand in terms of quality, quantity, design, locality and price. Thus anyone intending to go into business must first examine his market and find out all he possibly can about it. He must carry out a careful market research and base his business planning upon it.

Market research

There are many market research companies in existence who are prepared to undertake market surveys. They are mostly offshoots of advertising agencies who pioneered this form of research; some may still be attached to agencies, but many are now independent. Among the agencies who were pioneers in market research are The London Press Exchange, Pritchard Wood & Partners, G. S. Royds, J. Walter Thompson and W. S. Crawford's whose Market Research Section *Contimart* has recently become an independent organization.

Market research can be either a general survey of the market based on available information, or it can be a more detailed consumer survey – in fact both generally go together, but the market survey comes first.

Suppose that a well known manufacturer of razor blades is thinking of setting up a factory in Pakistan. His first requirement will be to know what competition exists already. Are razor blades being imported? If so at what price? Are they subject to import duty? How does their quality compare with his own?

Secondly he wants to know whether razor blades are being manufactured within the country and how many firms are making them. What is their total output and what proportion of the market does each manufacturer control? Is the output expanding?

Next he examines demand. What are the social customs? Do men favour wearing beards? Is it possible to change these customs – are they based (as for instance with Sikhs in India) on religious traditions? How are razor blades marketed? What channels exist in distribution?

All these and many other factors would be considered in a market survey, and would be equally applicable, with necessary variations, to any country. It would obviously require to be done by people on the spot, who are familiar with local conditions.

The next stage would be a consumer survey in which consumers are interviewed regarding their razor blade preferences, why they use a certain brand, how many blades they use a month, whether they would be prepared to change, under what conditions they would do so, such as reduction in price or longer durability.

On the basis of the information gained the manufacturer would then be able to build a picture of the market on which he could plan a possible marketing programme with estimates of sales, distribution costs, turnover, capital requirements etc. He would then be able to gauge the feasibility of the project. If he felt he could get a reasonable proportion of the market, say 20 per cent at first, he would have to estimate his chances of increasing this proportion through cost and hence price-reduction, through advertising, better sales and distribution methods, higher quality etc.

Much of the consumer information gained would be on the basis of 'sampling', that is, studying a representative section of the consumer market and extending the results as typical of the whole.

Design and packaging

Once a market has been established to exist, two important features present themselves. The first one is design, the second packaging. Even such a simple commodity as a razor blade is subject to variations of design. When safety razors first came on the market the blades were made with three circular slots to fit the razors. The original makers then tried to cut out competitors by changing the design of their razors so they only took their own blades. Other blade makers did the same. Today razor blades are designed to fit almost any razor. The profit made by a firm is not on the razors but on the blades. A razor lasts for a lifetime, blades constantly need renewal. It has now been realized that it is better to make all blades interchangeable rather than restrict their use to only one type of razor. Blades now sell on quality and price alone, plus fringe 'convenience' factors such as special packaging for easy blade-change and disposal etc, though such factors could be assumed, in the context of blades, to be an aspect of 'quality'.

This is only one simple aspect of design. One can take a hundred

THE MARKETING CONCEPT

examples. Considerable changes over the years have taken place in the design for instance, of typewriters, umbrellas, telephones, desk-lamps, cars, motor-cycles, crockery, cutlery, furniture, sewing-machines, kitchen utensils and equipment, railway carriages, buses, street lamps, liners, houses, aircraft, fountain pens and of course wearing apparel – in fact, in many product fields, the public has come to accept design change virtually every year. Changes in design are assumed to be made to improve consumer satisfaction, to save unnecessary cost, to increase convenience, to simplify manufacture or to conform to new materials. Unnecessary ornamentation has now been dispensed with: utility and economy have now been accepted as criteria of good design.

Packaging on the other hand has now become an integral part of marketing and even a form of advertisement. A colourful, gay, attractive and eye-catching package may help to sell a product. A dull and dowdy package may repel a customer. Even wrapping paper is now made in different colours and designs and used to advertise the shop it comes from the same applies to carrier bags. Special designers and commercial artists are employed to think out new ideas in packaging and presentation. Product display is also a part of marketing in which packaging plays its part. (See also p. 101.)

Coupons and stamps

A practice has grown up for some years whereby customers are bribed to buy a certain brand of product by promises of coupons in each package which can be collected and exchanged for goods. This practice has been frowned on by some manufacturers and attempts have been made to stop it as being unfair trading. Another practice, also censured by some, is to give away stamps with certain products, including petrol, which can also be collected and exchanged. Several firms have been set up to supply these stamps and arrange for their exchange. Certain firms refuse to join in any such forms of bribery, others have found it a valuable sales incentive. The large and well-established firms, whose brands have been recognized for many years, find little necessity for such practices. New firms, freshly entering the market, find them helpful in winning customers.

THE MARKETING CONCEPT

The marketing manager

Most manufacturers have a marketing department controlled by a marketing director or manager: his responsibilities are to handle the distribution of the product from the point where it leaves the factory. At the same time he has a responsibility to keep the production side informed, probably through the board of directors, regarding future markets. His job is not only to sell goods but to see that goods are made in such a way as to satisfy the needs of the consumer. He is therefore under obligation to feed back a constant stream of information regarding consumer needs and preferences, expanding and contracting demand, changes in taste, competition developments and market information generally.

Coupled with this, his job is to see that sales are kept at a maximum, that channels of distributions are constantly being increased and developed, that maximum availability of the product, in all possible markets, is maintained.

Division of markets

Markets can be divided in a number of ways of which the most obvious is territorial. They can also be divided in terms of buying power, social status, or mental outlook. A publisher has to consider markets in terms of mental attitude as well as territory. Books which may sell well in the older universities will probably not sell in the poorer part of an industrial town. A marketing department will be sub-divided in many ways and probably one section will be devoted to exports, which in its turn will be subdivided into territories. In a small firm so many subdivisions will not be possible and one man may have to handle many different aspects of a market. The important thing is to keep their divisions clear because each subdivision may require a different marketing emphasis.

Today such emphasis is being placed on the discovery of new retail outlets. Traditional habits of selling are being broken down and many retailers are broadening the range of goods they sell. Bookstalls, for instance, are now selling gramophone records, chemists are selling many things beside pharmaceuticals, 'drugstores' in America have for many years been acting as 'soda fountains' and 'snack bars'.

The multiple store

The multiple store was set up to simplify shopping for the customer by putting within his reach under one roof, in a great many locations, as many as feasible of the things he might need. The latest development of this is the self-service 'super-market' where customers help themselves and pay as they go out. These 'supermarkets' provide a useful outlet for branded products particularly if they develop into chains with shops in a number of different towns. They can then buy the goods in bulk and at suitably increased discounts which they may or may not pass on to their customers.

Fixed prices

An attempt has been made for some years for the manufacturers of well-known branded goods to insist that all retailers sell their goods at a fixed retail price. Anyone selling them at less may have his supplies cut off. In certain cases the 'supermarkets' have broken this enforcement, knowing that their bulk orders of the goods put them in a strong position. The smaller retailers, who cannot afford to give bulk orders, are thus put at a disadvantage. They dare not sell below the fixed price but find they are being 'undercut'. This is causing great dismay and even hardship. The law however has decreed that fixing prices cannot be upheld, because it is restraint of trade, and many of the smaller retailers may eventually be forced out of business unless they also lower their prices which, since they cannot obtain the bulk-buying discounts of the big retail chains, might drive many of them out of business. This is one of the less happy results of free competition. However, this is the economic trend at the moment and one which marketing policy must consider carefully. Obviously, retail price-fixing from the manufacturer's end, which is really a form of monopoly, will have to go; though its withdrawal may cause hardship to some of the smaller traders who cannot effect the economies possible to large-scale chain-stores whose discounts are much larger and whose overheads are spread more widely. In fact this may be the start of the gradual disappearance of the small to medium shop-keeper, unless he can effect economies and readjust in other ways to offset those of the chain-store and the supermarket.

THE MARKETING CONCEPT

Marketing overseas

Marketing overseas requires a lot of special study. It is no use thinking that because a product sells in England it will automatically sell overseas. Markets have to be carefully investigated and a study of the country carried out.

There are many well-established export houses who specialize in marketing British products: these include The United Africa Co., Ltd., Booker Brothers, James Finlay, Gillander Arbuthnot and many more. Having acquired a great deal of knowledge of overseas markets, where they have generally had establishments for many years, they can save British manufacturers a lot of trouble. But of course they expect high discounts for their services.

Another means of distribution is an agent who acts as representative of a manufacturer but whose job is merely to get orders and charge a commission on what he sells.

A manufacturer may choose to set up his own sales organization in an overseas country and finally may set up his own factories there and so save paying import dues. As a variation of the latter he may arrange for his product to be manufactured on licence by a manufacturer in that country who will pay him a royalty on the products he makes. Alternatively he may export parts only for assembly of the final product overseas, thus also avoiding payment of tax on complete products.

In all overseas selling good communication is essential, both for initial market assessment on the spot and for the continuing welfare of the business. Constant visits to the overseas market, by responsible people, to see that things are going well and to give assistance are essential. In the agreement under which the goods are marketed, no loophole should be allowed for exploitation, cheating or overlapping of territories of agents or distribution, also cancellation should be made easy if things are not going well. For manufacture abroad on licence it is essential that strict enforcement of quality specifications be made as well as checking of quantities, so that the good name of the product – and of the manufacturer – does not suffer.

Two excellent books on overseas marketing are recommended, which discuss the details of the process at some length. They are *Selling Overseas – The Principles of Export Marketing* by N. Deschampsneufs and *How to Sell Successfully Overseas* by A. & G. Tack.

CHAPTER 10

Science as an aid to management

Scientific method

Science, generally speaking, means the methodical investigation of facts and their correlation into working hypotheses. It is based on factual research. Research must however be directed and co-ordinated towards an objective. This objective is determined on the basis of induction. This means that known facts are used to formulate a tentative theory which is then used as a basis of experiment by the collection of further facts to prove its validity. The object of a scientific experiment is to isolate a situation from irrelevent influence and then apply stimuli from which facts can be deduced. For instance a metallurgist may believe that by adding certain ingredients to an alloy he can strengthen it sufficiently to withstand greater strains. He consequently isolates the alloy and then adds the ingredients after which he subjects it to certain tests which prove, or disprove, his hypothesis.

Science and business

Science is of necessity used widely in business on the technical side in such fields as development of new products, processes, production equipment etc. but it is now being used to a greatly increasing extent in the sphere of management and business economics. The difficulty of using science in the economic and business fields is that it is difficult to conduct isolated experiments to prove hypotheses arising from the observation of economic phenomena. Usually a number of different causes contribute to an economic or business situation, and it is difficult, if not impossible, to hold one set of causes in abeyance while one observes the effects of another. Thus economics is subject to a larger amount of controversy and difference of opinion than the physical or biological sciences, where experiments can be more rigidly controlled. Nevertheless a great deal of scientific investigation has been used in business which can be of considerable value to management, if rightly understood and if adequate reservations are made. We have already outlined, for instance, the use of statistical theory in market research in respect of 'sampling'. Science can also be used in the identification of business trends and the determination of optimum production.

One way in which experiments can be conducted in the business field is by the construction of imaginary business situations or 'models' and then varying the circumstances in accordance with calculated probabilities and mathematical principles. A simple example of this has been shown in Chapter 8. Such a model, as we will show below, is capable of considerable variation. The accepted way of showing a probability mathematically is to work out the number of chances in 100 it is likely to incur and then show it as a decimal. If there is a 60 per cent chance of something happening then its mathematical probability is shown as ·6, if 75 per cent as ·75. If the chances of making a profit of £1,000 are 55 per cent then we show our profit as £550.

Operations research (OR)

One of the most important applications of science to management today is what has already been referred to as operations research, the two main characteristics of which are (a) that it is an application of scientific method to business operation and (b) that its findings are a useful reinforcement to management common sense.

Operations research is not a specialist function of science but a general application of science to a number of different fields. It started during the second world war as a means of dealing with general strategic problems, and proved so useful in solving them that it has since been successfully applied to business. The problems it was originally applied to were those which apparently defied any solution by the specialists concerned – who, it was felt, because they were specialists, could only take a somewhat narrow view. This, in fact, is one of the dangers of scientific progress, that a specialist, because he confines his attention to only one set of phenomena such as biology, medicine or physics, may find it difficult to relate a problem to a wider set of circumstances, and therefore may sometimes miss an important factor in its solution. In war time the operational research teams consisted of groups of scientists deliberately chosen from a wide field of scientific enquiry, whose main qualifications were that they had been trained to use scientific method and research disciplines. They were then asked to forget their particular specializations and look at problems with an open mind.

A practical example

A classic example, often quoted, of the early application of operational research in war-time was the failure of the combined efforts of the navy and air force to curb the enemy submarine menace at a certain stage of the war. This menace, which threatened to cut off our food supply, was obviously acute and had to be overcome if Britain was to survive. The method of attacking submarines from the air was carefully examined. It consisted, at the time, of the practice of dropping delayed action depth charges from aircraft as near to a submarine as possible. These depth charges were automatically detonated by water pressure at a depth of 35 to 100 feet. The theory was that as soon as a submarine saw an attacking aircraft it would dive and the depth charge would catch it after it had submerged. Unfortunately, owing to the time it took the depth charge to sink, it was found that a submarine had time to get away far enough from the explosion to maintain its safety. Consequently a high proportion of depth charges were ineffective. The solution which emerged was to change the detonating device to explode the charge either when it touched the surface or it had sunk not lower than 25 feet. The result of this simple alteration was to increase submarine sinkages by 700 per cent and to enable Britain to bring the submarine menace to an end.

Some people might say that anyone with normal common sense could have worked out this solution and that it was hardly necessary to employ a team of high powered and expensive scientists to find it. The point is however that the solution had *not* been found by the naval or air force specialists whose main concern was with this problem, but by an independent group of observers who were able to bring scientific method and an unbiased viewpoint to the situation. (See *Decision and Control* by Stafford Beer (John Wiley 1966).).

No doubt human relations problems were involved and a certain resentment engendered by the introduction of 'boffins' to teach the services their business. Professional men tend to acquire a vested interest in their own techniques and to resent suggestions that they might be altered, as witness the opposition of the medical profession to the theories of Lister and Pasteur which revolutionized the practice of surgery and medicine. As Stafford Beer says: 'Thus without years of special research and development effort, but simply through breaking through a conceptual barrier in policy making and by studying the operational facts, a tremendous success is achieved'.

Operations research applied to business

'Finally,' continues Stafford Beer (ibid.), 'life is also considerably changed for those whose job it is to advise management on the detailed methods of working within a particular management policy.' Not only is industry full of specialists such as accountants, engineers, marketing experts, work study men, but management itself tends to become a specialized function restricted within certain hidebound policies and conventions. Operations research helps to break through these barriers of convention and question every operation objectively in relation to its purpose.

Many years ago a cartoon appeared, in a comic paper, of a company director dressed in the conventional morning coat and striped trousers of the day and wearing a top hat and a white moustache. He is looking up at a gigantic machine in a factory and saying to the works manager: 'Jones, we must cut down our expenses. What's that thing for?' The cartoon was funny, it was meant to be, but it may also have had some sense in it. In fact, there is probably a vast amount of equipment in many businesses which is obsolete and wasteful – but because it has been there for a long time nobody questions its importance. The same applies to many processes and routines. Somebody installed them years ago and they have become a tradition of the business, and nobody dares to alter them because they have grown up with them. The object of operations research is to examine everything dispassionately and see it in the light of innocence.

Questioning

The main function of operations research, however, is (a) to solve difficult problems and (b) to help managers make decisions. Discounted cash flow and decision trees (see Appendix B) are among the technique of operations research; so, even, is work study itself. In fact operations research takes over where work study ends. The basis of work study is questioning. Kipling wrote many years ago:

> I keep six honest serving men
> (They taught me all I knew);
> Their names are What and Why and When
> And How and Where and Who.

The same applies to operations research. But it also employs certain scientific techniques based on the laws of probability and statistics.

Variables

One of the main difficulties facing the manager of today is the number of variables he has to deal with, each of which interacts upon the other so that a variation in one or more factors will alter all the others and produce endless permutations and combinations. Where a company produces a number of different products, each product reacts upon the other and creates problems of inventory programming to ensure the optimum distribution and use of resources. Among the problems involved are: raw materials; labour utilization; power utilization; distribution; transport; delivery; cost; capital investment; marketing problems.

All these problems interact upon each other. If we spend more on one product, or on an aspect of one, we have less to spend on another. How do we keep our machines and labour fully utilized, saving cost on idle equipment and labour? How can we combine transport and distribution for several products in such a way as to ensure maximum efficiency with minimum cost?

Cybernetics

In Chapter 8 we considered a simple example of a typical small business. We assumed a lot of things which in practice might never

SCIENCE AS AN AID TO MANAGEMENT

have taken place. We made a model, on paper, and tried to draw from it certain conclusions which might be applied to a real business. This is called 'cybernetics', the original meaning of which is, in fact, the science of control and communication. It comes from the Greek word κυβερνητης (Kubernetes) which means a steersman or governor.[1] Cybernetics has come to mean the making of models or the contriving of mechanisms which imitate natural phenomena, such as a computer which imitates human mental processes. In fact the human brain is a highly complex and extremely compact computer which is continually sending and receiving messages from various parts of the body, correlating them and drawing inferences from them. It employs many thousands of nerve fibres through which pass electric impulses. The computer attempts to reproduce these functions electronically and is thus a product of cybernetics. The control element comes in through the means of the supply of information quickly on which decisions can be made. In fact the making of a model is involved in any control activity even though it may only be a mental model. We say to ourselves, 'If I do this, such and such will happen.' We imagine the result of our action, and then hope our forecast is correct. The degree to which it is correct will depend on the accuracy of our model.

Working model

In the business we described in Chapter 8 we took certain things for granted. These included our sales targets, our cost of raw material, our overheads, our ability to meet our sales targets and so on. In fact any one, or possibly several, of these factors might not have turned out to be what we imagined. Our sales targets might have been under- or over-estimated. The demand might have been more than we thought it would be, or possibly and more likely, less. Our sales costs might have been higher or lower, thus altering our figures for overheads or fixed costs. Our costs of raw material might increase or decrease. Postal and transport costs might have altered since we made our original estimates.

All these things have to be allowed for and our model, in order to

[1] The 'governor' on a machine which automatically controls its speed has been used as an illustration of cybernetics – it is a mechanism which automatically imitates the action of a controlling mind.

be accurate, must be a 'working' model allowing for all possible variations and every possible combination of variations. To work these permutations and combinations out mathematically would take an enormous amount of time, but a computer can do it and give us the answer to a number of diverse problems almost immediately. It can show us which is the 'optimum' or best of a number of different possibilities. We might, for instance, find it cheaper to manufacture a year's supply of products all at once, but against this we must reckon costs of storage and rate of dispersal. We might decide to pay our salesmen on commission only, but then we should probably have to pay a high rate of commission. We might decide to employ more salesmen, thus adding to our overheads, but probably increasing our sales. Finally, we might decide that, instead of buying our components from outside and assembling and packing them ourselves, it would be more economical to make them ourselves; but this would entail setting up a factory and investing in machinery, thus increasing our capital charges. All these are problems of operations research, just as the grocer's problem of what quantities of stocks to keep of each line he trades in, so as to ensure the optimum profit and the maximum saving in storage costs.

Queueing theory

One method which OR has developed to deal with stock control is called *queueing theory*. The simplest example is to consider two machines, A and B, which are linked by the fact that a particular product cannot be processed through B until it has been processed by A. If machine A works faster than machine B, unfinished products will obviously pile up between A and B; while if B works faster than A, a great deal of time will be wasted while B is waiting for A to 'catch up'. The ideal situation is that each machine will work at the same speed, but breakdowns often occur and these may upset the harmony. Probabilities can be worked out statistically to show, in a given period, how often problems occur, either when goods pile up waiting for B or when B is idle waiting for products from A. This investigation would be in the category of a stochastic exercise.[1] This means an exercise in which random

[1] The word 'stochastic' comes from the Greek στοχαζομαι which means 'to aim at a mark'. Though now obsolete, in English usage, it was fre-

variations can be calculated and to some extent foretold by the application of the laws of probability.

This process can be applied very effectively to network planning (see Appendix A) to determine minimum and maximum periods between one operation and the next, thus materially helping to determine the estimated time for a job which involves a number of interlocked operations. These might include large construction contracts for a building, a ship or aircraft. Delays in the construction of the Polaris submarine and the Concorde aircraft might have been avoided by such an exercise if carried out accurately. But operations research is at present very much in its elementary stages and a great deal of development will be necessary before it can be used with accuracy. Nevertheless, many millions of pounds have already been saved by the application of operations research techniques to problems of variation and delay, and for the control of factors which formerly had to be left to chance.

Stochastic method

Stochastic methods can be applied equally effectively to small businesses as to large ones. We have already referred to the grocer who has to decide which brands to stock, and in what quantities. In a large undertaking this accumulation of large stocks of raw material, of finished and semi-finished products can be expensive, and deviations from the optimum can cost a company many thousands of pounds.

A simple application of stochastic method might be useful to a municipal bus company wishing to work out the optimum number of buses to run on a series of different routes through the day. In the field of public transport it is obviously uneconomic to run buses which are more than half empty. On the other hand, great inconvenience can be caused if an insufficient number of buses are available when more are needed, so that large queues accumulate and people have to wait for long periods before another bus arrives to take them to their chosen destinations. Anyone who has waited for half an hour in London for a particular

quently used in the seventeenth and eighteenth centuries to mean 'conjectural'. It is now only used by scientists to mean 'planned chance'. See *Decision and Control* by Stafford Beer, Chapter 9.

bus while four or five almost empty buses of another number pass him by will appreciate the value of stochastic method. A similar problem arises in the case of international airlines.

Product variety

A related use of stochastic method or 'queuing theory' in stock control is for product inventory control. A product inventory, as its name implies, is a list of products marketed by a company. A good example of product inventory control was shown by a company of cigarette manufacturers which I was once called in to advise on certain training problems. The chairman, whom I had known in another company, had only recently taken over, On his arrival he had been horrified to find that the company, although not very large, was marketing something like thirty different brands of cigarettes. Many of these brands were selling not in millions, as do most of the better-known brands, but in a few thousands. In spite of the protests he received from many quarters, the chairman immediately set to work to cut down the number of brands by at least half and later to about a quarter. Though this meant cutting through brand loyalty and accepted custom, it was essential to ensure variety reduction and to save unnecessary duplication.

Since each brand had to have special packets printed, special advertising and special distribution channels, the addition to overhead costs made the whole operation uneconomic. By judicious education of consumers to accept substitution for their favourite brands, the company was able to maintain its sales at a very much lower cost.

In this case the need for brand variety reduction was obvious and hardly needed an operations research expert to point it out. But it should be noted that it was not until a new chairman was appointed, who was able to take an objective view, that anything was done to remedy the situation. The former management had grown used to the situation and had not bothered to question it.

In many companies, however, the need for modification of existing customs is not so obvious. Objective research is then required and stochastic methods need to be used to determine action to be taken for seasonal fluctuations, time schedules, market saturation points and other factors with an important bearing on profitability. (One exercise in the determination of profitability through product variation is shown in Appendix C: Linear Programming.)

OR teams may be expensive to install, but generally speaking they can pay for themselves in a year or so by the savings they can produce. OR contains two important factors:

(a) that it brings objective observation to bear upon a problem;
(b) that it makes use of scientific method and scientific techniques, such as statistical theory, cybernetics and network planning, to solve those problems.

But once again it must be emphasized that OR is not a substitute for management, it is merely a tool of management, a means of bringing under greater control those factors which cannot be accurately foreseen or which are not immediately obvious. But one thing must always be remembered in relation to the laws of probability which, as we have seen, are the essence of OR. They are not infallible. The larger the sample the greater is their chance of accuracy. In a sample of ten thousand throws of a dice the chances of an even distribution of numbers turning up is far greater than in a hundred throws. But exceptions sometimes happen and these have to be allowed for. What the businessman cannot afford to do is to count on their happening in his favour.

Statistically, extremes are important as well as 'means', as was proved by the man who was drowned while wading across a river of which, he was told, the average depth was only four feet! The vast business of insurance has been built up on calculating averages or means. Nevertheless it is the extreme against which we insure, namely that, out of the five thousand days on which our house is not burnt down, it may possibly be burnt down on the five thousand and first. In calculating the delays between machine A and machine B in the example we have given above (p. 148), what we want to know are the chances of maximum delay occurring so that we can, if necessary take steps to remedy the situation. We can, of course, only calculate future chances from past observed data.

For example we can take 200 runs and observe the distribution of delays. If we want to be more accurate we can observe 500 or even 1,000 runs. If we find the ratio of delays to runs the same in each case, say 1 to 20, we shall know we are not far wrong. We also need to know the *length* of the delays. This gives us some data to go on, from which we can calculate probable delays over any given period. We can then plan our operations accordingly. In the same way insurance companies calculate their risks on death claims by examining statistics over a given period in relation to age. This is particularly important in calculating the costs of annuities, which are based on length of life. The cost of a £100 annuity will be lower as age advances, and the insurance company is gambling on the holder living only to the average age. If he or she lives to be 100 the company loses; if they die earlier, the company wins and the wins and losses probably cancel out. Actuaries, for years, have been using simple stochastic methods, if we accept the definition given by Stafford Beer that a 'stochastic process... is one in which chance governs the particular selection of events unfolding in time...'

Decision theory

All this leads up to what is known as 'decision theory'; the object of which is to make decisions easier by cutting out risks due to chance as much as possible. In fact operational research actually uses chance, in the form of the laws of probability, to help in arriving at decisions. The words of Stafford Beer may need some clarification for the layman. They are:

> The foregoing discussion of the nature of prediction is set within the general theory of model-building... A methodical amalgam is required, having three separate aspects: a correct (that is homomorphic) identification of underlying structure and mechanism, a stochastic scheme of quantification and a knowledge of statistical interaction... Given the framework, the process of reaching the best decision is known as 'optimization', and the corpus of theoretical knowledge which bears on this is called 'decision theory'.

In simpler words, this means that in order to solve a problem we first have to make a model of that problem in our minds or on paper, and that model must contain all the structural characteristics of the real situation; it must, in fact be a product of correct 'simulation' in that it must contain all relevant factors (e.g. our 'model' business in Chapter 8). The quantitative data of the model must then be filled in, in such a way as to cover a number of possibilities the effects of which can then be calculated stochastically in relation to the various patterns of statistical reactions which arise. If, for instance we substitute different sales figures for those given in our 'model' in Chapter 8 they will alter the other statistics. A stochastic picture would consist of a calculation of the various probabilities attached to maximum and minimum sales, and these would affect other factors in the model such as capital requirements and charges, position of 'break even' point, cash position, profitability, etc.

We thus get not merely a working model, but a series of working models, from which we can choose the one giving us the optimum benefit – i.e. in which all the inter-relating figures, taken in relation to their stochastic probabilities, give us the maximum profit. In former days the vastness of the manifold calculations needed to work out all these figures would have been beyond the power of human accomplishment, at least within a reasonable time; today, the electronic processing mechanisms available have put them within our reach. (See Appendix E for a stochastic solution to stock control.)

Mathematics and management

It is not proposed in this book to enter into the ramifications of technicalities of the mathematical side of operations research. All that it is intended to show is how it can be called in by management to help them in making decisions. EDP (electronic data processing) cannot itself make decisions, still less can it carry them out. Both are the function of management. But obviously if EDP can indicate the optimum decision it can do much to simplify decision making. We may not be so very far from the position when, by the extension of electronic methods in inter-communication, which at present is management's main business, the actual implementation of decisions may also be effected electronically.

Basically, EDP itself is a system of communication processing, whereby information is sifted and analysed and correct conclusions are drawn, provided, as we have already noted, the information is itself correct and not distorted or inadequate to the purpose. It will still be somebody's job to make sure that the data is adequate and correct, but, as computerization increases, this too may be done by EDP. In fact computers may soon be capable, through appropriate linkages, to pick up relevant data at relevant points, and pass it on to others, with the result that the purely human element may be very considerably reduced even in the field of programming: that is preparing data in such a way that it can be handled by a computer. For example the output of a machine may soon be automatically recorded in such a way that it can be passed straight into a computer where similar data is available for comparison and correlation. The same could apply to the input and output of warehouses, loading figures for transport, or, at the other end of the production line, the receipt and issue of raw material.

Not long ago I saw a cigarette factory where three previously separate operations were all linked together in one machine, namely the manufacture, packaging and final packeting of cigarettes. The experiment was not entirely successful because it increased the chances of delay, should one link in the process break down. Where three machines are employed, if say a packeting[1] machine breaks down, cigarettes from the making machine can be diverted to another machine for packeting, whereas if all three are linked, the breaking down of one machine stops both the making and the packaging process. To overcome this difficulty may only be a matter of time and operations research. Operational research may well be leading us to an entirely automatic factory controlled by a press button switch, with certain built-in correctives to adjust systems to all possible emergencies. In fact it certainly appears that OR is not only transforming industry, but also the distributive trades, transport, hospital administration and many other corporate activities. It can obviously be used in canteens and restaurants, in supermarkets and multiple stores, in public transport systems and other public utilities such as power supply. It can be used equally well in simple, as in highly complex, operations.

The importance of concepts

To anyone who may find some of the ideas outlined in this chapter apparent irrelevant to the ordinary practice of business, it might be as well to touch briefly on some fundamentals of elementary philosophy which are also, whether we like it or not, fundamentals by which we live. Take for instance the idea of 'models'. Some 2,500 years ago Plato pointed out that none of us sees things as

---

[1] The correct name is a 'packing machine' but I use 'packeting' to distinguish it from the final process which I have called 'packaging'.

they are, but only as we think they are. We create an 'idea' or a concept of something and then act as though it were real. The more accurate is our concept, the more likely we are to act realistically. In business if we mistake a crook for an honest man we find our mistake an expensive one. In the same way if we over-estimate or under-estimate our sales we may lose a considerable amount of profit. We can never know a person completely. We only see the outside of him or her and we have to judge their real nature by a number of often unverifiable clues such as the way they talk, the way they act, or the way they answer questions. This emerges in personnel selection but it also emerges in everyday life. Few of us can even be certain that we know ourselves absolutely, and we often find ourselves acting in ways we would not have predicted: such behaviour may either be more base and cowardly or else far more courageous than we would have thought. In fact we make 'models' of ourselves and also of other people, as we make models or concepts of everything around us. Eddington pointed out some years ago in his *Nature of the Physical World* that the world as seen by the poet is an entirely different world to the one which is seen by the scientist.

A large number – if not all – the mistakes made in business are due to acting on faulty concepts or models. Even an accountant can often be mistaken about the solvency of a business, not because he is a bad accountant, but because accountancy by itself cannot take all the relevant factors into consideration, such as the character of the managers, or changes in economic or social conditions. A manager must be very much more than an accountant in that he must see a business from a far wider angle than merely profit and loss. He has got to consider a number of variables and he has got to predict future trends. He has got to see a business as a dynamic entity and not as merely a static entity, as an auditor sees it on audit day. It is to help the manager to predict the future within certain defined limits of accuracy, taking account of the variable factors, that OR has been developed and can be of inestimable benefit. Not only does the OR man constantly employ Kipling's six honest serving men (see p. 146), he also has to ask further questions such as 'What will happen if this is done?' or 'What will be the result of that action?'

Thus OR is not some mysterious new gimmick invented by management consultants to extort large fees, but is merely a logical extension of the ordinary techniques of living a normal life. It is an attempt to make the unforeseen a little more foreseeable, to bring the imponderables more within our grasp. It is based upon the instinct which makes a man take out an insurance policy or save money for his old age or his children's education. It is based on much the same sort of concepts or 'models' as a man makes in relation to the everyday world about him. We call a man shrewd who makes provision for all possible eventualities and uses his provision for his own advantage. Hitherto man has been at the mercy of chance, but science has now put it within the power of man to use chance itself and its laws in order to keep it under control and reduce its power to affect him adversely. This adds a great deal of power to man, particularly in the industrial world. It gives him more of that control of his environment which is the characteristic that distinguishes him from the lower animals.

As we have said before, a manager does not have to be a higher mathematician to control a successful business, any more than he has to be a qualified engineer. What he needs to know is *how* to use the specialist, be he mathematician or engineer, research and development expert, or operational research man, to help him make *his* business more efficient.

OR and human relations

One point already touched on which needs, perhaps, to be re-emphasized is that OR is almost bound to cause some degree of friction. It needs to be applied with great tact. All innovations are unpopular because they tend to disturb the accepted conventions and the even tenor of people's lives. It is the job of OR to question – and also to change – accepted conventions, and people tend to have a vested interest in these conventions. Their usual cry is: 'What the hell do these so-and so's know about my job (or this business) more than I do who have been in it for 20 (or 30 or 40) years? How dare they come and tell me what I'm doing is wrong?'

This attitude is very understandable, but it can also be very unprofitable. A man who is not prepared to accept change is not a good manager. Change is the essence of progress. Moreover it is just because the OR observer has *not* been in the business for 20 years that his view is worth listening to. He can see the business from outside, objectively and as a whole, in relation to external factors which may well have escaped the notice of the manager who has devoted his life to the business and possibly little else. It is difficult for most people to admit that they may be wrong. The best advice to a manager is that he should not assume that he must, in the first place, be right: in other words that he should keep an open and objective mind about himself and his own decisions and welcome advice and assistance where they may be helpful. At the same time this does not exonerate the OR man from the duty of putting forward his suggestions, not only as tactfully and politely as possible, but also with the clearest possible explanation of the grounds on which they are based. This may not always be easy, because many of his suggestions may be based on mathematical calculations with which the manager may not necessarily be familiar.

Most men are naturally suspicious of things they do not understand, and today, more than at any time in history, we are in need of interpreters and even a technique of interpretation of science to the ordinary layman. Such interpretation is vitally necessary in an age in which we are, to some extent, in the hands of the experts, who can make disturbing and far-reaching changes in the lives of ourselves and our children, often without our realizing it. This, once again, is a problem of communication and it needs more profound study and development than has hitherto been given to it. The experts themselves are often to blame for refusing to recognize the necessity of making themselves generally understood to those who may not know their particular jargon.

Where the layman is not suspicious of science he may well go to the other extreme and accept its findings without question, which may be equally dangerous. There are many pseudo-scientists today who deliberately exploit the veneration for science held by many laymen, and who go out of their way to invent long words and mysterious jargon to confuse and impress, rather than to clarify. Such people work on the principle enunciated by the Greek critic Demetrius some 2,000 years ago that 'what is clear and evident is likely to be scorned, just as men stripped naked. Mystery is spoken in allegory to excite such fear and awe as exist in darkness and night'. It is the obligation of the expert to explain himself, so that the truth can be apprehended by all and judged objectively and fairly. This will go a long way to dispel the prejudice of those who suspect innovation and to call the bluff of those who try to trade on obscurity.

CHAPTER 11

Management accounting

Basic control

Accounting has many limitations as a means of controlling a business, for it merely measures one side of the activities; those which can be assessed in terms of money. Obviously a business consists of many activities which cannot be measured in money; but without an accurate system of accounting a manager cannot tell whether his business is making a profit or a loss, or which activities are profitable and which are not.

It is just conceivable that a very small, one-man business could get along and even make profits, without some system of accounting, just as many householders manage without accounts, but if it did it would be, as the saying goes, 'rather by luck than good management'. Most people, even if they are not in business, find it convenient to have some idea of their annual quarterly or monthly expenditure, as compared with their income, particularly if they find themselves continually running into debt. Business accounting therefore is really only an extension of what most sensible people do in their own homes: namely, it is a record of expenditure and income from which to judge whether one is running into bankruptcy or building up reserves for the future which can be invested, if one so wishes to bring in further income.

Capital

To start a business, as we have stated, we require some capital to enable us to buy or rent the necessary equipment to start and continue the business. This equipment may be simple or complex, according to the nature and the size of the business. It may consist of stationery and postage stamps, a typewriter, a telephone and possibly an office: or it may consist of expensive buildings and machinery, consignments of raw material, rent of power, heating and light, of transport facilities and labour. As we have already seen, a distinction can be made between fixed and working capital, direct and indirect costs and so on.

The balance sheet

Basically all accounting systems start from the balance sheet, which is a statement of the condition of the business at the time it is drawn up. Most companies draw up a balance sheet yearly, but many draw up 'trial balances' more frequently: monthly, perhaps, or quarterly. In the 'model' business we considered in Chapter 8, quarterly balances would be more appropriate. A balance sheet, however, is merely an agglomeration of totals and by itself tells us only whether we have made a profit or loss over the period covered. To give us a clearer picture of where we stand, we need to break down some of the figures further: particularly the profit or loss figure, and for this we draw up a 'profit and loss' account or 'income' account to show how we have arrived at the figures shown in the balance sheet.

Profit and loss account

The profit and loss account is a record of day-to-day trading, the balance sheet shows the financial position of the company at a given date. The reason it is called a balance sheet is because it shows, on one side, our liabilities and, on the other side, our assets; and these must end up equal when profit or loss are included.

Double entry

The system of accounting in use today is known as the 'double entry' system, because it obliges the accountant to make two entries for every transaction. For instance if we buy £500 of raw materials we debit it to one side of our balance sheet and credit it to the other. If, from £500 of raw material we make and sell £750 of finished products we debit £500 on one side and credit £750 to the other, and to balance the transaction we then show a profit of £250.

By a convention of accounting what might appear to be assets are shown as liabilities: that is to say debts owed to the company by the accountant. The accountant is looked upon as the guardian of the company's finances to whom its assets are handed over for safe keeping. It is his job to show how these assets have been used if he cannot hand them back in cash. Thus if he is given £1,000 and is told to spend £500 of this on raw material: the £1,000 is shown as a liability and the £500 worth of raw material is shown as an asset. If the £500 is then converted into finished products which are sold at £750, the profit of £250 then features as a liability. Taking our business in Chapter 8, let us show a balance sheet at the end of the first year of trading, followed by a profit and loss account for the same year.

Balance Sheet at 31 December (1st year)

Liabilities		Assets	
Capital	£20000	Cash in hand	£16000
		Loss on trading	4000
	£20000		£20000

Profit and Loss Account (1st year)

Rent of premises	600	Sales for 2nd qtr	4000
Wages and salaries	4600	Sales for 3rd qtr	5000
Cost of raw materials	12000	Sales for 4th qtr	7000
Interest on capital	1200	Loss on year	4000
Advertising	1000		
Postage, lighting etc.	600		
	£20000		£20000

These are, of course, very simplified versions of these documents. Many other items would have been included which have been left out for the sake of clarity. For instance it is possible that not all suppliers' bills would have been paid by 31 December, in which case, in the balance sheet, these would have been shown on the left hand side as creditors and the cash on the right hand side would have been a larger sum. Also possibly at least one quarter's rent would have been paid in advance and this would have reduced the cash and added to the assets, since premises have a realizable value for sub-letting.

In the profit and loss account many items might have been included which are here collectively lumped under expenses.

Trial balances

We will now show quarterly trial balances, which lead up to the final annual balance sheet.

Liabilities		*Assets*	
1st qtr capital	20000	Cash in hand	18000
		Loss on trading	2000
	£20000		£20000
2nd qtr capital	20000	Cash in hand	13000
		Sundry debtors	4000
		Loss on trading	3000
	£20000		£20000
3rd qtr capital	20000	Cash in hand	11250
		Sundry Debtors	5000
		Loss on trading	3750
	£20000		£20000
4th qtr capital	20000	Cash in hand	9000
		Sundry debtors	7000
		Loss on trading	4000
	£20000		£20000

This shows our first year's loss as 4,000 as shown in Table B (see p. 123).

Now let us look at our profit and loss account for the 2nd and 3rd year.

On the 2nd year our final balance sheet is as follows:

Liabilities		*Assets*	
Capital	£20000	Cash	4000
		Debtors	12000
		Loss on 1st year	4000
		Loss on 2nd year	nil
	£20000		£20000

At the end of our 3rd year our balance sheet would show:

Liabilities		Assets	
Capital	£20000	Cash	3000
		Debtors	16000
		Loss on 1st two years	4000
		Less profit on 3rd	3000
			1000
	£20000		£20000

If instead of buying materials ready processed and merely packing them our business included its own factory and machinery, these would figure on the assets side of the balance sheet, and the cash figure would be correspondingly smaller. Meanwhile in the profit and loss account we should have to include a figure for depreciation. Factory and equipment wear out and have to be replaced one day. Where tax is paid on profit these depreciation figures are allowed for deduction at an agreed rate: say 5 per cent each year. Meanwhile reserves should be allowed for ultimate replacement and these reserves are shown in the balance sheet. If in twenty years a machine is written off and replaced it ceases to appear among the assets, but a new replacement machine must be added to them.

If a machine is sold, profit or loss on its depreciated value must be shown. If profit is distributed as a dividend it is shown in the balance sheet. Also in the balance sheet are shown reserves or sinking fund for repayment of debt. If, for instance, money has been borrowed on debenture its repayment must feature in the balance sheet but not in the profit and loss account, since this is a capital payment. The debt is part of the capital liabilities of the company, as are shares issued to shareholders who have lent it money in the first place. Since a company cannot buy its own shares (though certain shares are redeemable) they are not shown at their market value but only as debts to shareholders, which is merely a convenient fiction since no ordinary shareholder can reclaim from the company the amount he paid for the share. What he can do however is to sell the share to someone who is prepared to give a price for it, in return for a title to dividends; and naturally these shares on which companies pay higher dividends, command a higher price. If a company goes bankrupt and is 'wound up', shareholders may or may not receive compensation in accordance with the amount of assets available to pay off its debts and debenture holders. This, however, is a digression.

Change in values

One point to be remembered regarding accounts is that because many of the values they record refer to past transactions, and the value of money changes rapidly, as it has over the last few decades, these values tend to become unrealistic. Certain assets, such as land and buildings, may in fact appreciate in value, while others, such as machinery, could probably only be replaced at far greater expense than was originally incurred, which means that depreciation figured have to be drastically revised. Many firms today are spending a good deal of time and money reappraising the value of their assets in terms of depreciated money values, often with surprising results. This creates another problem for the accountant, which he cannot afford to ignore.

Business is dynamic not static

To return to our elementary explanation of accounting practice, we have now dealt with the theory of balance sheets and profit and loss accounts. These give a general picture – but only a very general one. If a business was a static entity or even a smooth-running mechanism which could ignore such things as market fluctuations and other constantly varying phenomena, everything would be fine. But business is a dynamic organism and the effective manager has to see it as such. Hence the need for operations research methods which we discussed in Chapter 9. But accountants can do a great deal for us; one of the most practical contributions is in cost accounting.

Cost accounting

Obviously we must know what our business is costing us to run and what our products are costing to produce before we can know what price we ought to charge and whether we shall make a profit. If we charge too high a price we shall limit our market unnecessarily, while if we charge too low a price we shall find ourselves in the red. What then is the optimum price at which we can command maximum sales and also make a reasonable profit?

The art, or science, of cost accounting is a comparatively recent development. It has been of enormous benefit to management. It is also an essential factor in a great deal of operations research, because it can supply some of the essential data which OR is able to work on to arrive at optimal decisions.

Unit cost and break-even point

In theory it should not be so difficult to arrive at the cost of a product. We take our total costs, both fixed and variable, over a period and divide it by our output. This should then be our cost. In our sample firm in Chapter 8 we took our fixed costs over three months at being £2,000, while our direct, or variable costs were £1,500 for 1,000 units selling at £2 each. This meant, as we decided, that we had to sell a maximum of 4,000 units or £8,000 worth per quarter to break even, that our cost per unit is $\frac{2,000 + (1,500 \times 4)}{4,000}$ = £2. This confirms our break-even point at 2,000 per quarter. Now suppose we increase our number of units to 5,000 our cost figure becomes $\frac{2,000 + (1,500 \times 5)}{5,000}$ which works out at $\frac{9,500}{5,000}$ = £1 9s. = £1 18s. 0d. This gives us a profit of 2s. on every unit or £500 on 5,000 units. Thus the greater number we can sell the larger will not only be our total profit but also our rate of profit per unit until our total production capacity has been reached. It is also probable that the larger the orders we can give to our suppliers, the cheaper will be their charges per 1,000 units, so here we make additional profit. The important thing to bear in mind here is that our fixed or indirect costs remain constant, while our direct or variable costs also remain a constant percentage of our selling price per unit. Once our capacity has been reached, however, our indirect costs will tend to rise; we shall have to rent larger premises, take on more labour, employ more salesmen and take on additional staff: this will raise the point at which we break even, so that we must draw in a new fixed cost line on our analysis graph and see where it crosses our sales line. This will show us at what point it is safe to take on additional fixed expenses without wiping out our profit.

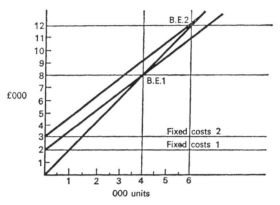

Figure 4. '000 Units sales per quarter.

In fact we can work it out arithmetically that if we increase our fixed costs by 50 per cent, bringing them up to £3,000 per quarter, our break-even point will be at 6,000 units, since

$$\frac{3{,}000 + (1{,}500 \times 6)}{6{,}000} = \frac{12{,}000}{6{,}000} = £2.$$

Provided therefore that our sales have passed 6,000 per quarter or 24,000 per annum (i.e. £48,000 worth) we are safe in adding to our overheads with the object of increasing our sales further.

Standard costing

The conventional way of calculating costs is what is known as standard costing. The object is to arrive at cost per unit. First all costs are considered, taken over a standard period, say a week, and based on a standard capacity of output of say 6,000 units per week. On this output we then calculate labour costs, material costs and overheads at a weekly figure. If we employ twenty men at £15 a week to turn out 6,000 units then the labour costs per unit are

$\frac{20 \times £15}{6{,}000}$ = 1s. If our overheads work out at £13,000 a year, then one week's overheads are £250 which we then divide by 6,000 so that we can allocate £$\frac{1}{24}$ or 10d. as the share of overheads borne by each unit. We now have a figure of 1s. 10d. Next we must allocate raw material and we find that from £500 worth of raw material we can make 1,000 units; this means our raw material is costing us 10s. per unit, so our total cost per unit is 11s. 10d. This gives us our basic standard cost per unit on which we can fix our minimum price to the trade. If we sell below this price we shall never make any profit. But in order to keep the business going we have got to go on selling steadily at a price which covers our costs and eventually gives us a profit. This is where we have to calculate our break-even point. This will come earlier or later according to where we fix our selling price and this depends partly on our assessment of the market. Let us say we fix it at £1. Then our gross profit, i.e. before the deduction of overheads (see footnote, p. 125), will be 20s. minus 10s. equals 10s. per unit. To find our break-even point we have to find how many units we have to sell before our gross profit per unit multiplied by our units sold equals our fixed costs. Now since our overheads work at £13,000 per year or £3,250 per quarter plus labour[1] costs at £3,900 per quarter the figure our sales have to reach before we can break even must be 14,300 units at £1 each. After that we are making a clear profit. Now since our average output is 6,000 per week, and if our sales department can sell all the units we make, we should break even in the third week and end the quarter with a turnover of £78,000 on which our nett profit should be £31,850.[2]

Suppose, however, that we only sell £30,000 worth in the first quarter. We shall then have two alternatives, either to go on piling up stocks, of which we may now have £48,000 worth of potential sales on our hands, or else reduce our production – entailing a reduction of our labour force thus cutting down our fixed costs. Even though we have made a profit on £30,000 minus

---

[1] We must count labour as a fixed cost over a short period though it may vary over a longer period as we shall see.

[2] i.e. £78,000 − £3,250 (overheads) + £39,000 (materials) + £3,900 (labour) = £78,000 − £46,150 = £31,850.

MANAGEMENT ACCOUNTING

£14,300 = £15,700 of sales we still have a disproportionate amount of unsold units on our hands to which we are adding at the rate of 6,000 units per week. We shall therefore have to revise our production in accordance with out market. In fact this shows the danger of not getting an accurate estimate of one's market first before going into production. Suppose we now decide to reduce our production figures drastically and cut down labour accordingly. Instead of employing twenty workers we now reduce our work force to five and reduce our weekly output to £1,500 worth, bearing in mind our accumulation of unsold stock. Our quarterly total costs will now appear as follows:

Overheads	3250	
Labour	975	
Material	9750	(13 weeks)
	13975	

Suppose that our sales for the second quarter increase to 45,000. Let us now look at the profit and loss account and trial balances for the first two quarters of our business:

1st Quarter

To raw material	15000	From sales	30000
To labour costs	3900		
Overheads (rent, power, etc.)	3250		
Profit on trading	7850		
	30000		30000

Assuming we started with a capital of £50,000, with equipment costing £30,000, our trial balance would be as follows:

Liabilities		Assets	
Capital	50000	Equipment	30000
Profit on trading	7850	Stock at cost	24000
		Cash in hand	3850
	57850		57850

MANAGEMENT ACCOUNTING

It will be noted that our surplus stock does not appear in the profit and loss account, since this only refers to our trading costs. It does, however, appear in our trial balance which is a record of our capital costs.

The cash in hand figure is arrived at by deducting our total expenditure, i.e. materials: £39,000, plus labour costs £3,900, plus overheads £3,250, plus our cost of equipment £30,000, from the sum of our original capital of £50,000 plus our revenue from sales £30,000 = £80,000. The result is £3,850 which, added to our stock in hand, at cost should equal our capital plus our profits.

For our 2nd quarter we get the following figures:

2nd Quarter

(Profit and Loss Account)

To raw material	22500	From sales	45000
Labour	975[1]		
Overheads (rent, power, etc.)	3250		
Profit	18275		
	45000		45000

Our trial balance now appears as follows:

Capital	50000	Equipment	30000
Profits on 1st qtr	7850	Stock in hand	11250
Profits on 2nd qtr	18275	Cash in hand	34875
	76125		76125

Here again the cash in hand figure is arrived at by adding our original capital to the profits from the first quarter and the revenue from sales for the second quarter, which make a total of £102,850. From this we deduct cost of material for the 2nd quarter namely £22,500 plus stock in hand at cost, £11,250 plus the quarter's labour and overheads plus equipment. We are now left with a substantial profit and also a reasonable stock in hand to which we can add as we wish. As our sales increase, however, we may need

[1] 5 men at £15 per week for 13 weeks.

168

to increase our labour, since our reduced labour force can only produce enough stock, when added to our stock in hand, for sales of £32,250. In fact, in order to keep our present reserves of stock we ought to aim at a sales figure of £60,000 involving a labour force of some sixteen men with an output of 4,800 units or so a week. If we achieve this target on our third quarter our trial balance will be as follows:

Capital	50000	Stock in hand	11250
Profits on 1st qtr	7850	Equipment	30000
Profits on 2nd qtr	18275	Cash in hand	58505
Profits on 3rd qtr	23630		
	99755		99755

and our profit and loss account:

3rd Quarter

To raw material	30000	From sales	60000
Labour	3120		
Overheads	3250		
Profit on sales	23630		
	60000		60000

Let us now suppose that we go back to our original labour force and a production figure of 78,000 units of which we manage to sell 70,000 in the final quarter of our first years trading.[1]

Our accounts will now appear as follows:

Profit and Loss for 4th Quarter

Cost of raw material	35000	Revenue from sales	70000
Depreciation on equipment	1500		
Overheads	3250		
Labour costs	3900		
Profit	26350		
	£70000		£70000

[1] We are assuming that it is possible to lay off and take on labour at short notice, which is not always the case. If it is not, then our need for forward planning becomes even more important.

MANAGEMENT ACCOUNTING

Our trial balance for the 4th quarter will now be:

Capital	50000	Stock in hand at cost	15250
Consolidated profits on first 3 quarters	49755	Cash in hand	82355
Profit on 4th qtr	26350	Equipment/£30000 Less depreciation 1500	28500
	£126105		£126105

Let us now review our position at the end of the first year's trading and draw up a final balance sheet and profit and loss account for the year. Obviously our profits have been considerable and we can decide to pay a reasonable dividend on our capital. We may also decide to use some of our cash in hand to purchase additional equipment. Let us suppose we pay a 20 per cent dividend on our capital (it doesn't matter whether it is ours or whether we borrowed it, a reasonable interest charge should already be included in our overheads) and also to purchase £20,000 worth of equipment. The maintenance of this equipment will probably add something to our overheads, and also, in further profit and loss accounts, a figure will have to appear for depreciation, at present however we will show it simply as an asset. Here, then, are our final accounts for the year, consolidating the figures for the four quarters.

Liabilities		*Assets*	
Capital	50000	Stock in hand at cost	15250
Profit on year's trading	76105	Cash	52355
		New equipment	20000
		Present equipment (less depreciation)	28500
		Dividends	10000
	£126105		£126105

Consolidated Profit and Loss a/c 1st year:

Expenditure		Income	
Purchase of raw materials	102500	From sales	205000
Overheads (rent, power, etc.)	13000		
Depreciation	1500		
Labour	11895		
Profit on year's trading	76105		
	£205000		£205000

It will be seen from our balance sheet that the value of our business has more than doubled in one year and that if our capital were issued in £1 shares, each share would be worth some £2·32. If the company were a public one, a purchase of 100 shares on the Stock Exchange at 46·2s would stand to receive a dividend amounting to 8·62 per cent on investment.

Auditing

These accounts have to be checked physically by the auditors where possible. The main checks are on: (1) stocks in hand at cost, (2) cash in hand and at bank, (3) amounts paid out to labour, (4) receipts for rent, light, power, etc., (5) equipment (which in normal accounts would be itemized under a number of headings such as buildings, machinery, vehicles etc.) Also separately itemized would be the general description of overheads such as rent, light, heat, salaries, fuel, power etc. Careful records must be kept of all money going out and all money coming in. This is why receipts for all payments are important as well as copies of receipts for payments-in. Where a number of items have to be kept in stock for daily or weekly requirements there must be a strict method of stock control to ensure that stock is properly received, issued and maintained. In a medium-sized business, say in the engineering industry, many hundreds, even thousands of different items may have to be held in stock including spare parts, tools, components, raw materials and stationery. There will also be a stock of finished products which will require continuous checking. Stock books will be kept showing intake and withdrawals, just as they will with cash.

Cash will be recorded in a day book where all transactions are recorded under a number of headed columns. For each column a separate book may be kept. One column will be headed 'ledger'. These items will be entered in separate ledger accounts of which one will be opened for every customer, and also for every supplier. The object of an accounting system is first to record and then to analyse.

Credit

An added complication of accounting, which was not shown in our sample accounts above, is the fact that payments are often not made immediately. This means that in most balance sheets an item is shown under assets of debtors and another under liabilities of creditors. In the profit and loss account these are counted as cash, since it is assumed they will be paid sooner or later. In the balance sheets debts owed to the company are shown as assets but, since they are not actually cash, our cash will be so much the less by our debtors' figure, and in calculating what our cash should be we have to deduct them from our liabilities, i.e. capital + profits, together with stock in hand, etc. But occasionally a time will come when 'bad debts' have to be written off because all chance of their recovery has vanished. This has to appear in the balance sheet since these debts can no longer be counted as assets. It will also be shown in the profit and loss account as a diminution of profits.

Budgeting

The important thing is that we now have, in money terms at least, some reasonably accurate record of our year's transactions. It will be seen that, had we budgeted our needs for labour and stock more carefully at the beginning, we should have saved ourselves the necessity for laying off and later taking on new labour at short notice. It also shows how dependant we are on market conditions in our forward planning. Unless we have a reasonably accurate estimate of our future markets we are completely in the dark as to our operating costs. Fortunately in this case we had adequate facilities for carrying excessive stock. If our capital had been less we should have been in trouble. The ideal is to aim at a smooth upward growth in labour requirement, not a see-saw movement as in this case. These two samples should have taught us some lessons in budgeting and forward planning, which we can now consider in the next chapter.

CHAPTER 12

Planning

Need for planning

In the several businesses we have considered, the need for sound forward planning has become abundantly evident, particularly for forward budgeting. It has also by now become clear that planning must be based on markets because it is no use going to the expense of producing goods and services which nobody will buy. Marketing obviously involves an element of risk, since only a monopoly can force people to buy a particular product because it limits the choice to one supplier – and even then the consumer generally has the choice of going without the product rather than paying the monopoly price. So planning must take account of these, and other, business risks and possibilities.

Suspicion of planning

Planning is a suspect word in some circles and particularly with Professor Galbraith who, in his recent book, *The New Industrial State*, claims that because large industrial corporations have to plan, often years ahead, before they bring out a new product, owing to the exigencies of developing mass production machinery, new tooling, dies etc., they have to manipulate the market by mass methods of advertising and sales promotion so that they can eliminate the element of chance. This is an extreme view and needs more evidence to prove it. A leading article in *The Times Business News* (4 December 1967) and an article by Samuel Brittan in the *Financial Times* (4 December 1967) both question the validity of Galbraith's argument. His argument is, in fact, that the large quasi-monopolistic corporations actually create their own market first, in order to sell their goods, and that this creation is a form of coercion and mass hypnotism: moreover because they have a virtual monopoly they can force the customer to pay what price they like. This is a matter of argument. But suffice it to say that for the ordinary businessman detailed forward planning is essential, and that it must start from the market.

Swedish example of planning

A good example of first-class planning has recently been demonstrated in Sweden, where it has finally been decided to change all traffic from driving on the left-hand side of the road to driving on the right. The planning actually took four years, though the idea has been considered for twenty years. Everything possible was foreseen and arranged for. The result was 100 per cent successful. One advantage the planners had was that the Swedish Ministry of Transport had complete power to impose its will on the public – but considerable imagination and enterprise were used in thinking out original ideas, including the recruitment of children to direct pedestrians on to crossings and also the practice, in schools, of children riding bicycles on the right-hand side; together with model exercises explaining how the new system would work.

Attention to detail

The essence of planning is attention to every possible detail in order to minimize chance. In business this is not so easy, because business is based on markets and markets are in varying degrees unpredictable. Not only do fashions and tastes change but new inventions may completely eliminate one market while suddenly opening a new one. In fact, as we have pointed out, innovation is of the essence of business and one of its main objectives. The plastics industry, for instance, has not only widened enormously the use of synthetic materials but has in many cases made old materials obsolete. The number of household objects which used to be made in a variety of materials such as wood, glass and various metals, and are now made of plastic is tremendous. The range of new products available to the buying public today compared with that available thirty years ago is enormous, and changes are taking place rapidly every year. This makes planning for the future extremely difficult because by the time our plans are completed they may already be out of date.

PLANNING

Budgeting and planning in the private sector

An independent private sector company, be it small, medium-sized or large, must take everything into consideration while eliminating risk as much as possible. We have seen how operations research can help in this. We have also noted the value of the 'break-even' chart and forecast accounting in our budgeting. A government budget, as we know, is a document showing what the government plans to spend over the coming year and how it intends to raise the money. A business budget does the same, but it extends over a longer period though it has to be broken down into shorter ones.

In the company we described in Chapter 8 we outlined one of the simplest types of business. Here the components of the final product were purchased outside and merely packed into boxes; nevertheless we had to produce a budget for future trading, based on a previous forecast of the market. We assumed the forecast was correct, at least as regards minimum sales. We also had to take into account our maximum capacity for production based on our capital resources. Our estimate of sales may have been conservative – it may also have been pessimistic. Our price policy may have been at fault. Had we fixed our price higher we might have sold less, though our nett profit per unit would have been greater. Had we fixed our prices lower, our break-even point would have been higher and possibly longer deferred. On the other hand, our sales might have been greater – had we power to increase our production. Thus the factors which go into planning may be enumerated as follows:

1. Market capacity;
2. Price policy;
3. Production capacity required;
4. Manpower resources;
5. Capital resources;
6. Cash flow;
7. Availability and cost of raw material;
8. Distribution arrangements;
9. Marketing structure;
10. Merchandising and advertising;
11. Profit policy.

All of these are variable, to some extent, and are thus open to various permutations and combinations. Our market capacity, for instance, will obviously vary with our price. But our price will vary with our costs. Manpower may or may not be readily available, taking account of the range of skills required. Our production capacity will vary according to several other variable factors including capital resources, raw material, labour skill and cash flow. Our capital resources may vary according to our ability to borrow money or the money we have at our disposal. Our distribution arrangements, as mentioned in Chapter 9, will vary according to our product and our resources: so will our marketing structure. Our advertising and merchandizing will vary with our resources and with our marketing structure.

Planning for the optimum

In making one over-all plan all these variables have to be assessed and combined. The trial and error method is costly and inefficient. We may waste a lot of time and money trying out different variations before arriving at that combination of them all which gives us the optimum solution. By planning we try to arrive at the optimum solution *before* launching into large capital expenditure. We may have to make certain experiments and construct a series of models on paper in which all variations are allowed for. The experiments may be included in our primary market research on the lines of those made for Rowntree's 'Black Magic' Chocolates. In this case, sample products were actually made and tried out on a section of the consumer market. There may be reasons for avoiding this, where an element of surprise or security are involved and possibilities of imitation exist. This is only one side of the highly complex planning process. The financial side is also vitally important once we have established that a market exists at a given price, so are quality and content; these, and the related operational factors, are interdependent. Though we have mentioned that quality and durability are necessary objectives in many products, they are not all essential to all products. Durability is certainly an essential of a motor-tyre – but it is not necessary in a cigarette or a bar of chocolate which is made for consumption!

Moreover there is such a thing as 'planned obsolescence,[1] that is

[1] A detailed consideration of this subject can be found in *The New High Priesthood* by Ralph Glasser (Macmillan 1967).

to say a deliberate policy whereby certain commodities are made to be replaced within a given period by models of newer design. In our planning this needs to be taken into consideration. There are, for instance, some people who like to change their car every year. This entails a policy of 'model changing'. A particular example of planned obsolescence is women's fashions, where most women scorn to be seen wearing long skirts when short ones are in fashion, and vice versa. But most products are made to last a reasonable time and nobody wants or can afford to keep on changing their washing machines, electric cookers, bicycles or television sets unless they are forced to. Nor can a manufacturing company afford to produce goods of inferior quality, even though immediately consumable – such as a detergent or washing soap. Quality must always be of such a standard that the product does what it is designed to do and anyone who produces goods below this standard, merely for the sake of cheapness, will lose his market however vigorously his products may be advertised. Thus, in planning our future production programme, we must make adequate provision for research and development to make sure that our product is up to the standard of quality which we claim for it and which the customer requires.

Servicing

Another requirement of planning, with many products, is adequate servicing. People who buy an electric or mechanical device, for which they are unable to obtain adequate spare parts or repairs if it goes wrong, will soon switch their custom (and persuade others to do so) to products whose manufacturers do provide adequate servicing. This is particularly important for goods supplied to overseas markets.

We have already, in Chapter 9, discussed the various alternatives in marketing and merchandizing a product, and these must be taken into account in our over-all plan. They have an important impact on our financial policy and budgeting.

Stock control

Stock holding is another important feature of our planning, and for this a special technique has been devised under the name of 'linear programming'. Briefly it consists of calculating the inflow and outflow of stocks and the optimum amount of stocks to be held, allowing for market variations and production capacity. Storage, as we have seen, costs money, and stocks are of many different categories of which raw materials and finished products are the most important. Where stores of raw materials have to be held for some time to mature, as in the tobacco industry, not only are considerable costs involved in warehousing, protection from deterioration, insurance and labour, but also in immobilization of capital resources which could be used in other ways. This, as we have seen, is an important factor in budgeting or financial planning. (For a more detailed analysis of stock control, see Appendix D.)

Long- and short-term planning

Planning must be both long-term and short-term. We must have an idea where we are going and what objective we hope to achieve in at least five years, probably ten or in certain cases much longer. We must think ahead continually – for business is dynamic. To see it as static is unrealistic and even a balance sheet can be misleading because, by the time it is published, the situation may have radically changed. Nevertheless it is some indication not only of the position of the company but also of its past development, since most annual balance sheets and profit and loss accounts give figures of the previous year's position for comparison with the present ones. What a balance sheet does not show is what is likely to happen in the future, except in so far as it may indicate certain reserves which have been put aside for certain specified developments.

The planning department

Most firms now have a separate planning department, whose sole occupation it is to be constantly looking ahead and working out details of future development of the business. This department acts in two capacities, first as advisers to the board, and second as instruments whereby board decisions can be broken down into detail, analysed and, if approved, put into action.

A planning department will be concerned both with long- and short-term planning. It should work closely with research and development, whose job it is to suggest improvements in the product or changes in production methods which may possibly even affect the structure of the business.

Organization change

In the *Harvard Business Review* recently, an interesting article appeared on successful organization change[1], in which details are given of the necessary factors involved in re-planning an organization. One of the most difficult, but also most important, is obtaining the co-operation of those involved in the changes. People are naturally conservative and resent changes in the accustomed routine. It is thus essential for the planning department to gain full co-operation from all managers in carrying out changes which affect them. In fact, where possible, it is highly advisable to include line managers in consultations so that they can feel involved in, and committed to, such changes.

One of the greatest dangers of setting up a planning department is the impression it can give that experienced departmental managers are being 'pushed around' and told their business by theoreticians who have little or no practical experience of the day-to-day problems of the business. This also emphasises the need for careful choice of personnel in the planning department. They should be people who are both acceptable and capable of establishing good human relationships, as well as intellectually equipped for examining situations objectively.

Short-term planning

In a paper read to a B.I.M. seminar in September 1966, Professor Ernest Dale, Ph.D., made the following point:

> Each executive must organize his own planning group and develop a plan for his own activities, then try to co-ordinate his plans with those of other departments.

The advantage of this is that each department then feels committed to carry out its own plans. The planning department then

[1] *Harvard Business Review*, May–June 1967, condensed by Larry E. Greiner in *Management Review* (the journal of the American Management Association), August 1967.

has the responsibility of co-ordinating the plans of each department with the full co-operation of each group. Obviously modifications will have to be made, but these will be by consent and not by imposition.

Individual departments must set their own targets and then see how they tie up with those of other departments. A departmental head is the best person to judge what his department can achieve, but, he must also take into account the interdependence of all other departments and be certain their targets integrate with his own. Thus the planning officer's job is primarily not one of imposition but of transmission of information and co-ordination of agreed targets. He must also be in a position to transmit information and advice to the board through the general manager or the managing director.

Long-range planning

The information gained in short-range planning can then be used in long-range planning. The object of any business must be growth – it cannot stay where it is; if it tries to do so it will slip back, because other more ambitious firms will leave it behind. It must therefore be fully aware of its own capacity and of the means whereby this capacity can be increased.

It may be that its range of products is too limited or that some of its capacity is being wasted. Is it fully using its raw materials, its manpower, its machine equipment, its capital resources, its buildings, its transport? It is carrying too much stock – or risking stoppages by running out of material? Is time being wasted in labour disputes? If so, why?

It is the planning department's job to investigate all these factors. It is also the planning department's responsibility to be fully aware of the competitive position, and the actual and potential share of the market commanded by the company. Is the market becoming saturated? Are improvements to the product possible? Can new markets be opened up or new channels of distribution found? Obviously the planning department must work closely with the marketing department as well as with the research and development department (R & D). In fact it must work closely with all departments including the costing and financial department.

The planning department should, in fact, be the nucleus of growth and development. But whereas the R & D people are mainly concerned with technical development, the planners are concerned with assessing whether or not new developments are feasible from a business point of view.

The R & D people may come up with a brilliant idea which may entail the entire re-equipment of the factory. The planning department have got to assess whether they can afford, after consultation with the financial side, to entail the capital expenditure required – and more important – whether they can afford *not* to make the necessary sacrifice. Supposing a competitor gets hold of the same idea and decides to go ahead with it? What will be the effect on the market? Will it make existing products obsolete and so make a big hole in the market? The pros and cons have to be weighed against each other and the chances assessed by stochastic methods (see p. 149). Thus short-term planning inevitably merges into long-term planning and it is difficult to draw the line between them.

Planning in a world situation

If a business is going to make progress it has got to see many years ahead and make its plans accordingly. Even to maintain the *status quo* many businesses have to plan ahead, as for instance in providing for raw material requirements. But in a highly competitive economy, such as we have today, no business can afford merely to stay where it is, it has always to be anticipating the future, and for this it must have the maximum information.

It may be said that international politics have nothing to do with business; but any business which could have anticipated the second world war and made appropriate plans, would have reaped considerable benefits. It could also have done considerable service to the country by helping it to be prepared, whereas history records it manifestly was not. It used to be said that the reason Germany nearly won the last war in its early days was because it had organized its industry, though ostensibly on a peace-time footing (which it was obliged to under the Treaty of Versailles) in such a way that it could very easily be switched over to making armaments. This was far from the case with Britain, though unrestricted by the Treaty of Versailles.

This was why many commanders of tank brigades whose strength should have been 150 vehicles, found themselves with only 3, as I well remember one tank brigadier complaining in 1939. I am not, of course, suggesting that industry should be constantly preparing for the next war! But a wise company should always have 'its ear to the ground' as to possible new events and developments which may affect its markets. The planning department should certainly be in a position to warn its board of directors of national or international developments which may require readjustment of policy or capital development, whether these developments are in the political, the military or purely the business field.

New developments

The vast development of electronics since the war, the new developments in atomic energy and aero-space exploration, affect not only the largest corporations but also the smallest. New components are required every day, and the small to medium-sized company, which can anticipate needs for such components, may well find itself in a very strong position when such new projects are launched. We have all seen many small companies grow from very insignificant beginnings to become vital contributors to the economy, through intelligent anticipation of needs which may not have been thought of twenty years ago.

Industrial and commercial intelligence is essential to forward planning – and I don't mean industrial espionage about which much is being written and said today. This is an ethical matter which I do not intend to discuss. It involves industrial security, which obviously cannot be neglected, and cases are certainly on record of businesses which have spent considerable sums developing a new product only to find that a rival has 'beaten them to the post' and collared their potential market. There are certainly times when speed is essential in developing new products, and this is a matter of judgment on the part of the planning department and the board, who have to assess the sacrifices necessary to get in first with something new – and such sacrifices may be considerable.

Once more we are thrown back on the analogy of a military or naval operation. Surprise can be the essence of success, in many cases, and this is something which has to be fully realized and weighed in both long- and short-term planning. For planning should never be so rigid it cannot be changed at short notice if necessary.

The smaller firm and planning

Long-range planning, or LRP as it is called technically, is not a luxury which can only be indulged in by the giant combines, though for them it is obviously a necessity, since many thousands or even millions of pounds can be involved in the launching of a new operation. The smaller firm, with less resources at its disposal, must carefully safeguard those resources against dispersal on wasteful or ineffective projects. It must also safeguard them against wastage through more effective planning by its competitors who may be waiting to capture their markets. Thus planning, whoever carries it out, cannot be neglected by the smaller firm. It is, therefore, advisable to make certain that somebody is available, if possible a competent team of experts, to plan operations ahead both on a short- and long-term basis. A knowledge of operations research is valuable in such a team or, if this is not possible, the advice of an OR consultant.

Many business men may think they are doing well enough as they are to be able to dispense with LRP, OR and other 'newfangled' techniques. They may be at the moment – but are they looking to the future? Are they conscious of the need for growth, for development, for adjustments to changing markets? And markets *are* always changing, as we have seen. The prosperous business man of today may well be the failure of tomorrow. That may sound depressing and pessimistic, but a study of economic growth and decline proves it only too abundantly true. The chemist round the corner believes he has a thriving business – and he may have, today. But supposing a rival sets up in his area who uses more up-to-date methods and who widens his range of business? Our prosperous chemist may well find his business declining. A business may not be threatened now, but it may be threatened later; it is therefore in its interest to develop to its utmost capacity, not merely to increase its profits but to keep out potential competition, or, if it arises, to be able to deal with it. No business can afford to 'live on its fat'. It must always be planning for the future, investigating new possibilities and new opportunities for growth.

Supposing our chemist learns that a new housing estate is being developed nearby, he may well consider moving his business to that area. He may consider extending his 'inventory' and 'plugging' certain products which are more profitable than others. Compare a chemist's shop today with one of 25 years ago; it carries nearly twice the range of products. Jesse Boot realized, nearly a century ago, that chemists need not be confined to selling prescriptions and patent medicines, and built up a vast chain store enterprise, though it is still primarily based on pharmaceuticals. In those days, 'planning' was unknown as a business technique, but Jesse Boot planned his operation and made sure it would be successful. But planning today needs science, because the business world is not only more complex but also more highly competitive.

What is our business?

A question often asked today and originated by Professor Peter Drucker (see *The Practice of Management*, Chapter 6) is 'what is our business?' – to which Drucker added 'and what should it be?' The simple answer, which Drucker quotes from Theodore N. Vail of the American Telephone and Telegraph Company, some half a century ago, is 'our business is service'. But that, for our purposes, is perhaps an over-simplification. The question is more commonly asked today in connection with diversification. In other words, is a company justified in multiplying the services it gives until it becomes a multi-service organization supplying everything from a pin to a jet-liner or a space-craft? There are obvious merits in specialization. Rolls Royce became the finest makers of aero-engines because they specialized in making internal combustion engines of the finest quality and craftsmanship. But note, when the turbine and the jet superseded the piston-driven engine, Rolls Royce immediately switched over a large proportion of their resources to making these new types of engines, with the same precision and craftsmanship as they had given to the original car and piston engines. In the same way a generation before they had switched from making luxury cars to making aero propeller engines. They were as fully up to date with their marketing as they were proficient in their precision engineering. They may have operated in a limited field, but today their products are sold and relied on throughout the world, and their profits have been consistently high.

Expansion

This is one form of expansion, but expansion within the same business. There is also lateral expansion, known today as 'expansion by acquisition' or 'take-over'. We have seen that this has happened with many companies, as for instance with Unilever and Dunlop and recently with the British American Tobacco Company, who have taken over Yardley Perfumeries and also Wiggins Teape, the paper makers. Almost every day we read in our newspapers of new 'take-over' bids, sometimes by firms who wish to buy up their competitors in order to gain a larger share of the particular market, sometimes by firms who wish to spread their interests to avoid including 'too many eggs in one basket'. The motive behind take-overs by cigarette-making companies is obviously the result of the cancer scare and the action taken by governments in both England and the U.S.A. to restrict cigarette advertising, on which cigarette firms rely to such a great extent for their sales promotion. Other firms feel that they have capital lying idle which might be utilized more profitably in other fields than those they have traditionally engaged in. Others believe they can utilize their sales and marketing machinery to include products other than their own. To many of these companies the answer to Peter Drucker's question is becoming increasingly difficult to determine, except in the general sense used by Theodore Vail.

Planning and take-overs

These take-overs are however, in almost every case, the result of long-range planning. They are based on an evaluation of the resources at the company's disposal and of their optimum utilization for profitability. The same principles can be – and are being – constantly applied to smaller businesses.

A friend of mine told me that he had recently made an offer of a quarter of a million pounds for a business similar to his own – a comparatively small engineering firm. I was somewhat amazed, because I knew that when he started his own business his capital was considerably less than this sum. Such transactions are taking place daily and it is not an unhealthy sign. In fact it is a sign of economic progress. There is still plenty of room for the small to medium-sized business, provided it plans its operations wisely and pays proper attention to its markets. When my friend started his business it was making marine engines. It is now making centrifugal pumps for which there is a far greater market. The marine engine side of the business has virtually lapsed. He employs about 300 people – yet he can afford to offer £250,000 for another business. In his case the answer to Drucker's question was originally: 'The wrong one', and by asking Drucker's second question: 'What business should it be?' he found the right answer. This emphasizes the need, already mentioned, of consistently asking pertinent questions and of doing everything possible to arrive at the correct answers, including where necessary the use of OR techniques.

Sometimes, as Drucker points out, we are too deeply committed to a particular business to be able to change it over-night. He quotes, as an example, the owner of a copper mine. If there is no demand for copper, he says, the mine will have to shut down. But he goes on rightly to point out that copper is used in a number of products and could probably be used in a great many more to advantage. Here is the challenge to management. It consists of answering another question, namely: 'Who is the customer?' Then we have to go on to ask the question of how we can reach him? We may also consider the point that if the price of copper is so low that it is no longer profitable for us to mine it, then would it not be worth switching to making copper-based products from the surplus of copper on the market, assuming that it is this surplus which has caused its price to fall so rapidly? Alternatively we could use the copper produced by those mines whose economy of production enables them to produce copper cheaper than we can.

What are we selling?

Another question which planning experts have to ask, simple though it may seem, is 'what are we selling'. A gas cooker maker, as Drucker points out, is not only competing with other gas cooker makers but with all makers of cooking devices whether electric, solid fuel, paraffin or (in Eastern countries) charcoal. I happened to be in Karachi when natural gas was first introduced there and this lesson was brought home to me. To the marketing man this question of 'what are we selling' may be of vital importance, and it may well be that on careful consideration he may find he is selling something quite different from what he thought, and that his competition lies in a different direction than he anticipated. This is the sort of question and answer the planning expert has to be continually considering. The answer, for instance, in the case of moulded plastics, would be an extremely complicated one, but from the planning point of view, the more complicated the better, because it gives far more scope for suggestions which may lead to far greater productivity. In moulded plastics, however, a number of different moulds will be required if our range of products is wide enough to cover all possibilities. What our planners have to decide is the optimum range of moulds to satisfy an optimum profit in the market. They also have to decide on the possibilities of standardization to reduce varieties of moulds to a minimum. But all this has to be based on as accurate a survey as possible of the markets for every product.

Planning tools

The planner today has many new tools at his disposal, and it is essential that he should use them to their best advantage. If he doesn't his competitors will. Value analysis is one of these tools; that is, investigation into the value of every operation carried out inside a business and what it yields. Job analysis is another, to determine what each man is doing, what are his exact functions and whether he is overlapping with someone else? Is he getting paid correctly in relation to similar jobs and the actual content of the job? Can his job be combined with that of someone else?

We have already considered network planning, linear programming, cost-control, manpower utilization, use of managerial ability, research and development and operational research. These are only a few of the new tools available to the manager to help him to improve his business and increase not only his productivity but also his profitability. And profitability, as we have seen, depends on providing a 'needed' service to the community.

Use of consultants

We have, in this book, covered a fairly wide range of business activities and discussed the various methods of control available to make a business effective. We have not gone into the technical details of these controls but we have added a bibliography where some of the standard works on these controls are listed, so that the reader can study them for himself in greater detail. We have tried, however, to indicate in what way these controls can help the average business man to run his business more effectively. Consultants are available, at a fee, to help him to apply them, if he feels they are too complicated, too technical or too mathematical for him to grasp; or he can hire specialists to help him.

The consultant has a useful role to play, as we have suggested, but his role is not to run a business, which is management's job, but only to advise on its improvement and perhaps to install new methods and train people to operate them successfully. Consultants, however, need to be carefully chosen and they now have two professional associations. The B.I.M. and the C.B.I. also run a joint panel of consultants whom they can recommend as reliable. Those who are thinking of calling in a consultant would be well advised to refer to one of these bodies regarding the best firms of advisers in any particular field. Consultants themselves are specialists in different aspects of business such as finance, production, personnel, marketing and so forth, and need to be selected accordingly. A consultant should possess considerable practical experience of business, of as wide a variety as possible, as well as theoretical knowledge of the latest techniques and developments.

Value of consultants

It is sometimes said that if consultants know so much about business why are they not in business themselves? The answer is that they *are* in business, and frequently a very lucrative business, that of consultancy itself. It is also sometimes said that consultants are merely failed businessmen on the basis of Bernard Shaw's dictum that 'those who cannot do, teach'. This is an unfair generalization, though it may apply to a small minority; hence the need to discriminate. The reason for the growth of the consultancy business is that management techniques have become so complicated and diverse, as the result of new research and scientific developments, that many managers find them difficult to grasp without a great deal of study and more time than they have at their disposal. It is therefore worth their while to use the brains and experience of the consultant, who is able to see a business from outside, objectively, to advise him where improvements are possible or where mistakes are being made. In future planning, for instance, a consultant can be of great assistance and may well see possibilities of development which a manager may have overlooked.

Conclusion

A book such as this is not designed – nor would it be capable – to act as a comprehensive compendium of detailed methods of good management. It is designed rather to stimulate thought and interest in certain new developments in management practice and to indicate where further information and guidance may be found. A manager is a creative agent, his job is a socially valuable one. He performs a service to the community by helping to organize resources in such a way as to benefit society, by helping its members to live fuller, safer, more comfortable and more enjoyable lives. It is not for him to decide what is good or bad for the community. The community must decide that through its own free choice of purchase within the limitations laid down by law. The businessman's job is to provide the community with those things which it desires at prices which it can pay. The measure of the manager's success is whether he makes a profit or a loss. If his profits rise too high, competition will step in to regulate them. For profits indicate demand, and business is there to satisfy it. Society has always recognized the dangers of monopoly and taken steps to curb them, through Anti-Trust laws in America and laws against Restraint of Trade in Britain. The chief monopolies today exist in state-owned enterprises, for which there may or may not be valid justifications: but this is a political matter which the community has to decide. There is however, still plenty of room for the small to medium-sized business provided its management is effective and is clear about its objectives. This book is a limited attempt to define what those objectives might be and to indicate how they may be achieved.

APPENDIX A

NETWORK ANALYSIS

Basically network analysis is a method of arriving at priorities in planning an industrial operation. The operation is broken down into stages and each stage is allotted a time limit based on past experience. Those operations which can be carried out simultaneously are shown as parallels, those which are consecutive follow a continuous line. Thus one may have say seven parallel lines composed of a varying number of events each of which is shown as a circle. The line between each circle is marked with a number denoting the number of days or weeks required between one event and the next. When the network of parallel lines is completed the total for each line is then calculated and the maximum time for the total operation is arrived at. The line showing utilization of the maximum time is shown in red and is the 'critical path'. Since all lines do not add up to the same total some parallel operations will have more time than they need, and will not in fact be 'critical'; certain jobs will have what is called a 'float' – that is to say they will have a margin of time left over after they have been completed; but if delivery of material is held up or workers are required for other jobs and there is delay in starting, this 'float' may gradually dwindle until the job becomes a critical one in which further delay will hold up the whole operation. Thus network analysis and critical path are not only a means of planning an operation but also of keeping a check that it is developing according to plan. The job may be building a new factory or launching a new product from the drawing board design to the final delivery and distribution.

The following is an extract from an article by Peter Hardie-Bick, then Head of Organization Division, United Africa Company of Nigeria Ltd. (now with Unilever, London), published in *Management in Nigeria*, July–August 1967. Much of the material for the article was drawn from a course devised by E. L. Buesnel for training Unilever personnel:

APPENDIX A

NETWORK PLANNING

Planning plays a major part in the success of every undertaking and is frequently management's greatest single responsibility. To co-ordinate large- and small-scale projects with optimum efficiency, making the best use of available resources, and to schedule and control a project to completion are vital aims.

How network planning was developed

The operational research work which has led to the present form of what is known as network analysis was carried out in the U.S.A. by the Dupont and General Dynamics organizations. In dealing with major development and construction projects these organizations had to co-ordinate the work of many departments. A system was needed which would:

1. Plan the most effective use of resources and diagnose potential bottlenecks and trouble areas.
2. Provide an efficient means of forecasting the completion date of a project, and the means of checking at all intermediate stages that the project would be completed on time.
3. Record in planned sequence all the activities for the completion of a project showing how the different tasks to be carried out would fit together into the project processes.
4. Enable all personnel concerned with the execution of the project to see graphically their relationship to the others, pinpointing responsibilities and improving communication and co-operation between persons and departments.

These objectives are much sought after, particularly in the field of government contracts where ability to achieve completion within defined target dates is a powerful bargaining factor. One of the first major projects controlled by network analysis was the Polaris development programme. This involved the employment of many subcontractors on the problems of developing the missile system to be used by submarines of the United States Navy. The completion time allowed for this project was reduced by more than two years and this has been shown to be the result in part of the application of a specially developed technique based on network analysis. The effect of this in reducing the cost of the project, and

APPENDIX A

on the improved tactical military situation which was the outcome of the early introduction of an advanced weapon system, emphasized the importance of this new management technique.

Commercial applications soon followed and it was found that the network idea had a profound effect on the thinking of planners at all levels. In the first place the emphasis which the new techniques placed on the interdependence of technical authorities helped to generate a spirit of team work. Second, the increasing complexity of major projects could at last be brought under control by a logical system of great effectiveness. The apparent inflexibility experienced in some planning systems in the past had been overcome by a clear expression of the relationship of activities at the initial planning stage. These relationships, when subsequently translated into a schedule, formed a basis for a simple and flexible plan of action with a clearly stated priority for each activity.

Most of the early network applications were in connection with large complex projects, but it was soon found that there was a need to simplify and standardize the approach to project planning even at relatively simple levels. This has led to the use of network diagrams to express visually relationships which might otherwise have been described in words. The clarity of this new form of communication has proved sufficient justification for its use, even in minor projects.

Network techniques

It will be helpful if at this stage some of the more common aspects of network analysis are briefly described.

Critical path method (CPM) is the most frequently used description of the techniques used for the simple time analysis of operations in network planning. The significance of this title will be explained later.

Programme evaluation and review technique (PERT) is a more advanced system used for time analysis where the uncertainty of target times is significant e.g., in scientific work.

Resource allocation is a technique using the network information to plan the deployment of scarce resources to achieve the desired results.

APPENDIX A

Multi-project scheduling (MPS) is a procedure for relating more than one project to the availability of a set of resources.

This article concentrates on critical path method which forms the basis for the other techniques mentioned and because it can readily be understood and put to practical use on a wide variety of small as well as large projects.

The critical path method

Networks are built up of activities. An *activity* is a job or task which consumes time and is represented on a network diagram by an arrow. At the beginning and end of each activity events are said to occur. The tail of the arrow indicates the beginning and the arrow head indicates the completion of the activity.

An *event* is a specific accomplishment in the overall project e.g., the completion of an operation. No event can be accomplished until all the activities which precede it are complete. As completion takes place at a specific point in time an event does not, therefore, consume time or resources.

The methods of linking activities and events to show their relationship to one another on a network diagram is governed by a set of rules designed to assist in the logical analysis of a project.

Figure 5a shows an activity expressed as an arrow and each event represented by a circle.

The arrow indicates the expenditure of time but generally, and this is dealt with in more detail later, the length of the arrow is not

Figure 5. Critical path method.

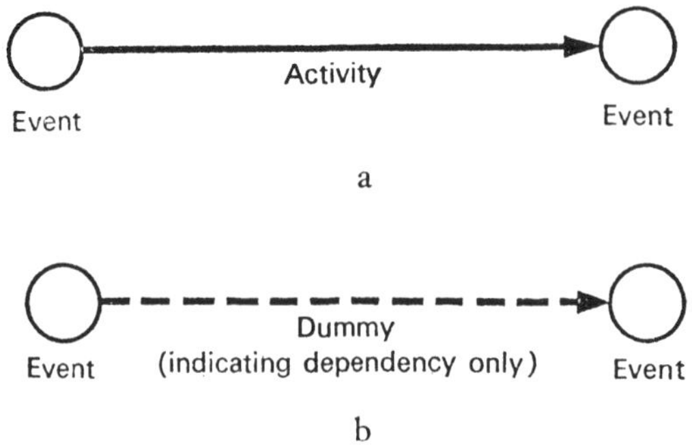

APPENDIX A

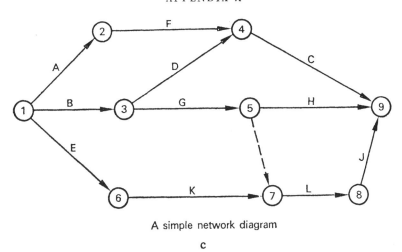

A simple network diagram

c

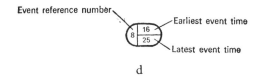

d

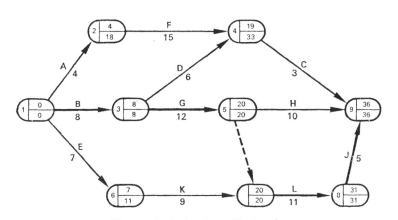

Time analysis showing critical path

e

APPENDIX A

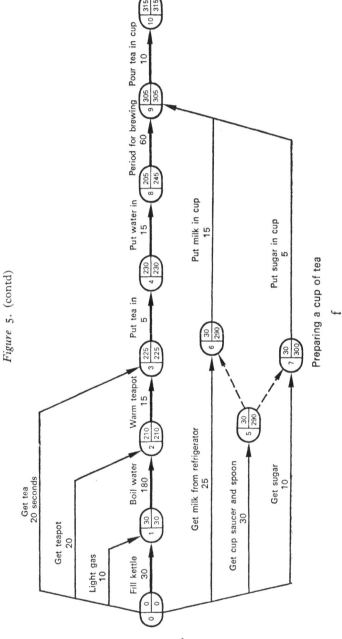

Figure 5. (contd)

APPENDIX A

related to the length of time taken by the activity because this would complicate the construction of the diagram. It would also complicate the valuable characteristics of this method under which the diagram can be easily revised to take account of new factors including changes while the project is proceeding.

The linking of one activity to another indicates the sequence in which they must take place. It is therefore essential that the sequence and logical relationship of each activity to the other activities as shown on the diagram is true to life. The network diagram should always express the desired practical sequence and relationships of activities.

In certain cases, although there is no inter-related time consuming activity between two events, the one event cannot be completed unless the other is complete. This is called a 'dummy' activity and indicates that the activity following the arrow head is dependent upon the completion of the activity immediately preceding the arrow tail. Examples demonstrating the significance of this type of relationship will be shown later.

The logic of the critical path method is best demonstrated in a simple network diagram as shown in figure 5c. The relationships expressed in words are as follows:

1. Activities A, B and E may be started at the beginning of the project.
2. When B is complete, D and G may start.
3. When A is complete F can start.
4. C can start when both F and D are complete and is a final activity.
5. H can start after G is complete and is a final activity.
6. K must follow the finish of E.
7. L cannot start until both G and K are complete.
8. J can start when L is complete and is a final activity.

The relationships of activities G, H, K and L should be studied because this shows the significance of the 'dummy' activity previously described.

The identification of individual activities in the example of figure 5c can be either by the code letter used for each activity or by the reference numbers of the tails and heads of the arrows. The latter is the normal method of identification of the activity and related positions of the events in the network. This is an important

APPENDIX A

feature even in medium-sized networks of 300 to 700 activities, where the location of individual activities in the network, once they have been taken out of their context, may prove to be difficult without some kind of positional reference.

Time analysis

The planning of the logical sequence of the activities in a project should be supported by a method of analysis which will enable accurate time estimates to be made. In the case of network plans the time analysis is more flexible and comprehensive than previous techniques have made possible.

An estimate, as accurate as possible, must be made of the time required to complete each activity. As will be seen a little later one of the great advantages of the critical path method is that it focuses attention on the activities where errors in estimated times could affect the total project time, and emphasizes the critical activities whose estimated times must be checked with great care.

It is vital that these time estimates should be as realistic as possible and that they should be made by those directly responsible for carrying out each activity. Unless additional resources are made available or the activity is modified, any attempt without the agreement of those responsible for the activity to reduce the estimated time to meet target dates will jeopardize the value of the network and may seriously affect the whole project.

The method of time analysis is simple and it will be made easier if each event is represented by a lozenge shaped symbol as shown in figure 5d.

Figure 5e shows the network diagram of figure 5c with the estimates of time recorded against each activity in working days and with the time analysis completed to show the earliest event time and the latest event time for each event.

Calculating earliest event times

The earliest event times are calculated by starting at the beginning of the network and adding the times shown for each preceding activity together. For example in figure 5e it will be seen that the earliest event time for event 8 is 31 days, comprising the aggregate time taken for activities B, G and L = 8 + 12 + 11 = 31 days,

APPENDIX A

because event 5 as well as event 7 must be completed before activity L can start.

In the case of more than one arrow head arriving at a single event the greatest of all the alternative times through the different paths is the earliest event time. For instance, in figure 5e it will be seen that on the path of events 1, 2 and 4, the aggregate time for activities A and F = 4 + 15 = 19 days, but that on the path of events 1, 3 and 4, the aggregate time for activities B and D = 8 + 6 = 14 days. Since unless events 2 and 3 are both completed event 4 cannot take place, the earliest event time for event 4 is 19, not 14 days.

Calculating latest event times

The latest event time is the latest time by which the event must be completed if the project is to be completed on time. This is calculated by working back from the final event in the network. For example, in figure 5e the latest event time for event 6 is calculated by subtracting the aggregate of times for activities J, L and K = 5 + 11 + 9 = 25 from the final latest event time shown for event 9 of 36 days to give a latest event time of 11 days for event 6.

In the case of more than one arrow tail arriving at a single event the lowest of all the alternative times through the different paths is the latest event time. For instance, in figure 5e, it will be seen that on the path of events 9, 4 and 3 the aggregate time for events C and D = 3 + 6 = 9. Subtracting this from the final latest event time of 36 would give a latest time for event 3 of 27 days. But on the path of events 9, 5 and 3 the arrow showing a 'dummy' activity between events 5 and 7 indicates that before event 9 can be completed, events 7 and 8 must first be completed. The latest event time for event 3 must therefore be calculated by working backwards from event 9 through events 8, 7 and 5 to event 3 and calculating the aggregate time of the activities which connect them J, L and G = 5 + 11 + 12 = 28 days, which substracted from the final latest event time of 36 for event 9 gives a latest event time of 8 days for event 3. As this is lower than the latest event time of 25 days for event 3 calculated for the path through events 9, 4 and 3, the latest event time for event 3 is 8 days as shown on the diagram.

APPENDIX A

Determining the critical path

Having calculated the earliest and latest event times for each event and inserted them on the network diagram we are now in a position to identify the critical path through the network. It will be noted from figure 5e that in some events there is a difference in the time allowed for the completion of the event, e.g. the earliest event time for event 2 is 4, and the latest event time is 18, leaving a period of 14 days during which the event may be completed. But for some events there is no 'slack' time whatever, where the earliest and latest event times are the same. All such events are critical and lie on the critical path because any change in the activities linking these events will affect the time taken for the completion of the project. In figure 5e it will be seen that the critical path lies from event 1 through events 3, 5, 7 and 8 to event 9, and that the project will take 36 days for completion.

Where events do not lie on the critical path, the difference between the earliest and latest event times is known as slack time. Any delay in completion of the event after the earliest time will not affect the completion of the project, provided the event is completed between the latest event time. This slack time varies between the different paths through a network and it is thus possible to produce a list showing the priorities of activities, both at the beginning and at any time throughout the project, classifying activities according to the flexibility of completion based on the earliest and latest times for the completion of each activity as shown on the network diagram. On a small network this list of activities can be produced without any special equipment. For a large network this could be a formidable task but this problem can be solved easily by the use of a standard computer programme which produces classified lists of network information very economically. Computer bureaux exist in most countries which are able to provide this service.

A network for making tea

To illustrate the principles involved it may be helpful to look at a familiar but trivial 'project' – making a cup of tea – a network for which (with the time in seconds) is shown in figure 5f. The following assumptions have been made in drawing the network:

APPENDIX A

1. That all ingredients i.e. tea, sugar, milk and water are available and to hand.
2. That sugar will be used in the tea and will be put in last.
3. That milk is needed and is put in the cup before the tea is poured in.
4. That the pot is to be warmed with boiling water.
5. That the project objective is 'tea poured out' (the final event).

This illustrates the importance of clearly defining the project objective, i.e. 'tea poured out' which is the final event. Had the project objective been 'tea consumed' a further activity would have been necesssary. Before, or in the course of, drawing the network diagram it is important to decide and record the assumptions and subsequent alterations in assumptions requiring modification of the network.

Figure 5f illustrates the function of 'dummy' activities. As is indicated by the dotted lines on the diagram, activity 'putting milk into cup' and activity 'put sugar into cup' cannot take place until activity 'get cup, saucer and spoon' has been completed.

Drawing network diagrams

The more complex the project, the more complex the network diagram becomes, and at first sight it may be difficult to comprehend and disentangle, a little frightening though it may be in its apparent complexity. It is usual to draw a rough layout of the network as a first step, putting in all the events and activities without showing times. It is important that the rough layout is revised to ensure that all the arrows point from left to right so that none point backwards, which could give a misleading impression! The spacing or positions of some events and activities may have to be re-drawn on the diagram to achieve this. The aim is to draw all events and activities in such a way that their logical sequence is maintained and so that the diagram is as tidy and comprehensible as it can be made. Having considered and modified the rough diagram accordingly, the network diagram can then be drawn and time estimates and brief descriptions of activities added as shown in figure 5f.

One of the problems in drawing network diagrams is to decide the amount of detail to be included. This becomes clearer with

APPENDIX A

experience, but it is important to decide at the outset what the purpose of the network diagram is to be – i.e., who is to use it and how it is to be used. The detail required will depend on the level of responsibility and the degree of involvement of the persons who will use the network. In some cases it will be sufficient to combine a number of events and activities and show them as early as possible in the network. At each event point it is essential to consider which activities can start at this point and which must be completed.

The benefits to management:

Improving team work

The evolution of a rational approach to project planning is by no means a panacea, but it highlights the problems of team work and leadership which have tended to be obscured by the technical complexity of present-day operations.

Management roles in the field of projects need to be carefully defined. A network diagram avoids friction by stating the advantages of co-operation explicitly. Network analysis itself creates a need for teamwork, and brings specialists together in a spirit conducive to constructive thought. The leadership of such a team should be settled fairly and objectively. The discussions leading to the construction of an agreed plan in this form must be objective, at least in connection with the plan. Thus it is clear that a team selected to co-ordinate the execution of a project must accept the discipline of the network. The roles of the team members and their relationship to one another are assisted by the process of developing and using the network technique.

Experience of the technique suggests that intermediate-level communications between departments can be improved by this means.

The earlier planning can start, the better for any project. The rational approach suggested in this article can do little but emphasize the importance of an early appraisal of a new project in an objective form. The form of the appraisal is significant because it gives management another yardstick to gauge the degree of certainty of the outcome of a particular course of action. At the same time the value of a network as a medium of communication both to contributors to a project and to interested potential

APPENDIX A

supporters should not be underestimated. The simple factual layouts used are easily understood.

Controlling and progressing of projects

During the progress of a project it is often necessary to measure the achievements to the point of review and sometimes to state revised objectives. A clear statement of the relationship of activities assists in this, and the effect of the delay in the arrival of a shipment of rolled steel joists for example, can be clearly appreciated. In addition the opportunities for mitigating the effect of the late delivery of items should be more clearly seen in network form than by other means.

Progress reporting is closely linked to control, and there is a need in most cases for close control and intelligent co-ordination of activities. The need for an understanding of rapidly changing situations is vital in project management work, and frequently the situation must be made apparent to a group of managers who may be in a position to correct a deteriorating situation. The visual impact of a network diagram is considerable in these circumstances.

The use of thickened arrows in the diagram to indicate completed activities and the proportional thickening of semi-completed ones are satisfactory methods of updating a network diagram in use on the job. In addition, colour codes can be used to indicate departmental responsibilities, and fresh time information can be inserted from time to time in a different colour from that used in the printing of the original network. New issues of a network can be provided if the original is made to reproduce easily, and these can be circulated to contributing departments from time to time. The beneficial effect of this on departmental performance and in the efforts made by individual sections to achieve results in critical areas is often remarkable.

The use of resources

Having established the time required for the completion of the project using defined resources, the question arises as to whether it is possible and desirable for the time to be shortened by the use of extra resources if they are available, and whether extra costs should be incurred using extra resources which would be justified by

APPENDIX A

greater over-all savings as a result. The critical path on the network will disclose immediately which are the most critical activities on which more resources must be used to shorten the completion time for the project. Before deciding to commit extra resources the effect on the other activity paths on the network must be calculated and studied in case other activities not on the critical path become the limiting factors in the time required to complete the project. In this case calculations will have to be made using the network to show whether it will be economical to use extra resources to dispose of the additional limiting factors. As a result of these calculations and a decision to use extra resources, a new critical path may be established before the project commences. Similar calculations may be made while the project is proceeding if reasons arise for using more resources, or if the resources on which completion time has been estimated are reduced.

If there are insufficient men or if there is insufficient equipment the project will not go through on time. In such cases a compromise will be necessary and new calculations will be necessary using the network analysis to determine the optimum use of the available resources.

Theoretically it is possible to re-calculate all revisions to a project using a network analysis, but in practice the amount of work involved in addition to the original calculations may well make the calculation costs outweigh the advantages unless a computer can be used.

Repetitive project work, such as repair and overhaul of plant, may be considered as a special case for detailed examination of resource requirements. Deciding the minimum team of fitters may for example have a critical effect on the duration of the overhaul of process equipment. Since the work is repetitive, every year or so the co-ordination of tasks will be refined so as to make minimum peak demands on craft labour without extending overhaul time. The effect of using network analysis to help management in the task of determining these optimum labour requirements can be considerable.

Review techniques in connection with projects of all sizes are necessary to management in their role of taking responsibility for the control of the tasks involved and their cost. Techniques of this kind, based on networks, are currently in use to help management to control both short- and long-term projects.

APPENDIX A

Initiating network analysis

In introducing network analysis into an organization it is important to obtain the understanding and backing of top management through their awareness of the benefits to be derived. It is desirable to run a short training programme within the organization to give everyone who will be concerned a knowledge of the principles and advantages of networks. The initial use of the technique on simple projects may be extended to more difficult operations as experience of and confidence in the technique increase. The importance of defining the completion point of each project will be apparent. It is, for example, essential if the technique is used for the preliminary development of repetitive manufacturing processes that when these have been properly developed, standard production control methods should take over.

APPENDIX B

TREES OF DECISION

(Extract from an article by David T. T. Frost, of David Frost Associates, Management Consultants, in *Management Today* July/August 1966)

The paramount creative function of management is taking decisions. Although decisions vary greatly in their size and significance, all the way from minor points of marketing or information policy to major plant expansions or product diversifications, they all can be taken on a scientific basis. The subjective element will never be eliminated. But it can be brought under control.

This is demonstrated by the simple case of a group of consultants faced with the choice, when they started business this year, of whether to take office space in London or Manchester. The sum involved was relatively small. Adequate office space in London would cost £30,000 for the freehold, against £20,000 for equivalent offices in Manchester. The principles, however, were exactly the same as if £20 million or £30 million were involved. There was one special factor. The effective life of the project (during which the premises would retain their market value) was ten years. At the end of that period the partners planned to disband for academic jobs.

They judged there to be a 60 per cent chance that assignments during the first three years of operation would be concentrated in the South-East, and a 40 per cent chance that initial work would be mainly in the North and Midlands; an 80 per cent chance that business would stay concentrated in the same region during the subsequent seven years, and therefore a 20 per cent chance that heavy bookings would switch the emphasis to the other area after three years (expressed as probabilities, these subjective assessments read 0·6, 0·4, 0·8, 0·2). Relocation expenses after three years were estimated at £5,000 in time, transport, office staff changes and loss of business during the change. Thus a move from London to

APPENDIX B

Manchester would involve a net £5,000 inflow of cash, resulting from a change to cheaper premises, while a move from Manchester to London, would involve an additional cash outflow of £15,000.

Money could be borrowed at 8 per cent per annum. But the partners had investment opportunities that could be expected to yield 20 per cent before taxation, or 12 per cent after taxes. The firm could expect a residual annual income (after associates' salaries and administrative expenses) of £5,000 after tax if offices were located in the area of major business. This would be reduced to £3,000 if consulting opportunities mostly came up far away from the offices, increasing transport, mailing and telephone expenses. The simplest tool for making such a decision, and the most widely used in industry, is payback. This means ignoring the above carefully thought out, but admittedly subjective, probabilities and settling for the most likely annual cash inflow at each location – £5,000 in London and £3,000 in Manchester. On this basis the decision would have been for London with a payback period of six years compared to 6·7 years for Manchester. A more sophisticated method, essential for a project committing large resources, is the 'discounted cash flow' technique – again, this could have been relied on entirely, as follows:

	London	*Manchester*
Cash outflow now, in Year 0	− £30000	− £20000
Annual cash inflows of £5000 for London and £3000 for Manchester in Years 1 to 10 inclusive, as discounted at the opportunity cost rate of 12 percent	+ £27801	+ £18151
Sale of offices at the end of Year 10, for £30000 in London and £20000 in Manchester when discounted at 12 per cent	+ £10566	+ £7044
Net present value	£8367[1]	£5195[1]

[1] To arrive at the discounted figures, present value factors were read from *The Capital Budgeting Decision* by H. Bierman, Jr. and S. Schmidt.

APPENDIX B

The decision for London reached on the basis of payback would have been reinforced by use of this superior technique, which takes account of the time value of money (£1 today is worth more than £1 to be received in ten years time) and of all anticipated cash flows. Payback analysis ignores expected flows of cash beyond the time when the initial investment is paid back. But could straightforward financial analysis cope with all factors or probabilities that might

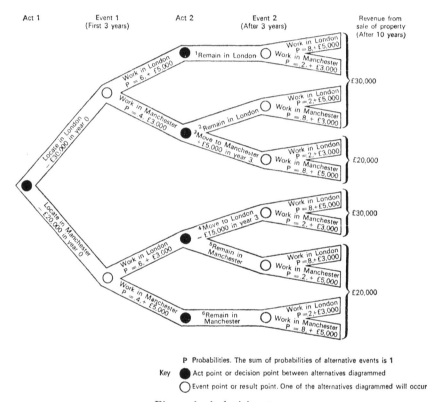

Figure 6. A decision tree.

affect the outcome? If payback and discounted cash flow provided an inadequate basis for decision-making the consequences could have been catastrophic. So the partners decided to draw up a plan that would provide a sequence of acts and events and take account of probability.

APPENDIX B

For example, following through from the £30,000 decision to locate in London (the first *act*), the first *event* was to work for three years – either mainly in London (the 0·6 probability) for a £5,000 cash flow, or in Manchester (the 0·4 probability) for a £3,000 cash flow. If the first alternative occurred, there was no question about *act* 2 – the partners would decide to remain in London. The next *event* would be either to continue working mainly in London after three years (the 0·8 possibility) or to see the balance shift heavily to Manchester. This was represented diagrammatically by a decision tree (see figure 6, p. 208).

Organizing the facts and estimates in this way revealed the necessity of making conditional decisions about future acts along the branches of the tree before decision on the current course of action, that is, which of the two major boughs – London or Manchester – to follow. It was intuitively obvious that, just as the partners would stay in London after three years if the bulk of initial business was there, the same would apply for Manchester. However, if they started off in London and initial work was concentrated in Manchester, they would have to decide in mid-1969 between London and Manchester – and vice versa.

These decisions demanded calculation of the net expected value in mid-1969 of the events flowing from each alternative act. In each case every possible annual cash inflow that would result from each act was multiplied by its likelihood of occurrence. This produced a duly weighted cash inflow estimate which was then discounted back to mid-1969 values. To these were added the values of expected proceeds, similarly discounted, from the sale of assets in mid-1976. The expected mid-1969 expenditure attaching to each act was then deducted. This gave the expected value at that date of each of the six possible acts.

This table (2a, p. 210) showed that Act 2.3 (move from London to Manchester after finding initial work to be concentrated in the North and Midlands) had a higher expected value than the alternative Act 2.2 (remain in London in spite of initial heavy bookings in the Manchester area). So the conditional decision was to move to Manchester in mid-1969 if the consultants decided in mid-1966 to locate in London *and if* business during the first three years proved to be mainly in the North. Similarly, Act 2.5's expected value superiority of that to Act 2.4 made the consultants decide to remain in Manchester in mid-1969, if they had located

TABLE 2

A

Act	Expected annual cash inflows	Discounted value of annual cash inflows	Discounted value of proceeds from sale of offices	Expenditure attaching to Act	Expected mid-1969 value of Act
2.1	0.8 × £5000 + 0.2 × £3000 = £4600	£20993	£13569	£0	£34562
2.2	0.2 × £5000 + 0.8 × £3000 = £3400	£15517	£13569	£0	£29086
2.3	0.2 × £3000 + 0.8 × £5000 = £4600	£20993	£9046	£5000	£35039
2.4	0.8 × £5000 + 0.2 × £3000 = £4600	£20993	£13569	(£15000)	£19562
2.5	0.8 × £3000 + 0.2 × £5000 = £3400	£15517	£9046	£0	£24563
2.6	0.2 × £3000 + 0.8 × £5000 = £4600	£20993	£9046	£0	£30039

B

Act	Expected Annual cash inflows	Discounted value of annual cash inflows	Expected subsequent proceeds in mid-1969 money	Discounted value of subsequent proceeds	Expenditure attaching to Act	Expected value of each Act
Locate in London	0.6 × £5000 + 0.4 × £3000 = £4200	£10125	0.6 × £34562 + 0.4 × £35039 = £34753	£24737	(£30000)	£4862
Locate in Manchester	0.6 × £3000 + 0.4 × £5000 = £3800	£9161	0.6 × £24563 + 0.4 × £30039 = £26753	£19043	(£20000)	£8204

210

APPENDIX B

there in mid-1966 *even if* assignments were concentrated in the South-East during the first three years of operation. With these sums a simplified tree was drawn (see figure 7, below).

The immediate basic decision on location could now be made. This involved calculating the net expected present value of events flowing from each alternative act. Once again, each possible annual inflow of cash resulting from each act was multiplied by the likelihood of that inflow's occurrence, and the weighted inflow estimates were discounted to their present value. To these were added the present values of the mid-1969 expected values calculated above, after weighting these by the appropriate probabilities; then the purchase price of the offices that attached to each act was deducted to give the expected value (table 2b, p. 210).

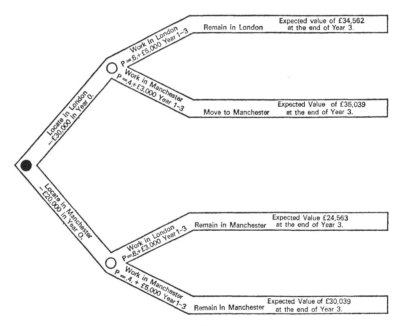

Figure 7. A simplified decision tree.

This result turned the discounted cash flow findings almost completely upside down. It showed that the firm should go to Manchester and remain there *wherever it won its major business throughout the ten-year proposed life of the consultancy*. Reliance on

APPENDIX B

'decision trees' took account of quantified estimates of likelihood of events and led to a contrary decision correct on the facts, estimates and judgments given.

The only missing element is that of caution. A fairly young and poor group could hardly afford to eliminate this factor, which was taken into account by using another technique, that of utility analysis. This method of allowing for the fact that a bird in the hand may be worth two or more in the bush is required when dealing in sums which are significant relative to assets: it can often reverse decisions made on trees alone – just as in this case trees reversed a discounted cash flow finding. In the example given, however, the tree finding held true.

Trees do not replace managers' judgment. But they allow such judgment based on experience to be fully utilized rationally and consistently. Large and vital businesses must rely on formal procedures and systems for efficient organization and operation. The same is plainly true for decisions.

APPENDIX C

LINEAR PROGRAMMING

The chief difficulty of understanding linear programming which faces the non-mathematical layman is that most books on the subject plunge straight into somewhat complicated mathematical calculations. These tend to suggest that the subject can only be understood by higher mathematicians. This is therefore an attempt to present the principles of linear programming in a simple and non-mathematical form.

The object of linear programming, like most operations research techniques, is to arrive at the optimum use of a number of variables. A simple example of this, given by Robert Dorfman in his chapter entitled 'Linear Programming: a graphical illustration' in Edwin Mansfield's *Managerial Economics and Operations Research* (Norton & Co., New York, 1966), is an automobile factory which can produce both commercial trucks or lorries and passenger motor-cars. There is obviously a limited capacity for the production of each type of vehicle. This limitation is imposed by the limited capacity of four operations: (1) sheet metal stamping; (2) engine assembly; (3) final car assembly, and (4) final lorry assembly.

The output limits of each of these departments is given in the table below:

	Cars	*Lorries*
Stamping department	25000	35000
Engine assembly	33333	16667
Final assembly	22500	15000

From these figures we can calculate a large number of varying combinations. These can be represented as lines on a simple graph (see figure 8, p. 214). For instance if 15,000 cars were made, this would use up 60 per cent of the metal stamping department's capacity, leaving 40 per cent for trucks. This 40 per cent would

APPENDIX C

be sufficient for 14,000 trucks. Obviously the number of combinations varies from 25,000 cars and no lorries to 35,000 lorries and no cars. This can be represented by the straight line on the graph (figure 8) stretching from 25,000 on the vertical ordinate representing cars to 35,000 on the horizontal ordinate representing

LINEAR PROGRAMMING GRAPH
Cars and Lorries

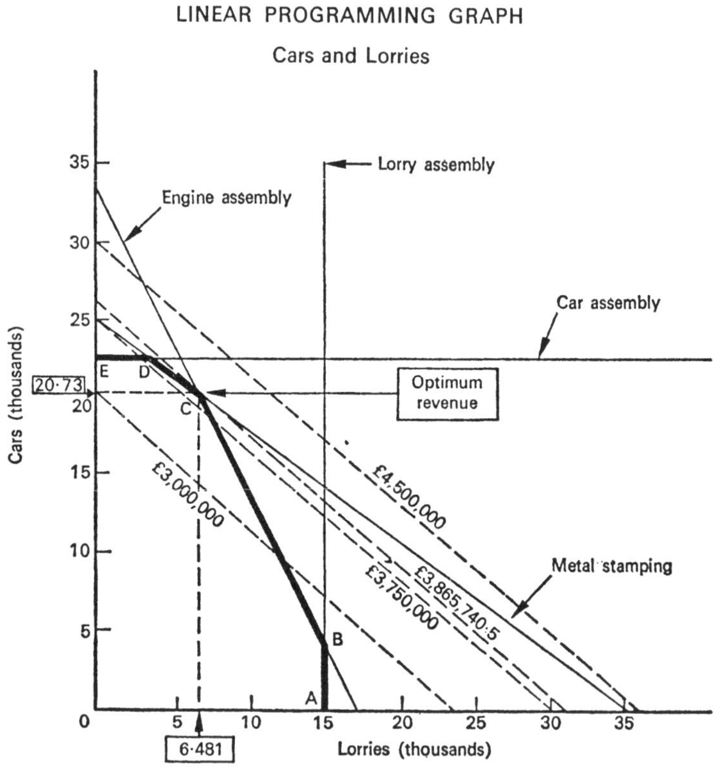

Figure 8. This diagram has been adapted from *Managerial Economics and Operations Research*, edited by Edwin Mansfield (W. W. Norton & Company Inc, New York).

lorries. There are however three other limiting factors which have to be considered as well as the capacity of stamping: engine assembly, car assembly and lorry assembly. We can however plot these limitations in the same way as we plotted stamping capacity. The final assembly figures are represented by vertical lines (cars)

APPENDIX C

and horizontal lines (lorries) based on the maximum assumed capacity for car assembly as 22,500 and lorry assembly as 15,000. These operations are carried out by two different departments the capacities of which are independent of each other. We now have to decide the optimum profitability of our two operations combined, taking into account the limitations imposed by the capacities of each department and we assume that the profit on a car is £150 and on a lorry £125. This means that the net revenue of the factory for a month will be £150 multiplied by the number of cars produced plus £125 times the number of lorries produced. Thus 15,000 cars would yield a net revenue of £2,250,000 and 6,000 lorries would yield a revenue of £750,000, making a total of £3,000,000. Since other combinations of cars and lorries will yield the same figure we can plot this revenue as a dotted line stretching from 20,000 on the vertical line (which would yield this revenue if only cars and no lorries were made) to 24,000 (which would yield this revenue if only lorries and no cars were produced). Parallel revenue lines can be plotted for combinations of net revenue of amounts greater or less than £3,000,000. It will be seen from the graph that the optimum revenue taking into account the limitations of the four departments of the factory is £3,865,740·5. This is achieved by seeing where the boundary lines of the figure ABCDE touch the highest revenue line. The figure ABCDE shows the total possible combinations of output within the limitations of the capacity of each of the four departments already mentioned above. The relative output of cars and lorries to produce this optimum figure are 20,730 and 6,481 respectively.

This is obviously a very simplified illustration of the use of linear planning. Normally the variations would be far more complex and would be worked out by algebraic formulae and equations which can be passed through a computer for rapid solution. Linear programming can be applied to a number of different problems in business where choices have to be made between combinations of varying factors from which an optimum solution is required. In this case we have applied it to a comparatively simple problem of 'product mix'. It can also be applied to choice of markets, stock-holding problems, transport problems and many others. It is a valuable mathematical management technique which can greatly aid a manager in decision making.

APPENDIX D

STOCK OR INVENTORY CONTROL

Inventory control is another name for stock control. All stock whether of raw material, components, spare parts or finished goods, have to be entered on an 'inventory' which is a record of incoming stocks, outgoing stocks and stocks held. Two important costs are involved in stock control apart from the actual cost of the materials which involves an immobilization of capital before the stocks are disposed of: one is the costs of purchasing new stocks and the other the costs of holding stock. In an average manufacturing business these may add up to a considerable figure. In the case of holding stocks for instance the holding costs alone often amount to about 25 per cent of the total value of the stock, while the purchasing costs of new stocks may amount to about 12½ per cent. Where stocks may run into several thousands of pounds these figures can be substantial.

Among items included under holding costs are the following:

	per centage
Interest on capital immobilized (say)	7
Rent of space occupied	3
Insurance	1
Damage and deterioration	2
Obsolescence	5
Handling costs	2
Loss and Pilferage	2
Stock taking and record keeping	2½
Total	24½

The figure for obsolescence may seem high, but in certain industries new developments and designs often make existing stocks obsolescent very quickly, and it is a common feature of many businesses to find themselves holding considerable stocks of components which they know they will never use because they

APPENDIX D

have been superseded by a later type. This particularly applies, for instance, to electrical or electronic appliances.

Among purchasing costs on new stocks we may list the following items:

1. Requisitioning from various departments (often in anything up to ten copies of the requisition form may be required).
2. Soliciting bids for tenders.
3. Selecting the vendor.
4. Issuing the purchasing order (this will also have to be issued in sextuplicate or more).
5. Progress follow up (to make sure of deliveries on time).
6. Receiving and inspecting.
7. Placing in storage.

The two vital problems in stock control are (1) how much to order, and (2) when to re-order. Hitherto the average practice or rule of thumb method has been to arrive at a figure by trial and error of the total requirement of stock over a given period and then to fix a safety margin (or buffer stock) below which the stock should not be allowed to fall. When the safety margin is reached a new order is made, to bring the total stock up to what is believed to be the necessary figure. Allowance obviously has to be made for delivery time, so that if our safety margin is 1,000 units, representing two months' usage, we have to re-order when our stock falls to 2,000 if delivery time is two months, then, if delivery time proves accurate, we shall have just reached our safety margin by the time the new stocks arrive.

The trouble about this rule of thumb method is that it is open to considerable variation and also to guesswork and difference of opinion. One department may use up stock faster than another and may insist on high margins of safety. The one thing above all others which a supply manager has to avoid, if possible, is running out of stock at a crucial moment. Imagine the chaos when a large contract has to be completed on a certain date, with penalty clauses for non-delivery, if the production department responsible for completing the order finds that the stores have run out of stocks of a vital component and that it will take perhaps two or more months to get in a further consignment. On the other hand, the supply manager must be constantly watching both his holding costs and also his purchasing costs, because the more times he purchases in a year

APPENDIX D

the more he will be adding to the total costs. It will be seen that the supply manager's job is by no means a sinecure and that he has to be on his toes all the time, particularly as, even in many medium-sized firms, he may be handling an inventory running into several thousand different items. There is also to be taken into consideration the discounts granted by the supplier on bulk orders. Often a manufacturer of components will complain that it is not worth his while to tie up capital in producing a comparatively small order. 'Short-runs', as they are called, are not economical and the costs of a short-run order may be disproportionately high both to the supplier and the purchaser. There is also the question of lack of proper standardization. The production side may order, for instance, a wide variety of screws or bolts, where in fact one or two standard sizes and types might be equally effective. This may call for a modification of design, but it might result in considerable savings in purchasing and storage.

In order to simplify the control of stocks, operations research men have come up with a mathematical formula which in certain firms has cut inventory costs by as much as 50 per cent. This formula is called the Economic Ordering Quantity or EOQ. On paper it can be written $Q = \dfrac{2Ucp}{ch}$. This equation means that the optimum ordering quantity, Q, is equal to the square root of twice the number of units (U) required over a planned period multiplied by the percentage purchasing costs (cp), divided by the holding costs (ch). Having arrived at your EOQ you determine the intervals between re-ordering by dividing U by Q.

In his chapter on stock control in *Operational Research in Management*, edited by Eddison, Pennycuick and Rivett, J. C. Beresford gives this formula in a slightly different form, namely $Q = \dfrac{2h_1 D}{h_2}$. He defines D as 'the total demand known or forecast over the planning period; while 'h_1 is the cost of raising one order' and 'h_2 is the cost of holding a unit in stock'. A mathematical reader, who understands calculus, is referred to Mr Beresford's article for the calculations by which this formula is arrived at.[1]

---

[1] See *Operational Research in Management* by R. T. Eddison, M.A., K. Pennycuick, B.Sc., Ph.D., and B. H. P. Rivett (The English Universities Press Ltd, London 1962). See also *Modern Production Management* by Elwood Buffa (Wiley & Sons) and *Management Economics and Operation Research* (Norton, New York) pp. 203–205. (See bibliography).

APPENDIX D

The average non-mathematical manager would, however, do well to consider whether the cost of installing or hiring an operational research mathematician might not well be offset by the savings of applying such a system to his inventory control.

SELECT BIBLIOGRAPHY

ALFRED, A. M., *Discount Cash Flow and Corporate Planning*, London: Woolwich Polytechnic.
BARNARD, CHESTER, *The Functions of the Executive*, Harvard University Press, 1958.
BATTERSBY, A., *Network Analysis for Planning and Scheduling*, Macmillan, 1964.
BEER, STAFFORD, *Cybernetics and Management*, English Universities Press, 1959.
BEER, STAFFORD, *Decision and Control*, New York: Wiley & Sons, 1966.
BIERMAN JR, H. and SCMIDT, S., *The Capital Budgeting Decision*, Macmillan, 1966.
BROWN, WILFRED and JACQUES, ELLIOTT, *The Glacier Metal Papers*, Heinemann, 1965.
BUFFA, ELWOOD S., *Modern Production Management*, 2nd edition, New York: Wiley & Sons, 1965.
CHASE, STUART, *The Power of Words*, London: Phoenix House, 1955.
CHURCHMAN, C. W., et al, *Introduction to Operations Research*, Wiley & Sons and Chapman & Hall, 1957.
DESCHAMPSNEUFS, N., *Selling Overseas, Business Publications*, 1960.
DRUCKER, PETER, *The Practice of Management*, Mercury Books, 1961.
FOLLETT, MARY PARKER, *Dynamic Administration*, New York: Harper Bros 1941.
GLASSER, RALPH, *The New High Priesthood*, Macmillan, 1967.
JACQUES, ELLIOTT, *The Changing Culture of a Factory*, Tavistock Publications, 1951.
LOCKYER, K. G., *Critical Path Analysis: Problems and Solutions*, Pitman, 1966.
MACMURRAY, JOHN, *Reason and Emotion*, Faber & Faber, 1935.
MANSFIELD, EDWIN, ed., *Managerial Economics and Operations Research*, New York: Norton & Co., 1966.

SELECT BIBLIOGRAPHY

MAYO, ELTON, *Human Problems of an Industrial Civilization*, Macmillan, 1933.
MAYO, ELTON, *Social Problems of an Industrial Civilization*, Harvard University Press, 1945.
MCCLOSKEY and TREGETHEN, *Operations Research for Management*, John Hopkins Press, 1954.
MCGREGOR, DOUGLAS, *The Human Side of Enterprise*, McGraw Hill, 1960.
OGILVY, DAVID, *Confessions of an Advertising Man*, Longmans Green, 1963.
PENNYCUICK, K., EDDISON, R. T. and RIVETT, P., *Operational Research in Management*, English Universities Press, 1962.
RIVETT, P. and ACKHOFF, R. L., *Manager's Guide to Operation Research*, New York, Wiley & Sons, 1966.
TACK, A. and G., *How to Sell Successfully Overseas*, Kingswood: World's Work, 1963.
TAYLOR, FREDERICK W., *Scientific Management*, New York: Harper Bros, 1947.
WADDINGTON, C. H., *The Scientific Attitude*, Penguin Books, 1941.
WOODGATE, H. S. *Planning by Network*, Business Publications Ltd, 1964.

INDEX

Accidents 13, 37
Account executive 105
Accountants 18, 88, 155
Accounting (Accountancy) 2, 4, 15, 19, 24, 37, 47, 158
Accounts (*see* 'profit and loss Accounts')
Achievement 73, 78, 80
Acquisition (*see* also 'Take-overs') 128, 186
Actuaries 152
Adaptation 41, 58
Adler, Alfred xii
Administrative Staff College 63
Advertising 7, 16, 19, 20, 24, 101, 102-108, 120, 122, 136, 137, 138, 150, 174, 176
Africa 12
Agents 141, (advertising) *see* 102-108
Aircraft 1, 107
Airlines 150
Alfred, A. M. 129
Ambition 23, 80
American Management Association 64
American Telephone Telegraph Company 185
Americanization 77
Analysis 5, 23-24, 54, (Utility) 212
Anglo-American Productivity Council 52
Anti-Trust Laws 190
Arkwright, Richard 7, 8
Anxiety 76, 78
Armed Forces (*see also* Army) 72
Army 19
Asia 12
Assessment (character) 44-45, 73
Assets 8, 160-162, 172

Association 94, 101
Asquith, H. H. (Lord Oxford) 111
Atomic Energy 183
Attitudes and attitude surveys (*see also* Opinion surveys) 71, 87
Auditing 25-26, 155, 171
Authority 6, 32, 35, 65, 66
Autocracy 54
Automation (*see also* Mechanization) 89, 154
Availability of consumer goods 132, 134, 135, 139
of materials 97, 176

Background, social and economic 5, 41
Balance Sheet 25, 31, 159-162, 170, 179
Bankruptcy 19, 60, 163
Banks 13
Bartlett, Sir Charles 77
Beaujolais 133
Beer, Stafford 145, 149
Behavioural sciences 83
Beresford, J. C. 218
Bierman, H. 129, 207
'Big Five' Banks 13
Biology 143
'Black Magic' chocolates 101, 177
Blacksmiths 18
Blake, Robert R. 44, 60, 82
Board of Directors 1, 26, 27, 28, 32, 62, 78, 139, 179
'Boffins' 145
Bolton 7, 8
Bonuses 46
Book trade 139
Booker Brothers Ltd. 141
Boot, Jesse (1st Lord Trent) 185
Brain, human 147

INDEX

Brainstorming 115
Branch Managers 32
Brand and brand names 11, 29, 132-133, 134, 137
'Break-Even Point' and Charts 119, 125, 153, 164, 176
Bribery 138
British American Tobacco Company Limited (B.A.T.) 64, 112, 186
British Institute of Management (B.I.M.) 64, 189
British Leyland and Motor Holdings Limited 14, 112
British Overseas Airways Corporation (B.O.A.C.) 110
British Rail Corporation 2
Brittan, Samuel 174
Brown, Wilfred (Lord Brown) 55-56, 70, 77
Brunner Mond 78
Budgetary Control and Budgeting 2, 9-10, 24, 87, 90, 174, 176, 179
Buildings 8, 171
Bulk buying 140
Bulk distribution 135
Burroughs Wellcome 133
Business Economics 4
Business schools 63
Buyers 18

Cadbury Bros. 76, 78 133
Capital 2, 6-17, 23-26, 86, 114, 117, 120-129, 146, 158, 160-162, 167-171, 179, 181, 186
Capitalism 53
Capitalist 6
Cash flow 176, 207 208
  position 120-126, 153, 160, 168, 171
Cashiers 18
Centralization 70
Cerebos salt 133
Chain stores 185
Chairmanship 57, 79

Change 156, 203
Character 5, 6, 42-45, 75
Chase, Stuart 94
Chemical products 109
Chemist's shop 185
Chicago University 61
Church, the 66
Cigarettes and cigarette making 11, 28-31, 135
Civil Service 70
Classless society 38
Coal Board, National (*see* National Coal Board)
Coats, J. & P. 133
Combinations (*see also* Permutations) 116, 215
Combines 116
Commissions 125
Commitment 82
Common-sense 20, 21, 50, 60, 61, 85, 116, 131, 143, 144
Commonwealth Development Corporation 12
Communication xii 32, 54, 55, 72, 73-75, 78, 80, 93-97, 141, 153, 157, 202
Community 19, 21, 22, 52, 53, 72, 190
Company Secretary 28
Competition 3, 22, 108, 136, 140, 188, 190
Components 117, 118, 171, 183, 216
Computers and Computation 58, 87-90, 147, 154, 200, 204
Comradeship 75
Concepts 154-155
'Concorde' aircraft 149
Confederation of British Industry (C.B.I.) 97, 189
Conference leading 79
Confidence 79, 110, 133
Confucius 75
Conservation 49, 59
Consolidation 23
Co-operation 35, 37, 55, 66, 67, 72, 75, 79, 92, 180, 192, 202

INDEX

Co-ordination 181, 203, 204
Consultants 60, 61, 62, 71, 85, 96, 155, 184, 189, 190, 206
Consultation 32, 55, 56, 57, 69, 71, 78
Consumer Finance (*see also* Hire Purchase) 17
Consumer Surveys and Research (*see also* Market Research) 90, 100, 111, 136, 137
Consumers 2, 22, 101, 107-8, 131
'Contimart' 136
Contingencies 126
Control 1-4, 18, 19, 23, 50, 53, 56, 67, 81, 82, 95, 112, 114, 124, 158, 189
Control, Cost (*see* Cost control)
Controls 1, 3, 5, 6, 17, 36, 90, 189
Copper 187
'Copy' (Advertising) 106
Corbusier, Le 99
Costing (*see also* Cost accounting) 37, 47
Coupons, gift 138
Cost accounting 11, 85, 86, 87, 90, 163-164
Cost control 2, 36, 59, 165-166, 188-189
Costs 2, 10, 11, 15, 118-125, 138, 146, 159, 166, 204
   distribution 137
   fixed 118, 125, 126, 147, 166n
   holding 216, 217
   production 126
   variable 118, 164
Cotton industry 7
Courage 4, 5, 41, 62, 74
Courses, training 63-65
Courtesy 51, 75
Crawford, W. S. & Co. 136
Creativity 69, 81
Credit 8, 120, 121, 172
Creditors 25, 160
'Critical Path' 47, 58, 59, 86, 95, 191-205
Crompton, Samuel 7-9, 17, 24, 103
Crystal Palace 100

Customer (Consumer) Relations 98, 107
Customers 20, 21, 187
Cybernetics 146-147, 151

Dale, Professor Ernest 180
Davies, John 97-98
Daybooks 172
Debentures 13, 162, 163
Debts 162, 163, 172
Decentralization 31, 32, 70
Decisions (*see also* Decision-making & Decision Theory) 5, 16, 55, 62, 78, 88, 129, 146, 206, 212
Decision-making 5, 78, 97, 129, 152, 208, 215
Decision Theory 95, 152-153
'Decision Trees' (*see also* Decision-making) 129, 130, 146, 206-212
Deflation 12
Delegation 61, 79, 80
Delivery 146, 217
Demand 3, 9, 15, 16, 114, 139, 147, 190
Demetrius 157
Democracy 54
Depreciation 162, 163, 170
Depth charges 144
Deschampsneufs, N. 141
Design 97, 98-101, 137, 138, 218
Deterioration 10, 16, 86, 179, 216
Determination 17
Developing countries 12
Development, management 40
Developments (*see also* research and development) 12, 16, 181, 183, 216
'Dexion' 16
Diminishing returns, law of 126-128
Diplomacy 75
Directors (*see also* Board of Directors) 25-29
Disagreements 32
Discipline 48, 66

225

INDEX

Discounts 117-118, 134, 140, 218
Discounted Cash Flow (D.C.F.) 128, 146, 207, 211
Discretion 23
Discrimination 5
Discussion 69, 79, 87
Display 101, 138
Distortions (of facts) 71, 72
Distribution 17, 24, 134, 136-137, 150, 154, 176, 181
  costs (*see* Cost of distribution)
Diversification 13, 26, 185, 206
Dividends 6, 11-13, 128, 162, 170
Division of labour 18, 87
Domination 75, 78
Donkeys 69
Dorfman, Robert 213
Double entry 159
Double talk 75
'Double Diamond' beer 133
Drive (*see also* initiative) 17
Drucker, Professor Peter xii, xiii, 20, 21, 59, 66, 83, 94, 185, 186-188
Drudgery 67
Drug stores 139
Dunlop Rubber Company Ltd. 186
Dupont Organization 192
Durability 137, 177
'Dynamic Group' (also 'T' Group) 45
Dynamic nature of business 3, 155, 163, 179

Economic Ordering Quantity 218
Economics, Business 4, 142
Eddington, Sir Arthur 155
Efficiency 19, 114, 116, 131
Education 4
  for management 5
Effort 80
Electronic Data Processing (E.D.P.) 153
Electronics 183
Emerson, Ralph Waldo 7
Engineering 47, 171, 185
Enjoyment of work 67-69

Enterprise, free 6, 22, 131
Enthusiasm 75
Environment, Control of 156
Equipment 2, 24, 86, 146, 158, 167, 170, 171
Espionage 183
'Esprit de corps' 73
Estimates, Sales 30
Executives (*see also* Managers & Management) 26
Expansion 25, 112, 128, 186, 206
Expenses 10, 161, 209
Experience 5, 16, 26, 38, 63, 69, 85, 130
Experiments (*see also* Glacier & Hawthorne) 142, 177
Exploitation 22, 108
Expression, Freedom of 70

Factories 29, 30, 32
Factory manager 29
Fashions 175, 178
Fear 5, 76, 78
Feasability studies 100, 100n, 137
Fertilizers 127
Film Production (Advertising) 105
Finance 12, 14, 24, 135
Financial Control 2, 3, 9-13, 15, 16
  Department 181
  Director 31
  policy 178
Finished products 172-173
Finlay, James & Co. 141
Fishmongers 10
Fixed costs 118, 125, 126, 147, 164, 166n
Fixed prices 140
Flexibility 40, 200
'Float' 191
Florence, Professor Sargant xi
Fluctuations (*see* Variations and Variables)
Follett, Mary Parker xiii
Forces, Armed (*see also* Army) 72
Ford, Henry (Junior) 21, 58, 61, 83
Ford, Henry (Senior) 8, 17, 21, 58, 59, 61, 117

INDEX

Forecasting (*see also* Budgeting and budgeting control) 2, 90, 135, 176, 192
Foreman (*see* Supervisors)
Foundation for Management Education 63
Free enterprise (*see* Enterprise, free)
Freedom 70, 73
Freedom of expression 70
Freud, Sigmund xii
Frost, David T. T. (Consultant) 206

Galbraith, Professor J. K. 102, 174
Gantt, Henry xi, 87
Gaussian Probability Curve 90, 91
General Electric Co. (U.S.) 114
General Manager 1, 18, 46
General Meetings 25
Germany 56, 111, 182
Gilbreth, Frank B. 87, 116
Gillander Arbuthnot & Co. 141
Glacier Experiment & Glacier Metal Co. Ltd. 54-57, 70, 77
Glasser, Ralph xiii, 177
'Go-slow' tactics 11
Gothic Architecture 99
Government 11, 12, 22, 110, 186
Graduates 38
Greengrocers 10
'Grid', Management 44-46, 48, 61, 82, 87
Grievance procedure 48
Gross Profit 119, 125n
Groups and Group Psychology 37, 67
Growth 181, 185
Guedalla, Philip xiii
'Guinea-pig' Directors 26
Guinness (Brewers) 110

Haig, John (Whisky) 133
Hall, Sir Noel 63
Hand-outs, Press 107
Harris, Frank 103

Harvard University Business School 50, 61, 63
'Hawthorne Experiment' 49, 50-51, 61
Hardie-Bick, Peter 191
Head Office 32
Henley (*see* Administrative Staff College)
Hierarchy, Management 39
Hire Purchase 10, 17
Hitler, Adolf 54
Holding companies 26
Holding costs
 (*see* Costs, holding)
Homomorphic identification 152
Hospital Administration 154
Human relations and relationships xii, 45, 48, 49, 76, 156
Human resources 81
Humanities xii
Humility 6, 60
Hunches 6
Hypnotism 102, 175

Idealism 59
Ignorance 76, 108
Image, Public 106-107, 110-111, 132-133
Imagination xi, 4, 5, 17, 41, 69, 81
Imperial Chemical Industries Ltd. (I.C.I.) 2, 12, 15, 64, 70, 87, 112, 133
Imperial Tobacco Co. Ltd. 15
Import Duties 11, 136
Incentives 34, 36, 46, 68-69, 73
Increasing Returns, Law of 127
Increment, 'unearned' 6
India 7, 136
Individuality 73
Induction Theory 142
Industrial Finance *see* Finance, Industrial
Industrial Psychology 4, 54, 76
Industrial Revolution, *see* Revolution, Industrial
Industrial Society (formerly Industrial Welfare Society) 64

INDEX

Information 1, 3, 15, 30, 48, 53, 57, 62, 88, 92, 93, 97, 106, 130, 137, 139, 153, 181, 182, 206
Ingenuity 69, 81
Initiative 63, 69, 71, 73, 79, 114
Innovation 112, 114, 115, 116, 156, 157, 175
Institute of Marketing and Sales Management 64
Institute of Personnel Management (I.P.M.) 64
Institute of Production Engineers 64
Institution of Works Managers 64
Insurance 2, 10, 151, 152, 179, 216
  companies 13
Integration 80, 82
Integrity 5, 42, 43, 62
Intelligence xii, 5, 6, 38, 41, 42
  commercial 183
Interdependence 66, 181, 193
Interest 6, 26n, 128, 216
International Harvester Company 61
International politics 182
Interpretation 157
Intuition (*see also* Hunches) 5
Inventions 7, 113, 175
Inventories, and their control 146, 150, 185, 216, 218
Investment 12, 30, 146, 171, 207
Issues of 'right' 13

Jaques, Elliot 56, 70
Jargon 157
Job analysis 59, 188
Job rotation 63
Joint Consultation 55-57, 93
Judgment 28, 130, 212
Jung, C. G. xii, 111
Junior Board 62
Junior Management 39-40, 87

Kellogg's corn flakes 133
Kent, George & Co. Ltd. 14
'Kia Ora' fruit squash 133
Kipling, Rudyard 42, 146, 155

Knowledge 4-6, 100, 130
Kynoch 70, 117

Labour 6, 8, 16, 24, 55, 146, 159, 168, 169, 171, 172, 177, 179
  Management relations 52, 55, 76, 78
  Division of 18, 87
  Charges 11, 171
  Troubles 11, 38, 58, 71, 78
Language 94
Large scale economies 113
Laws of Probability (*see* Probability, Laws of)
Leadership 5, 35, 38, 42, 66
Ledger 172
Leisure 73
Lever Bros. Ltd. (*see also* Unilever) 78
Lever, William (1st Lord Leverhulme) 8, 59, 76
Liability 160-162, 172
Liability, Limitation of 12, 25
Licence, Manufacturing under 141
'Liebfraumilch' 133
'Line' Management 48
Linear Programming 179, 188, 213-215
Lister, Lord 83, 145
Loans 6, 10, 12
  Long-term 12, 126
Locality 15
London Graduate School of Business 63
London Press Exchange (L.P.E.) 136
Long-range Planning (L.R.P.) 179, 181-190
Loss, losses 2, 8, 15, 52, 158, 160, 190
Loyalty 72, 75
  brand 133, 150
'Lufthansa' 111

McGregor, Douglas 66-67, 66n, 73, 80, 80n, 81, 83

INDEX

Machinery 8, 9, 29, 148, 159, 162, 163, 171
McMurray, Professor John 66, 77
Maintenance 10, 170
Management xi, xii, 4-9, 16-20, 39, 40, 47, 66, 72, 78, 100, 153
  ability 24, 25
  development 39, 40
  education, training 5
  'grid' (*see* Grid, management)
  Man xii, 72
  Personnel (*see* Personnel Management)
  Recruitment 40-42
  Techniques (*see* Techniques of Management)
Manchester 129, 209
  School of Business 63
Manpower allocation and utilization 95, 97, 135, 188
Mansfield, Edwin 213
Manufacturing 16, 18, 112, 237
Marconi 83
Marketing (*see also* Markets) 7, 16, 19, 20, 24, 97, 105, 135, 136, 138, 146, 176, 178, 181
  concept 23, 131, 136
  control 2
  manager 139
  Overseas (*see* Overseas marketing)
  policy 133, 135
Markets 2, 3, 17, 23, 24, 131, 135, 139, 166, 167, 172, 174, 175, 176, 177, 181, 184, 187, 215
  analysis, assessment 21, 22, 97, 141
  Research 4, 88, 100, 105, 117, 136, 143, 177
  Overseas (*see* Overseas markets and marketing).
Marks & Spencer 19, 110, 135
Marx, Karl and Marxism 6, 7, 21-22, 53
Massachusetts Institute of Technology (MIT) 63
Mass-consumption 108

Mass-production 58, 104, 108, 131, 174
Materials (*see* Raw materials)
Mathematics 95, 153, 157, 213
Maugham, W. Somerset 24
Mayo, Professor Elton xiii, 49
Mechanization (*see also* Automation) 69, 127
Media (advertising) 104-105
Medicine 143
Medium-sized business 171, 183
Meaning, of words 94-95
Merchandizing 176, 178
Merchant banking 13
Merit-rating 46
Method study (*see also* Work Study) 36, 47, 87, 115-116
'Meccano' 16, 132
Microfilms 97
Middle-men 134
Mind (electronic and human) (*see also* Brain) 88-89
Misconceptions 69
Misunderstanding 76
'Models' 98, 143, 147, 154-155, 177
Model-changing 178
Mond, Alfred (1st Lord Melchett) 59
Money 8, 31, 34, 158, 172, 176
Monopoly 22, 133, 140, 174, 175, 190
Morale 45, 72
Morris Motors 14
Morris, William (Viscount Nuffield) 8, 14, 17, 21, 59
Montgomery, Field-Marshal Lord 72
Motivation & motives xii, 34, 69
Motor cars 21, 108, 213-215
Moulton, Jane 61
'Mule', spinning 7
Multi-project scheduling 194
Multiple stores 140, 154
Mussolini 54
Mystiques 85

INDEX

Napoleon 1, 54
National Coal Board 2
National Institute of Industrial Psychology (NIIP) 55
Needs 20-21, 24, 103, 114, 131, 186
Negotiating machinery 47, 55
Network analysis and planning 47, 58, 95, 149, 151, 188, 191-205
'New Deal' programme 49
New Lanark 76
New products 9, 17, 22, 183
Nigeria 191
Nitrogen 127

Objectives 4, 19-20, 23, 33, 44, 54, 66, 69, 80, 81, 82, 106, 131, 190
Obsolescence 216
 planned 109n, 177-178, 177n
Ogilvy, David 105, 106
Older men 40
One-man business 14, 24-25
Opinion polls (*see also* attitude surveys) 91
Operational groups 78, 80
Operations (Operational) research and control (OR) 4, 36, 59, 85, 86-88, 95, 96, 100, 143-157, 163, 176, 184, 187, 188, 218-219
Opinion surveys (*see also* Attitude surveys) 48, 49, 71, 111
Opinions (importance of) 71, 74
Opportunities 63, 114, 185
Optimum and Optimization 15, 143, 146, 148, 149, 152, 153, 164, 177, 186, 188, 204, 213, 215
Ordinary shares (*see also* Shares) 13
Organization 7, 81, 115, 180
 and Methods (O & M) 115-116
Organizational problems 57-58, 70, 84
Organism, business as an 34
Output 166
Overdrafts 15, 31, 122, 126
Overheads 10, 11, 126, 140, 147, 148, 166, 166n, 170, 171

'Overproduction' 109
Overseas markets and marketing 124, 139, 140, 141
Owen, Robert 76

Packaging 101, 137-138, 154n
Packard, Vance 102
Pakistan 136
'Paper work' 36
Participation 69
 Labour (in management) 55, 56
Partnership 12, 14, 25
Pasteur, Louis 83, 145
Patents 118, 124, 132
'Paternalism' 51, 76
Paxton, Sir William 99
Pay 51
'Payback' 129, 207, 208
People (treatment of) 50
Permutations and Combinations 146, 148, 177
Personality 42, 46, 69
 assessment of 73 (*see also* Personnel assessment)
Personnel Management and Control 19, 36, 46-47
 Assessment 97
 Department 46, 48
Philosophy 154
Physics 143
Pigou, Professor A. C. 108
Pin-making 18
Planning 23, 36, 90, 96, 169n, 172, 173, 174-190, 191, 192, 202
 Department 179, 180-183
Plastics 175, 188
Play (and work) 67
Poetry xii
'Polaris' Submarine 149, 192
Policy 27, 48, 112, 206
Power supply 146, 154, 159, 171
Precision engineering 185
Prediction 152, 155
Prefabrication 100
Preference Shares 13
Prejudice 54, 69
Prestige 15, 35, 73

INDEX

Price 11, 20, 22, 108, 117, 122, 163, 176
Prices, Fixed 140
Priorities 23, 86, 200
Pritchard, Wood & Partners 136
Private Companies 12, 14, 25
Probabilities 88, 143, 153, 206
Probability, Laws of 90, 91, 146, 149, 151, 152
Procedure (at meetings) 57, 79
Product Mix 215
  Variety 150
Production Capacity 32, 176, 181, 214
  Department 29, 154
  Methods 17
  Planning and Control 13, 86, 205
  Manager/Director 29, 30, 31, 117
  Needs 30
  Economics 131
Productivity 37, 50, 68, 69, 90, 92, 188
Products, new (*see* New products)
Proficiency 37
Profit 2, 5, 8, 10, 11, 15, 16, 19, 21, 37, 52, 53, 114, 115, 118, 120, 122, 124, 126, 128, 155, 158, 164, 166, 190
Profit and Loss Accounts 25, 121, 159, 160, 161, 162, 167, 170, 172
Profitability 15, 22, 48, 70, 86, 88, 100, 128, 131, 150, 186, 188, 215
Programme Evaluation and Review Technique (PERT) 193
Programming 88, 96, 154
Project Appraisal 202
  Planning 202
Promotion (Personnel) 37, 39, 46, 79
Promotion, Sales 133, 134, 174, 186
Protection, of Consumer 108
Prototype 109

Pseudo-scientists 157
Psychoanalysis 45
Psychological factors 11
Psychology xii, 34
  Industrial 4, 76
Public Address System 93
Public Company 25
Public Relations 22, 52, 106, 107, 111
Public Schools 42
Publicity 106
Punishment 81
Purchasing 19, 135
  Costs 216, 217
  Orders 217
Purchasing Power 8, 12
Purpose, sense of 78

Quality 20, 107, 110, 132, 136, 137, 141, 177, 178
  Control 4, 13, 22, 36, 47, 85, 91, 108
Questioning 146
Questionnaires 71
Queuing Theory 148

Raleigh bicycles 133
Raw materials 2, 6, 7, 8, 9, 24, 31, 121, 146, 147, 149, 154, 159, 181-182.
  Cost of 176
Razor blades 136
Receipts 171
Recruitment 40-42
Refrigeration 10
Registrar 25
Rent 10, 15, 160, 171, 216
Replacement 9, 162
Reporting 32
Reputation (*see also* Image) 107
Research, see under Research and Development, Market Research, and Operations Research
Research and Development (R & D) 97, 100, 115, 142, 156, 178, 179

INDEX

Resentment xii, 52
Reserves 2, 9, 10, 12, 122, 162
Resources 6, 9, 179, 181, 186, 192, 203-204
   human 81
Respect 5
Reponsibility 32, 35, 43, 44, 62, 73, 80, 81, 82
Responsibility of management 4, 45, 27-28, 38, 62, 93, 192
Restraint of trade 190
Retailers 16, 112, 134
Revenue 31, 120
Revolution, Industrial 54, 57
   New Industrial 57-58
Right, Issues of 13
Risk 10, 130
Rockefeller, John D. 58, 77
Roethlisburger, Professor Fritz 49
Rolls-Royce 22, 105, 116, 185
Roosevelt, President F. D. 49
Rosenwald, Julius 21
Rotation of crops 127
Rotation, job 63
Rowntree 101, 177
Ruskin, John 99

Safety 36, 37
St. Pancras Station 99
St. Paul 66
Salaries 10, 46, 122, 171
Sales 2, 104, 118, 120, 147, 155, 164, 176
   Administration and Control 3
   Costs 134
   Department 30-31, 166
   Director/Manager 30-31, 104
   Force 3, 16, 148
   Supervisor 30
Salesmen 3, 4, 125
Sampling 88, 91, 109, 137, 143
Satisfaction in work 68
   of customer 131, 132, 138
Savings 6, 24
Schmidt, S. 129, 207n
Schweppes 106

Science, and Scientific Method 61, 65, 142-143, 151, 156, 157, 185
   Fiction 89
'Scientific Management' 11, 87
Scott, Gilbert 99
Sears, Richard 21
Sears, Roebuck Co. 21, 71, 103
Seasonal Markets (*see* Markets)
Secretary, Company 28
Securities 10
Security (Commercial) 183
Security (Personal) 73, 80
Selection (Personnel) 37-42, 46, 130, 155
Self-assessment 45, 82, 87
Self-control 54, 67, 79, 81, 84
Self-reliance 79
Semantics 94
Services 22, 52
Services, Armed 39
Servicing 178
Shareholders 12, 13, 25, 26, 27, 162
Shares 12, 13, 25, 26
Shaw, George Bernard 67, 103, 189
Shell Co. Ltd. 64, 112
Simplification 13, 115-116
Simulation 98, 152
Sincerity 75
Singer Sewing Machines 133
Sinking Fund 12, 162
Sleeping partner 26
Small business 1, 13-17, 18, 46, 110-114, 117, 118, 126, 134, 140, 183-187
Smith, Adam 18, 87
Soap 32, 133
Social Psychology and Research 4, 82
   Economics 4
   Factors 11
Social Sciences (*see also* Behavioral sciences) 82
Social Studies 73
Society, Classless (*see* Classless society)

INDEX

'Span of Control' 39
Specialists and Specialization 4, 47, 100, 117, 143, 156, 185, 189
Spinning 'Mule' 7
Stability, Emotional 41, 43
Staff 2
  Control 2
  and line Management 47
Stamps 138
Standard Costing 165-170
Standard Oil of America 58, 77
Standardization 13, 188, 218
State control 22
State-owned enterprises 190
Statistics 4, 87-93, 146, 149-152
Status 35, 39
Stochastic Methods 148-153, 182
Stock 31, 168-169, 171, 172, 181
  Control 2, 24, 171, 178-179, 216
Stock Exchange 13, 25
Storage 9-10, 15, 86, 148, 217
Stores Control (*see also* Stock Control and Storage) 19
Streamlining 99
Subliminal Advertising 102
Submarines 144
Subsidiary Companies 27
Substitution 150
Suggestion 101
'Sunlight Soap' 133
Supermarkets 135, 140, 154
Supervisors and Supervision 30, 32, 35, 36, 37, 38, 40, 49, 56-57
Supply 47
  Department 31
  Manager 31, 218
Surpluses 10
Suspicion 53, 76, 174
Sweden 175

Tack, A. & G. 141
'Take-overs' 27, 129 186
Targets 19, 82, 120, 126, 147, 181
Target-setting 82
Taste 139, 175
Tavistock, Institute of Human Relations 55

Taxation 6, 11, 29
Taylor, F. W. 87
Team & Teamwork, Management 40, 69, 74, 79, 193, 202
Technical knowledge 24, 37-38
Techniques of Management xi, 4, 17, 61, 65, 85, 87, 116, 190
Technological development 14, 58, 99, 114
Television 105
Temperament 74
Tenacity 4
Tenders 217
Tennyson, Alfred Lord 66
Tesco 135
Texas, University 61
Theories 'X' & 'Y' 80-82
Theory 6, 83
Thompson, J. Walter 136
Time 10, 193-200
Tobacco 10, 11, 28-31, 178-179
Top management 62-65, 74
Toys, Constructional 117
Trade Marks 132
Trade, Restraint of 190
Trade Union Congress (TUC) 53
Trade Unionism 51-53, 56-57, 78
Trading losses 15
Trainees, Management 38, 63
Training 13, 37-38, 47, 49, 53, 84, 205
  for management 4-5, 63-65, 79-80
  within Industry (TWI) 85-86
Transport 16-17, 19, 31, 127, 146, 149, 154, 159, 215
Trends 5, 92, 140
Trial balances 159, 161-162
Tube Investments Ltd. 18
Turnover 124-128, 135

Understanding 75, 77, 78
Unearned increment 6
Unilever Ltd. 14, 15, 26, 70, 86, 87, 105, 112, 133
Unique Selling Proposition (USP) 105

233

INDEX

United Africa Co. Ltd. 141, 191
United States of America (USA) 38, 58, 70-71, 77, 108, 113, 139, 186, 190, 192
U.S. Navy 192
United Steel Co. 112
Universities 1, 38, 42, 139
Utility Analysis 212

Vail, Theodore N. 185, 186
Value Analysis 188
Values, Changing 163
Variable costs 118, 164
Variables 146, 155, 213
Variations, in demand 3, 23, 177
Variations, Human 35
Variety, Products (*see also* Product Mix) 150
Vauxhall Motors Ltd. 76
Versailles, Treaty of 182
Voting rights 13

Wage fixing and Wage negotiation 11, 55
Wages 7, 46

Walls (Ice Cream etc.) 14
Waste 13, 19, 36, 37
Welfare 46, 47
Western Electric Co. 49, 50, 61
'Which' magazine 108
Whitehead, Commander Edward 106
Wholesalers 112, 117, 134
Wiggins Teape Ltd. 186
Wishful thinking 54
Wood, General Robert 21
Words, meaning of 94-95
Work 7, 67-68, 80-81
   conditions of 51
   measurement 36, 47
   study (*see also* Method Study) 13, 85, 115-116, 146
World situation 182
Wright Brothers 83

'Y' theory *see* Theories 'X' & 'Y'
Yardley Perfumery Co. Ltd. 186
Yorkshire 75